THE BAHAMAS

25° N

Statute Miles

10 0 10 20 30 40 50 60 70 80 90 100

N

I0605401

SAN SALVADOR

ONCEPTION

RUM CAY

LONG ISLAND

SAMANA CAY

CROOKED ISLAND PASSAGE

CROOKED Is.

Fortune Is.

PLANA CAYS

MAYAGUANA PASSAGE

MAYAGUANA

ACKLINS ISLAND

CAICOS PASSAGE

Mira por vos

CASTLE ISLAND

CAICOS ISLANDS

TURKS Is. PASSAGE

TURKS Is.

BUS NK

Hogsty Reef

LITTLE INAGUA

GREAT INAGUA

Matthew Town

20° N

TORTUGA Is.

Monte Cristi

WINDWARD PASSAGE

HISPANIOLA

75° W

20° N

A HISTORY OF THE BAHAMAS

A
HISTORY OF THE
BAHAMAS

by

Michael Craton

Collins
ST JAMES'S PLACE, LONDON

First Impression November 1962
Second Impression June 1963
Second Edition 1968

CONTENTS

LIST OF MAPS

LIST OF ILLUSTRATIONS

This book was begun with a secret fear that the chief problem would be the scarcity of material. Now, four busy years later, it can truthfully be said that the reverse has been the case. Not that the exploration of the shelves of books and mounds of documents has been an easy task. Bahamian historiography is beset by peculiar hazards. The chief papers, in London and Nassau, are separated by 4,000 miles of ocean, and those in the Bahamian capital have not been calendared or arranged. There is neither an archive department nor an adequate museum in the Bahamas; the excellent collection of Bahamiana in the Nassau Public Library is inadequately catalogued and difficult of access; the Bahamas Historical Society has not fulfilled the high hopes of those who launched it in 1959. Moreover, in the Bahamas it is difficult to be impartial. The islands are not innocent of factions, each with its favourite myths.

Perhaps, then, it is not surprising that this is the first general history to be published. Brief synopses, of varying degrees of inaccuracy, have appeared in several guide-books; but longer works seem to have been doomed in embryo. In 1903, James Wright found himself bogged down in the records and his projected history became an indigestible study of the brief emancipation period. Mary Moseley was said for years to be preparing a definitive history, but she died with it unwritten and the 1926 guide-book is her only monument. In the 1950s, the House of Assembly engaged the distinguished historian Hilary St. George Saunders to write an Official History. After two research assistants had worked in London for two years, he came to Nassau to compose the book and died six weeks later.

In writing this book I have tried to be as independent as possible. I would, however, like to offer sincere thanks to the Speaker of the Honourable House of Assembly, Asa H. Pritchard, for permission to use the library of the House, and to the Secretary of the House, George Johnson, for considerable help; to the overworked librarians of the Nassau Public Library, especially Miss Griffin, for their cheerful assistance; to the Development Board for the use of photographs; to the Director of Public Works, Richard Rae, and the ex-Director of Town Planning, William Lowes, for several ideas; to my colleagues, Lewis Morgan, for the end-paper maps, and Cecil Bethel, for some whimsical suggestions, and to Gillian Bain for reading some of the proofs. Several pupils and colleagues, particularly Julia Smith, gave invaluable assistance with the Index.

Possibly it may seem ironic that it is an Englishman who should write the first full history of the Bahamas and its people. I would, however, like to regard this book, which has been my master so long, as some repayment for six enjoyable years in the Isles of June. All too often I have been conscious of my lack of absolute certainty in research. When exploring virgin territory, rivers glimpsed here and there must be mapped with some confidence, even if later travellers find them described inaccurately or even flowing in different directions. I would therefore like to issue a general apology for any errors or distortions, and express the hope that they may, by stimulating others to controvert them, at least advance the study of this fascinating and neglected subject.

Nassau, April, 1962

PREFACE TO THE SECOND EDITION

Since this book first appeared, the Bahamas have attracted more and more attention from the outside world. A new edition, therefore, is both necessary and timely. Each return visit reveals such changes that one is constantly amazed how well the islands retain their incomparable allure; yet in the last five years, nothing has come to light to require drastic changes in the earlier part of the text, even of interpretation. Apart from minor corrections of fact or emphasis, only the last chapter, dealing with recent events, has had to be recast entirely. An independent viewpoint, as in 1962, has been jealously guarded, with debts to many friends but no master; with apologies, where necessary, to all.

Waterloo, Canada, June, 1967

I

Beginnings

The Bahama Islands form an enormous archipelago, extending south-east from the Manzanilla Bank off Florida some 590 miles to Great Inagua, near Cape Nicholas, Haiti. At their widest they stretch 380 miles from the Cay Sal Bank off Cuba to San Salvador, at the edge of the Atlantic. Few people have bothered to count the islands, but there are said to be 29 islands, 661 cays (pronounced "keys") and 2,387 rocks. The total land area has been computed recently at 5,400 square miles—rather more than the island of Jamaica, or half the area of Wales.

Some 30 of the islands and cays of the Bahamas have people living on them, though the population is very unevenly spread. Well over half the estimated population of 138,000 lives in Nassau on the small island of New Providence, which, with an area of only 58 square miles, has a population density of over 1,400 to the square mile. Over the remaining area, the density is roughly ten per square mile. Andros, the largest island by far with the area of 1,600 square miles, has a population of barely 7,000. Besides Nassau, with its 86,000 people, there are only two settlements—Freeport and Eight Mile Rock in Grand Bahama—with more than a thousand inhabitants.

The reason for the sparseness of the population of the Bahamas is the poverty of their terrain. The islands are almost completely flat; the highest hills, in Cat Island, are hardly more than 200 feet in height and in most islands there is no land more than a hundred feet above the sea. Both for this reason and the porosity of the rock, there are absolutely no rivers or streams. The soil is fertile but extremely thin, and lodged in shallows and "banana holes" in the harsh limestone rock. In some areas the ground is so split by interlocking caves and potholes up to sixty

11

feet deep that it is impossible to traverse, let alone farm. Fresh water is found, but only close to the surface, resting by some quirk of nature on the underlying salt water. Wells drilled too deep or worked too hard produce brackish or salt water. "Ocean holes", small lakes of salt water subterraneously connected with the ocean (and usually, of course, referred to as "bottomless"), are common, often far inland.

This harsh, often almost lunar landscape is moderated by the climate, one of the finest in the world. Insulated from the North American continent by the Florida Channel and yet cooled in summer by the North East Trades, the Bahamas suffer neither extremes of heat nor cold. Although the summer months are humid, the temperature rarely rises above 90° and the lowest winter temperature on record is 49°. The average for the five coolest months is an ideal 70°. Rainfall varies from 40 to 60 inches a year, but frost and snow are unthinkable, though a few freak snowflakes once fell—in 1798. Well do the islands merit the title given them by a nineteenth-century visitor, "The Isles of Perpetual June".

The chief scourge of the Bahamas, mercifully rare, is the hurricane. This savage tropical cyclone, which can unleash winds of up to 150 m.p.h. over an area up to a hundred miles wide, usually germinates in the Atlantic east of the Lesser Antilles, before travelling, in a crescendo of ferocity, steadily in a north-westerly direction. Serious hurricanes sometimes reach the eastern seaboard of the United States, before petering out in the latitude of Bermuda, or even farther north. The average track of all hurricanes, which have been accurately plotted for over a hundred years, passes directly along the axis of the Bahama Islands. Nearly every other year some islands are ravaged by one of the dozen or so annual West Indian "tropical storms", picturesquely nicknamed in alphabetical series by the Pan-American Weather Bureau. Nassau, however, when lashed by "Betsy" in September, 1965, had not suffered a hurricane since 1929.

The best way to see the Bahamas is from the air. Many astronauts have traversed the Bahamas in circumnavigating the stratosphere, thus enjoying the grandest view of all. During their flights, flashing through space at 17,500 m.p.h. a hundred miles or more above the earth they have seen the whole Bahamas chain stretched out beneath them, and admired the jewel-like myriad of colours which are the islands' chief claim to magnificence—the cobalt of the deep ocean and the deep purple of the reefs; the lighter spectra of the banks, turquoise and emerald, gold, yellow and silver with the underlying skeins of sand; the drabber greens and grey of the islands and their surrounding rocks.

From sea level the islands are far less impressive; long, tree-fringed strands almost unrelieved by background hills. Columbus spoke admiringly of the vegetation, but he was pleading a special cause. Palm trees, which give some islands a truly "South Sea" air, are not abundant, having been imported into the islands in recent times. Only in sophisticated Nassau on New Providence and other well-developed settlements in Eleuthera and Grand Bahama, does vegetation luxuriate. Only there can one imagine the Bahamas almost an earthly paradise; with whispering web-like casuarinas and fantastic silk cotton trees; the rainbow hues of crotons and creeping vines; poinciana and poinsettia with their unreal reds; bougainvillea in purple and salmon pink and the equally gaudy hibiscus and oleander. In orchards grow a confused abundance of exotic fruits; pineapples and grapefruit (once known as "the forbidden fruit"); sea-grapes, soursop and sapodilla; mangoes, guavas and a hundred others. At night the air is drenched with perfume and by day the trees are alive with humming-birds. Everywhere bright lizards scurry among the sunsoaked rocks and in gentle captivity in Nassau and wild in Inagua and South Andros are the pink flamingoes, most beautiful and least functional of birds.

Out to sea, under the transparent water of the reefs are natural gardens of coral more beautiful than any on land. Because of the absence of rivers with their cloudy sediments, Bahamian waters are the clearest in the world. The ocean floor can be seen, as through crystal, in 60 feet of water. Here for the skin diver and explorer with a water glass is a wonderful new world; corals of all shapes and colours, waving fronds and multicoloured fishes. It was a far-sighted step when, in 1957, the House of Assembly declared a large portion of the necklace-like chain of the Exuma Cays a Bahamian National Park.

Geologically the Bahamas are so simple that they have never attracted an expert study. Basically consisting of Tertiary limestone modified by vigorous coralline action, the actual sequence of their formation is still open to speculation. There are still some geological features that await explanation.

Nowhere in the Bahamas is any rock but limestone found, and borings at Cay Sal and other places have found it to be a bed many thousands of feet thick. Clearly the archipelago is a projection of the American limestone "fore-lands" found in Florida and Yucatan; the outer crust of older rocks. Unlike the two great limestone peninsulas, however, the Bahamas appear to be the relics of a great submarine mountain range. The islands and banks are the flattened peaks: the deep channels are vast valleys, dropping in some places 10,000 feet to the ocean floor.

The basic limestone was laid down as windblown deposits in the long geological period known as the Tertiary, between 75 thousand and one million years ago. Gradual, almost infinitesimal, subsidence produced a sea-girt plateau, fretted by waves into islands and divided by great canyons such as the Florida Channel, the Providence Channels, the Tongue of the Ocean and the Crooked Inland Passage. The superficial undulations and insignificant hills would be the result of dune-like formation during eras of great cyclonic disturbance. Most of the present aspect of the Bahamas, however, has been produced in geologically recent times, by coral formation during the four glacial and interglacial epochs.

The Bahamas are in fact true coral islands. The external limestone, worn razor-sharp by the sea and honeycombed inland with potholes and caves, contains coral fossils to a considerable depth. The climate and waters of the islands are ideal for coral building. There is ample sun and absolutely no sedimentation. The water temperature never drops below the coral minimum of 70° and is almost invariably in the ideal range of 75°-85°. Currents carry the food necessary for the hungry corals, salinity is in the ideal range of 25-40 parts per thousand and there are huge areas of shoal water shallower than the maximum coral depth of 150 feet.

With all factors favourable, all three types of coral reef formation are found in Bahamian waters: fringe and barrier reefs and coral atolls. Fringe reefs, which are formed near coasts

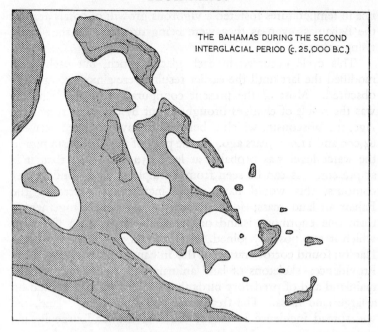

THE BAHAMAS DURING THE SECOND
INTERGLACIAL PERIOD (c. 25,000 B.C.)

at the outer edge of platforms cut by waves, are extremely
common in the Bahamas. Nearly all Bahamian islands are fringed
by such reefs on their ocean side, good examples being found
off the north of New Providence and to the east of Great Exuma.
Barrier reefs, separated from a mainland by a wide lagoon, are
naturally less common, but can be discerned in the line of reefs
at the northern edge of the Little Bahama Bank, the western edge
of the Great Bahama Bank and the outer fringe of the Bight of
Acklins. Of genuine atolls, where reefs encircle a central mass
which has since subsided leaving a circular lagoon, there are only
two examples in the Bahamas; the Hogsty Reef and Cay Sal Bank.

R. A. Daly in his *Glacial Control Theory* of coral formation
pointed out the significance of glacial shifts upon coral building.
During each of the Ice Ages the level of the water in the oceans
of the world dropped by as much as 300 feet below its present
level as the glaciers advanced. Each time the glaciers retreated,
their melted water gradually filled the oceans until they were as
much as 150 feet above the present level. The accompanying

rise in temperatures fostered a vigorous growth of corals around the Bahamas, even as they were being drowned by the slowly rising waters.

This cycle occurred in each glacial epoch, but each cycle modified the last until the earlier results were almost completely obscured. Most of the present configuration of the Bahamas was the result of changes brought about by the most recent Ice Age, the Wisconsin, which is believed to have occurred between 64,000 and 11,000 years ago. At the peak of the Wisconsin period the water level was probably at least 250 feet lower than it is at present. As can be seen from a simple study of underwater contours, this would have vastly increased the area of the Bahamian land mass; joining most of the islands together to form one enormous island or peninsula larger than Cuba, to which it was possibly joined. A few years ago, the late Robert Hanlon found corroboration of this in banana holes on tiny New Providence; skeletons of land animals now found only on the mainland and of predatory birds that could only have existed on a large land mass. The freshwater turtles of Long Island, the widespread incidence in recent times of the landborne iguana and perhaps even the New Providence raccoon, point to this also. Strangely enough, the earliest inhabitants also seem to have had a legend of a land mass joined to the mainland. Peter Martyr in 1511 recorded that "the natives themselves declare that there is such a tradition transmitted to them by their ancestors. Little by little, violent tempests submerged the lands, and separated them one from another by arms of the sea."

The process was, of course, far less cataclysmic than the legend. Imperceptibly the waters rose, no faster than the corals grew, until the Bahamas were as we know them today; rock-strewn, coral-rich and murderous to uninformed navigators.

Nor, despite the legend, was Man a witness to the process. There were no men on the mainland to migrate to the Bahamas as Neolithic Man first trudged into Britain by way of the Straits of Dover during the last Ice Age. The Bahamas, which modern man has found almost the perfect natural habitat, remained unsullied by *homo sapiens* well into historical times.

II

The Lucayans

In the timeless sweep of the geological history of the Bahamas the modern inhabitants are but visitors who arrived this morning. Whether they are the coloured majority, descended from anonymous African slaves of the seventeenth and eighteenth centuries, or the white descendants of Adventurers and Loyalists, no family can claim a history of more than three hundred years in these islands.

Who then were the first inhabitants of the Bahamas, and from where did they come? Probably they were the Siboneys, the obscure and primitive fisher-folk who migrated down the Florida and Yucatán peninsulas and hopped the cays to Cuba, Haiti and Jamaica, where their scant remains seem to indicate that they became in time the slaves of later Indian migrants. Certainly it is less far from the Florida coast to the West End of Grand Bahama and the northern end of Andros than it is from Key West to Cuba.

In 1952, Dr. J. M. Goggin explored a prehistoric "midden" in a cave at South Hill, Andros, where he found shell implements and aboriginal crania. But he failed to find a definite habitation site and was forced to conclude that the Siboneys were either very few in number or visited the Bahamas but temporarily. Perhaps the northern islands of the Bahamas were once peopled thinly by this fragile aboriginal tribe. But in the absence of more certain archaeological evidence we may never know. Unfortunately the Siboneys did not carve in either wood or stone.

As late as 1926 there were tantalizing rumours that the interior parts of Andros were inhabited by a lingering tribe of primitives. In that year Miss Mary Moseley hoped that an aerial survey would clear up the riddle. Today, long after the tribe has been exposed as a myth, and when airplane flights and aerial surveys have become commonplace, we can echo her feelings to hope that the exciting new science of archaeological research from the air will help us to find the ancient village sites for which Dr. Goggin searched in vain.

Columbus noted that the "Indians" he found in the southern Bahamas, who called themselves Lucayans, had several characteristics common to the *Guanche* inhabitants of the Canary Islands, the last land that the explorers had seen. Some later writers went as far as to suggest that the Lucayans came from the Canaries, and thus originally from Africa, down the North East Trade Winds in canoes. The slightest research into the customs and characteristics of the Lucayans, however, proves that this intriguing theory does not hold water.

The Lucayans were Arawaks. They were cousins of the Indians whom the Spaniards found in Cuba, Haiti, Puerto Rico and Jamaica, practising a culture which the anthropologists call Tainan. Their descendants may still be found in some numbers in the back country of Venezuela and the Guianas.

Crossing from the South American mainland to the islands of the Lesser Antilles, the peaceful Arawaks were probably forced onwards by the pressure of the fierce Caribs. Certainly by the time they reached the islands they were raided and then invaded by this cannibalistic people, whose chief aim was the murder of Arawak men and the enslavement of their women. Even the Carib religion promised the courageous warrior a paradise where he would be served by Arawak slaves; just as the coward was doomed to a hades in which he would be a slave to an Arawak master.

In the search for peace the Arawaks pushed ever onwards in their dug-out canoes. By about the year A.D. 1000, while the Norsemen were touching at Greenland and Labrador, they had reached Haiti. From there they settled Cuba and Jamaica, and some time later they came to the southern Bahamas, the last wave of their great migration. By this time they were known as *Lukku-cairi* or "island people". Their mainland origin was forgotten.

The Caribs were still not far away. By the time of the Spanish discovery in 1492, they had conquered the whole chain of the Lesser Antilles, giving their name to the sea which it encloses, and they were plaguing by raids Puerto Rico and the eastern end of Hispaniola. In the Bahamas the Lucayans were very conscious of the Caribs, and some men had probably come in contact with them. "I saw some with scars on their bodies", wrote Columbus, "and to my signs asking what these meant, they answered in the same manner, that people from neighbouring islands wanted to capture them and they defended themselves; and I did believe, and do believe, that they came there from the mainland to take them prisoners."

The Lucayans had no iron and were so ignorant of its use that they grasped the sharp Spanish swords in their bare hands. Generally they carried no weapons and they were so unskilled in the uses of bows and spears that they were easy prey for the bloodthirsty Caribs.

But for the advent of the Europeans, the Caribs might have pursued the Arawaks to the shores of the Atlantic and finally destroyed them there. As it stands, it is the Lucayan Arawaks, not the Caribs, whom we have to regard as the first certain Bahamians.

To put together our knowledge of the Lucayans is like completing a jigsaw puzzle with pieces missing. Although, as Peter Martyr said, they spoke a language that was "soft and not less liquid than Latin", and there are some sixteen Arawak words and their derivatives in the modern English dictionary (avocado, barbecue, buccaneer, canoe, Carib, cannibal, cay, guava, hammock, hurricane, iguana, maize, manatee, perogue, potato and tobacco), the Arawaks had no written language. Archaeological remains are also scanty in the extreme. Except for the excavation of a Lucayan village at Rose's, Long Island, the results of which can be seen in an excellent diorama in the Smithsonian Institute, Washington, there has been hardly any systematic work in the archaeological field. Studies of Lucayan artifacts by such specialists as Theodore de Booy, W. K. Brooks and H. W. Krieger, while valuable, have been piecemeal, and except for a few pieces in the Nassau Public Library and others in a private museum on Watling's, what remains there are, are scattered or have been lost.

A full collection would contain a fairly complete selection of Arawak artifact types. Most of the finds have been made in roughly a dozen caves, stretching from Bimini to Inagua, and in the so-called "banana holes". Usually the finds are associated with Arawak skeletons, indicating some sort of burial rite. In Bimini, for instance, a perforated stone pendant and a coral religious *zemi* were found in 1912. Pottery, which de Booy studied in detail in the Caicos Islands and presumed was not used elsewhere by the Lucayans, has been found in recent years in the Hamilton Caves, Long Island and Salt Pond Hill Cave, Inagua. The fragments found indicate crude designs of interlocking rings, nucleated circles, hoof-shapes, incised broken lines and, in one case, moulded figurine heads. Obviously some of the vessels were thin-walled, but simple lugs took the place of handles.

In the Hartford Cave, Rum Cay, crude petroglyphs have been found of fish, semi-human and purely decorative designs. Hardstone "celts", locally known as "thunderbolts", are quite common and there are several examples of mealing stones. Hardwood arrow-heads have been discovered in Eleuthera and wooden bowls with handles in several islands. The supposed find of a large canoe complete with paddles at Mangrove Cay, Andros, unfortunately cannot be authenticated.

Perhaps the most interesting finds have been the half-dozen Lucayan *duhos*, ceremonial stools of stone or wood. The best example, found in the Hamilton Caves in 1935, has a curved backrest of madeira wood. Most of the *duhos* bear a faint resemblance to a turtle, but one recently found at Guana Cay, Watling's, is said to be modelled on the Bahamian iguana, now extinct on that island.

A systematic cataloguing of all Bahamian archaeological discoveries by a team of experts would doubtless allow certain new conclusions to be made about the distribution of the Lucayans, their customs and the amount of intercourse between the islands. As it is we have to rely almost completely on the more formal work that has been done on the village-sites, middens and caves of the populous islands of the Greater Antilles and the studies still being made of the Arawaks surviving in South America. Through these researches we can infer much that applies to the Lucayans, though life in the less fertile Bahamas must have been considerably harsher and more dependent upon the sea. Since there is no suitable native clay, all pottery had to be brought from overseas. Other goods which had to be brought into the islands: gold ornaments, hardwoods and hard stones like nephrite and jadeite, would also have been correspondingly scarce. Besides this, some crops suitable to the larger islands would have been missing in the Bahamas. In one crop, however, the islands seem to have been outstanding. Because of the Bahamas black loam found in Watling's, Rum Cay and Long Island, these islands seem to have produced the best cotton known to the Arawaks.

The Lucayans were a race of primitive farmers and fishermen in what Europeans might have called the New Stone Age, or Neolithic, stage of development. "All of them go about naked even the women", wrote Columbus on the day of discovery, "although I saw but one girl, all the rest being young men, none of them being over thirty years of age; their forms are well proportioned, their bodies graceful and their features handsome. Their hair is as coarse as the hair of a horse's tail and short. They wear their hair over their eyebrows, except a little hank behind, which they wear long and never cut. Some of them paint themselves black (they are of the colour of the Canary Islanders, neither black nor white), some paint themselves white; some red, and some with whatever they find; some paint their faces, some their whole body, some their eyes only; and some their noses only."

Peter Martyr was able to say more than Columbus about the Lucayan women. "It is alleged", he wrote, "that the women of the Lucayan islands are so beautiful that numerous inhabitants of the neighbouring countries, charmed with their beauty, abandon their homes, and for the love of them settle in their country. It is also said that the islanders of the Lucayan archipelago have more civilised morals than those who live farther from the cultivated regions of Bimini and Florida."

The faces of the Lucayans were broad, almost oriental in appearance, and their foreheads were usually flattened in infancy by the tying to them of flat boards. This strange practice was not only designed to add distinction to their looks. The thickened bone which resulted was proof against enemy blows, and sometimes even against the sharp swords of the Spaniards. Often the Lucayans bound their slender limbs with bands of cotton thread, which wasted those parts in an unsightly manner.

If the Lucayans wore clothes, they were limited to a loincloth of leaves or dyed cotton cloth, though Peter Martyr described a kind of trousers which the young women wore once they were no longer virgins. Men as well as women loved ornament and besides daubing themselves as Columbus described, they wore tattoo marks and sometimes necklaces, bracelets and head-dresses of shells, bones and feathers. Very occasionally they would wear a droplet of gold in a nostril.

In character the Lucayans were an admirable people, in sharp contrast to the harsh and often greedy Castilians. By all accounts they were gentle and generous, lovers of peace and simple pleasures. As Peter Martyr said, "They seem to live in that golden world of which the old writers speak so much, wherein men lived simply and innocently without enforcement of laws, without quarrelling, judges and libels, content only to satisfy nature."

"They are so ingenuous and free with all they have", wrote Columbus to his sovereigns, "that no-one would believe it who has not seen it; of anything that they possess, if it be asked of them, they never say no; on the contrary they invite you to share it and show as much love as if their hearts went with it, and they are content with whatever trifle be given them, whether it be a thing of value or petty worth. I forbade that they be given things so worthless as bits of broken crockery and of green glass and lacepoints, although when they could get them they thought they had the best jewel in the world."

The Lucayans loved singing and dancing, both of which they called *arieto*. On festive occasions, such as the marriage of a chief, there were tribal chants and recitals of songs; dances for men and women, separately and occasionally together. At these times, much beer made from maize or cassava was drunk.

The Arawaks had a well-developed ball game, called *batos*. For this there was a special field attached to each village, complete with stone slabs or stools for spectators. The two teams were of equal size but might contain any number, up to thirty a side. Both men and women played. The ball, which was made of a hard elastic substance, perhaps rubber latex, was hit from side to side, kept in the air with head, shoulder, hip or knee. Hands were not used. As in Volley Ball, one side was penalised if the ball fell to the ground in its area. In the larger islands at least, villages sometimes played against each other. Next to the singing, dancing and drinking of village festivals, the Arawaks liked their ball game best.

It was the Arawaks of Cuba who first demonstrated to the Spaniards the strange custom of smoking tobacco, or *cohiba* as they call the plant. *Tabaco* was the name which they gave to their strange Y-shaped pipes. We do not know for certain whether the Lucayans smoked, but Columbus described a leaf which he found a Lucayan carrying between two of the islands in a canoe as one obviously valued by the natives.

The Indians smoked rolled tubes of leaves like cigars, which the Spaniards at first mistook for lighted firebrands carried between the teeth. They preferred their pipes, however, which were often smoked ceremonially. The two branches of the Y-shaped tube were inserted in the nostrils and the smoke, or snuff, inhaled so deeply that the smoker fell into a stupor. Within a very short time the Spaniards picked up the habit of smoking, though not to the point of intoxication, and in a few years the drug was popular throughout Europe. The insidious effects of this addiction might be termed the Arawaks' Revenge!

The houses of the Lucayans were circular with a conical roof, in shape very much like those of Kaffir *kraals* in South Africa. Although no mud or brick was used, their construction was strong enough to withstand all but the highest winds. First of all a tall centre pole was set up, around which was planted a circle of shorter, slimmer poles. These, when interwoven with canes, vines and withies, formed the wall, in which a space was left as a doorway. The roof was thatched with palm.

Furniture in the huts was very sparse. It consisted of treasured earthenware pots, a stool or two and a hammock for each member of the family. These *hamacas*, made either of cotton net or dyed cotton cloth, were a novelty to the Spaniards. Within fifty years they had been adopted by sailors throughout Europe. Prior to 1492 all European ordinary seamen at sea had slept where they could; on deck in fine weather, or on the bilge-washed, roach-run timbers below.

Arawak villages were never large. The "city" of Cubanacan in Cuba, where Columbus expected his ambassadors to find the gilded palaces of Kubla Khan, consisted of fifty squalid huts. In the less populous Bahamas the largest village which Columbus saw contained only about fifteen houses. In other places families lived by themselves.

The chiefs of the Arawaks were called *caciques*, whose importance depended on the area over which they were head. It is unlikely that the Lucayans were as well organised as the Indians of Haiti, who were divided into five "kingdoms" and whose *caciques* were very noble savages indeed. As Sven Loven says, there is no evidence that Lucayan *cacicazgos* extended beyond the boundaries of the village. But Lucayan *caciques* were certainly more privileged than their fellows, though like them they hunted, fished and worked in the fields. After the harvest the *caciques* received all the crops in royal granaries, allocating the food to each family as required. Although legal disputes were rare, the *caciques*' word was law; and besides being rulers they were often the priests.

On ceremonial occasions the *caciques* were magnificently attired. Andrés Bernáldez describes some of the *caciques*' ornaments which Columbus brought back to Spain in 1496 with which to impress the sovereigns: . . . "crowns, masks, girdles, collars, and many woven articles of cotton, and in all of them the devil was represented in the shape of a monkey or owl's head, or other worse shapes; some carved in wood, some made of cloth of the same cotton, or of a precious stone. He brought some winged crowns with golden eyes on their sides, and especially a crown that they said belonged to the *cacique* Caonabo, which was very big and tall, with wings on its sides, like a shield and golden eyes as large as cups weighing half a mark, each one placed there as if enamelled in a very strange and ingenious manner, and the devil too was represented in that crown; and I believe that so he appeared to them, and that they were idolators and regarded the devil as lord."

The size of the Lucayan settlements was determined by the availability of food. The Arawaks appeared to eat very little, and Ferdinand Columbus noted that the amount a Spaniard would consume in a day would last the average Arawak a whole week. But having such poor soil for cultivation and no metal except gold for fish-hooks and spears, this abstinence was more from necessity than choice. The Lucayans grew maize, yams, sweet potatoes and cassava, from which they made *yucca* bread by drawing off the poison. All these crops were new to the Spaniards, although they knew cotton, which the Lucayans grew extensively, from the Arabs. It must be remembered that modern West Indian food plants, such as coconut, sugar cane and banana, are not indigenous and were imported from Africa by the Spaniards.

Their land the Lucayans cultivated in the immemorial manner still practised in the Out Islands. First the land was cleared by burning the underbrush. The root crops were grown in earth mounds, but maize was planted in fields or in the pockets of soil found in the honeycombed rocks. The women did the planting, carrying a bag of water-soaked grain and a pointed stick as a "dibber". Later on, the children acted as scarecrows to protect the growing corn.

A kind of rabbit which the Lucayans called *utia*, similar to the agouti still found in the Turks Islands and Jamaica, was the only land mammal native to the Bahamas. These, which the Indians prized highly as food, they hunted down with their *alcos*, a species of small, barkless yellow dog, which on occasion they roasted and ate also. Michele de Cuneo, who accompanied Columbus on the Second Voyage, tried these *perros mudos* and declared them "none too good". Indeed, considering that they were forced by food shortage to eat also the iguana, the yellow snake and the manatee or sea cow, it is perhaps surprising that the Lucayans, unlike the Caribs, did not resort to cannibalism to supplement their meat supply.

The Lucayans sometimes snared parrots with nooses and pigeons with fibre nets. But their most abundant source of food was, of course, the sea. The middens in Arawak village sites are always composed largely of mollusc shells and the bones of fish and turtle. The conch was probably as much a relished food to the Lucayan as it is to the present-day Bahamian. Fish were caught with nets, with cotton lines and hooks of bone or turtle shell or with bone-tipped harpoons. The Lucayans may also have copied the Cubans in employing a captive sucking fish to land the bigger fish.

Naturally enough, the island people were completely at home on the sea. Columbus noted how fearlessly they swam, even a league out from shore, and how expertly they handled their canoes. These dugouts varied in size from one large enough for a single rower to an outsize specimen seen in Jamaica 96 feet long and 8 feet in the beam. Such a canoe could carry as many as 150 rowers, and with each man plying his paddle shaped like a baker's shovel, could outrun the fastest European sailing ship. Each man carried a small calabash for bailing in case the rather unstable craft were overturned or swamped.

Dugouts were usually made from the trunk of a single silk cotton tree. First the selected tree was felled by fires cunningly placed at its base and then hollowed out by the same method. Only in the finishing were stone adzes and chisels used. Since they were constructed so laboriously, the Arawaks' canoes were their most prized possessions and on them they lavished their highest arts of carving. "Every *cacique* has a great canoe for himself", Columbus reported to Bernáldez, "in which he takes pride as a Castilian gentleman is proud of possessing a fine, big ship. They have their canoes carved and painted both bow and stern with ornaments so that their beauty is marvellous."

Some examples of the Arawaks' skill in wood and stone carving have come down to us and many more are doubtless to be discovered. But perhaps their finest work has been destroyed. All their most elaborate ornaments incorporating gold were melted down by the Spaniards, who used the weak excuse that they were idolatrous to camouflage their own cupidity.

At first the Spaniards were unwilling to concede that the Arawaks had any religion at all. Columbus gave this as a reason for believing that they would readily become Christians. But later inquiries showed that they had a highly developed religion, some aspects of which have persisted in backward areas to the present day.

As with the Maori people of New Zealand, the priests were the guardians of the tribal mythology and in the absence of a written language handed it down in songs. The Arawaks had an account of the origin of the world and its inhabitants that would sound no more ludicrous to a Hindu than the biblical version of Genesis. Originally all mankind had been shut up in one cave and the sun and stars in another, in the charge of an ever-watchful guardian. Once the guardian slumbered. The sun and its minions sprang into the sky and a select body of men and women, under the command of the hero Guagugiona, stepped into the light of day.

To these first people the sight of the sun was taboo. Those who dared to risk its awful glare were turned into animals, birds or trees. Thus was the earth filled with living things. The ocean and its denizens were created when a calabash full of water and bones was accidentally overturned.

The Arawaks believed in two supreme gods, one male, the other female. They also believed that man had a soul and would go after death to a paradise called *coyaba* where drought and hurricane, pain and sickness would be forgotten in an eternity of feasting and dancing. Perhaps for this reason and because of the harshness of the mundane world, they held life in rather low esteem. With apparent callousness a sick relative would be taken out into the bush and left in his hammock to die. A sick *cacique*, as a mark of respect, would be hastened on his way to *coyaba* by strangling.

Perhaps the most sinister and persistent aspects of the Arawaks' religion was the belief in spirits or *zemis*. These resided in sacred trees, in carved images or in the relics of the dead. Sickness or misfortune was the work of malignant or displeased *zemis*. Good fortune was a sign that the *zemis* were pleased. Naturally enough, the spirits had to be kept in a good frame of mind, and the greatest public festivals were held to propitiate the tribal *zemis*, or simply in their honour.

On these occasions everyone would dress in their finery and the *cacique* would lead a parade beating a wooden drum. Gifts of cassava were offered to the *zemis* and preserved as charms against the four chief scourges of the Arawaks' existence: fire, hurricane, sickness and the Caribs.

The myths and prophecies handed down by the Arawak priests from generation to generation were rich and varied as only a spoken folklore can be. Among the prophecies was one, similar to another held by the Aztecs of Mexico, that said a race of demi-gods would one day reach them from across the great eastern ocean. They would be clothed in armour and armed with the thunders and lightnings of the skies. Against them, as against the *zemis*, there could be no resistance. Only meekness and conciliation could avert a worse destiny.

III

Columbus

In the Middle Ages each of the maritime peoples of Europe had its legends of islands in the west. Imagination competed with credulity and the primitive map-makers took their choice. The Irish told tall stories of the sixth-century monk St. Brendan, who was said to have discovered three low-lying islands; Lovo, Capraria and San Borondon. Later they believed firmly in the island of Hy Brasil, which some men of Bristol in 1480 sought in vain. The Arthurian legend had its Lyonesse beyond the Scillies and Brittany its lost Atlantis. A German cartographer of 1436 penned in an island roughly in the position of Newfoundland and called it Stocafisca. In Portugal and Spain the imagined island to the west was Antillia, which seven Portuguese bishops were said to have colonised in the eighth century and sundry stray sailors to have visited later.

Ironically, no whispers of the actual discoveries of the Norsemen beyond Iceland, which culminated in the finding of Vinland (Massachusetts?) by Leif Ericson in A.D. 1000, reached the countries to the south of Scandinavia. But then it is improbable that the Norsemen themselves were aware of having discovered anything but an unattractive archipelago of sub-arctic islands. They certainly were not looking for Asia, and never sailed as far south as the Bahamas.

The first of the nine islands of the Azores was discovered around 1430 when some Portuguese boats were driven far to the west in a storm. Although the prevailing westerlies in that latitude discouraged casual exploration from the Azores, there came evidence that there were yet more lands farther to the west and south. Occasional freak storms blew strange berries and twigs on to the shores of those islands and a pilot called Vincente picked up a piece of carved wood. There was even a rumour of two bodies with flat oriental features being washed up at Flores. However, with ships returning yearly to Lisbon from farther south around Africa with valuable cargoes of ivory, gold dust, Malagueta pepper and slaves, such trifles were ignored. They awaited the inquisitive genius of Columbus.

Cristoforo Colombo was the son of a middle-class Genoese weaver who learnt his apprenticeship at sea as well as at the loom. In 1476, quite by chance, he landed in Portugal, joining his younger brother Bartholomew in his map-making shop in Lisbon. During the eight or nine years he was in Portugal, Columbus learnt to make excellent maps, sailed as far afield as Africa and Iceland, married the daughter of one of Prince Henry's captains and conceived the magnificent foolishness of his "Enterprise of the Indies".

No contemporary portrait of Columbus exists, but features common to all descriptions are his piercing blue eyes and strong jaw, the visage of a man of single-minded determination. Already by 1484, he was impatient with the slow progress of the Portuguese search for the East by way of Africa. He had a suggestion to make to King John II, or anyone who would listen, about as fantastic as the notion in 1884 that men could fly. He wanted practical men to believe that the quickest way to the East, shorter even than the closed land route through Constantinople, was by sailing west.

Much nonsense has been written about the difficulties experienced by Columbus in convincing the world that his *Empresa de las Indias* was practical. Learned men since the Ancient Greeks, and ignorant seamen who had seen ships and land disappear over the rounded world's rim, believed that the world was a sphere. If this was so, it followed that Asia could be reached either by travelling east *or* west. Columbus's task, following up a treatise written by the Florentine Toscanelli in 1474, was to convince wealthy patrons that Cipangu and Cathay could be reached "in a few days with a fair wind" by sailing west. Undercutting the most optimistic estimates, he calculated that Japan was a mere 3,000 miles from Lisbon. In fact, the air-line distance is over 11,000 miles. Columbus was thus attempting to convince the sceptical world of a fallacy, a fact conveniently forgotten by those who know that the result of his error was the rediscovery of America.

John II was impressed with Columbus, but not to the extent of giving him official support. The king had already financed an unsuccessful voyage to the mythical island of Antillia beyond the Azores, and with the successful return of Bartholomew Diaz from the Cape in 1488, he shelved any idea of a Portuguese venture to the West. In fact, Vasco da Gama discovered the sought-for route to Asia for Portugal in 1497, and when the unknown world came to be divided in 1493, the Portuguese were given the African and eastern parts and the Spaniards the West.

After Portugal, Columbus's best hopes lay with neighbouring Spain and in 1485, after the death of his wife, he left Lisbon for Palos, near Cadiz. Intermittently for six years Columbus followed the Spanish Court as it went from city to city throughout Spain. During this time his brother Bartholomew approached Henry VII of England and Charles VIII of France. Neither of these monarchs, however, was interested in the Great Enterprise and unwittingly gave up to Spain the chance of a sixteenth-century American empire.

Spain, since 1474 under the joint rule of Ferdinand of Aragon and his wife Isabella of Castille, had become by this time the first of Europe's new nation states, the creation of which brought the Middle Ages to a close. Although she had as yet no fixed capital city, all power within Spain was centralised. All affairs: agricultural, industrial, commercial, military, naval and mercantile, were concentrated under royal authority. Later on, when Spain expanded, it was naturally the central authority of the state which controlled all aspects of colonisation.

But when Columbus arrived at Palos there was still one outstanding barrier to Spain's expansion. For centuries the War of Reconquest had been going on to drive the Mohammedan Moors from the Spanish mainland, and at this very time the campaign to expel them from their last stronghold, Grenada, was reaching its climax. Although Isabella was attentive to Columbus and provided him with a small pension of 12,000 *maravedis* a year, all energies and wealth were concentrated on the matter in hand. It was not until April 1492, three months after the fall of Grenada, that Isabella gave Columbus, now 41 years old, the aid he sought.

It was thus hardly a coincidence that the expulsion of the Moors was followed so soon by the discovery of America. The *Reconquista* was followed naturally by the age of the *Conquistadores*.

Isabella gave Columbus roughly the equivalent of £10,000 to outfit his expedition, provided the caravels *Niña* and *Pinta* of about sixty tons each, and declared that the mariners engaged would be on the royal payroll. Much more valuable in the event of success were the Articles drawn up on April 30, 1492. *Don Cristóbal de Colón* as he was styled, was to be hereditary "Admiral of the Ocean Sea" and Viceroy of all the lands he discovered, to possess a tenth of all their produce and to have the option of an eighth share in any trading voyage.

Columbus chartered his famous flagship *Santa María*, a Galician *não* of about 100 tons burden, from Juan de la Cosa of Santona. He recruited 90 men as crews for the three ships, with the brothers Martín and Vicente Pinzón as commanders of the *Pinta* and *Niña* respectively. With the exception of the two Italians and a Portuguese, most of the men were drawn from Palos and the other towns of Andalusia. Contrary to one myth, they were a well-balanced and seamanlike crew; not the rakings of the local jails.

After ten weeks of preparation, Columbus set sail from Palos at dawn on August 2, 1492. Wishing to avoid the westerlies which he knew blew steadily in the Azores, he set course southwards to the Spanish islands of the Canaries, where the North East Trades begin. After a pause of three weeks at Gomera while the *Niña*'s lateen mainsail was changed to square rig, the fleet finally set out across the uncharted ocean on September 6.

The story of the 33-day voyage has been told and retold many thousands of times. Considering its success and lack of incident, the most remarkable fact was the faultiness of Columbus's navigation. On his only attempt at a celestial "fix", he placed the *Santa María* in the latitude of Labrador—an obvious error. Even in dead reckoning, Columbus overestimated the fleet's progress by ten per cent, so that the "faulty" record he gave out to hearten the crew was nearer to the truth than that in his private log.

Despite several false alarms occasioned by low clouds, the fleet caught no sight of the legendary Antillia. Instead, on September 16, they became the first sailors to venture into the mysterious weed of the Sargasso Sea, for nineteen days expecting at any moment it would thicken into an impenetrable mass. The easterly wind was so constant that the men began to fear that they would never beat back to Spain against it. In one day they sailed no less than 182 miles. But still there was no sight of land.

On the night of October 8, great flocks of migratory birds were seen against the moon, and Columbus ordered a change of course to WSW. to follow them towards land. Upon this chance hung much in history. Had the fleet continued on its westward course, it would probably have made landfall in northern Eleuthera. Sailing through Hole-in-the-Wall and the Providence Channels into the Gulf Stream, it would have been carried north along the seaboard of North America. These parts might have been settled first by the Spaniards and not the English.

Unknown to them, however, the three small ships were now scudding towards the southern Bahamas. On October 10, after 31 days at sea, mutiny flared up on the flagship. No sailors had ever been so long out of sight of land and lived to tell the tale. Even Columbus, whose soft words had kept the muttering seamen at their posts up to that time, must have begun to wonder when Cipangu was to come into sight. He promised to turn back if land were not sighted within three days.

Immediately things began to look brighter. On the 11th, the ships picked up unmistakable signs that land was near; a branch with flowers on it, a piece of cane, a fragment of carved wood. That night was one of excitement in the fleet.

At 10 p.m., before moonrise, with the three ships dashing along before an easterly gale at more than nine knots, Columbus thought he saw a light ahead, "like a wax candle rising and falling". Two crew members claimed to see it also. But they were all mistaken. The *Santa María* was still about 35 miles from land; nor would Lucayans have been fishing in 3,000 fathoms on such a turbulent night. Nevertheless, the imaginary light was the basis of Columbus's own successful claim for the 10,000 *maravedis* a year promised by Isabella to the first man to sight land.

The reward properly belonged to Rodrigo de Triaña, forecastle lookout on the *Pinta*, which had stretched ahead of the other two ships. At 2 a.m., he sighted a dark line of land about six miles ahead, with a sliver of sand gleaming silver under the

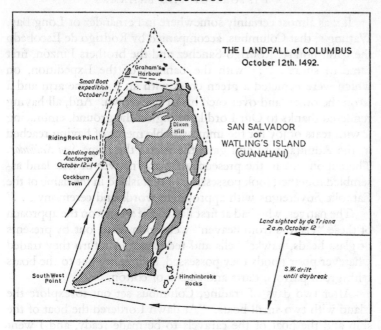

THE LANDFALL of COLUMBUS
October 12th. 1492.

Graham's Harbour

Small Boat expedition October 13

Dixon Hill

SAN SALVADOR
or
WATLING'S ISLAND
(GUANAHANI)

Riding Rock Point

Landing and Anchorage October 12-14

Cockburn Town

Land sighted by de Triana 2 a.m. October 12

S.W. drift until daybreak

South West Point

Hinchinbroke Rocks

moon, and shouted the momentous words, "Tierra! Tierra!"

The fleet hove to and tacked until daybreak, when it was seen that they were off the south-east corner of a small island almost surrounded by a reef. Putting on sail, the three ships searched the western side until they found a gap in the reef, and there they landed.

The island at which the Spaniards landed, called by the natives Guanahani, was without doubt the island of Watling's, since 1926 officially called also by the name given it by Columbus: San Salvador. And yet around this fact has raged more bootless controversy than any other in Bahamian history. Advocates have been found for Grand Turk, Cat Island, Rum Cay, Samana Cay and Mayaguana as the landfall of Columbus. But the arguments of Muñoz (1793), Captain Becher (1856) and Rudolf Cronau (1890), reinforced by the researches of S. E. Morison put forth in his excellent biography of the explorer (1941), prove conclusively that it was Watling's and none of these which first saw the Spaniards.

It was almost certainly somewhere in Fernández or Long Bay, Watling's, that Columbus, accompanied by Rodrigo de Escobedo the royal notary, Rodrigo Sánchez and the brothers Pinzón, first came to shore . . . "with the banners of the Expedition, on which were depicted a green cross with an F on one arm and a Y on the other, and over each his or her crown. And, all having rendered thanks to Our Lord kneeling on the ground, embracing it with tears of joy for the immeasurable mercy of having reached it, the Admiral rose and gave the island the name *San Salvador*. Thereupon . . . in the presence of many natives of that land assembled together, took possession of that island in the name of the Catholic Sovereigns with appropriate words and ceremony . . ."

The natives, who had at first fled to the woods on the approach of these "visitors from heaven" were soon lured out by presents of glass beads, hawks' bells and red caps. In return they traded whatever poor goods they possessed, swimming out to the boats with green parrots, darts and skeins of cotton.

After two days of trading, Columbus set out to explore the island with two small boats. "At dawn I ordered the boat of the ship and the boat of the caravels to be made ready, and I went along the island in a NNE. direction, to explore the other parts of the island, namely that which lies to the east. I was afraid to do this on account of a great reef of rocks which entirely surrounded the island, although there is within a harbour wide and deep enough to shelter all the vessels in Christendom; but the entrance is very narrow. True, there are some rocks within this harbour, but the water is there as smooth as a pond. I went to see all this this morning in order that I might be able to give an account of everything to Your Highnesses; and also to find out where a fort could be built. I discovered a piece of land which looks like an island, although it is not one . . . in two days it could easily be cut off and converted into an island."

In 1890, Cronau made a systematic exploration of Watling's Island following the details given in Columbus's Journal. He entered the placid expanse of water within the reef at the north end of the island, now known as Graham's Harbour, and noted the rocks described by the discoverer. He also saw the promontory selected as the site of a fortress, which had in fact since been cut off from the mainland by the action of the sea. On the islet formed he found a rusted eighteenth-century cannon, showing that someone had concurred with Columbus in choosing the spot for defence. Cronau also drew attention to the fact that Columbus described San Salvador as having a large lake in the interior, a feature uniquely possessed by Watling's among the islands which claim the first landfall. The only remaining controversial point was that Columbus gave the impression of seeing islands in many directions from San Salvador. In fact, the nearest land to Watling's are two islands, one 20 miles to the SW. and the other 35 miles to the WSW.; both, in fact, over the horizon.

It was to the former island, now known as Rum Cay, which he christened more nobly Santa María de la Concepción, that the Admiral and his fleet set sail in the afternoon of October 14. He was guided onwards by the enthusiastic signs of the natives, who probably mistook his inquiries for gold and great cities as requests for directions to other islands and settlements such as theirs. It did not at first occur to the simple Lucayans that the Spaniards attached far more value than they to the small gold ornaments which they wore. Nor, for that matter, does it seem to have occurred to Columbus that the Lucayans whom he took from San Salvador and other islands as guides, hostages and exhibits for the sovereigns, had any just cause to object. "They ought to be good servants and of good skill," he wrote, "for I see that they repeat very quickly all that is said to them; and I believe that they would easily be made Christians, because it seemed to me that they belonged to no religion. I, please Our Lord, will carry off six of them, so that they may learn to speak . . ."

From Rum Cay on October 16 the fleet sailed 22 miles to an island which Columbus had seen in the west. Actually, he had at first thought it a chain of islands, since the tops of the low hills appeared first over the skyline, spread out in a chain. This was Long Island, which he named Fernandina, and along the 60-mile shore of which he coasted for three days. He went ashore at native villages in the north and south near the modern settlements of Burnt Ground and Roses and there he obtained that commodity so valuable in the Bahamas, fresh water. But although the mariners caught their first sight of hammocks, tobacco, indian corn and a tree that had "branches of different kinds all

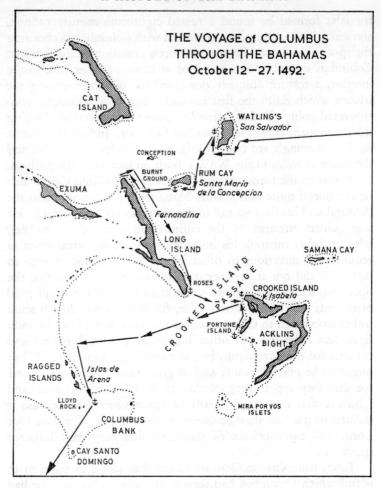

THE VOYAGE of COLUMBUS
THROUGH THE BAHAMAS
October 12 – 27. 1492.

CAT
ISLAND

WATLING'S
San Salvador

CONCEPTION

BURNT
GROUND

RUM CAY
Santa Maria
de la Concepcion

EXUMA

Fernandina

LONG
ISLAND

SAMANA CAY

ROSES

CROOKED ISLAND PASSAGE

CROOKED ISLAND
Isabela

FORTUNE
ISLAND

ACKLINS
BIGHT

RAGGED
ISLANDS

Islas de
Arena

LLOYD
ROCK

MIRA POR VOS
ISLETS

COLUMBUS
BANK

CAY SANTO
DOMINGO

in one trunk" in Fernandina, gold was noticeably lacking. This
time the Spaniards understood that it was to be found in large
quantities towards the south-east at a place the natives called
Samoete.

Without delay they set out across the deep Crooked Island
Passage and came to Long Cay, which Columbus called Isabela.
For four days he ranged up and down the shores of Fortune and
Crooked Islands, seeking a way through the shoals of Acklins

Bight to the gilded cities he felt must lie beyond. Columbus and his captains went ashore again and he described in glowing words the verdant pastures, the marvellous flocks of birds, the strange plants and the iguana which they tracked and killed. The Bahamas were far more lushly wooded then than now, but Columbus certainly exaggerated in his enthusiastic descriptions of the islands. The southern tip of Long Island he named Cabo Verde and the southern point of Fortune Island, Cabo Hermoso. This was all propaganda for the sovereigns.

Daily the explorers hoped to find some outlying inhabitants of Japan, light-skinned and richly attired as in the pages of Marco Polo. Everywhere, however, they found the same poor savages, gesticulating cheerfully ever onwards towards the phantom gold. Now they pointed to the south-west, shouting "Colba" (Cuba), and Columbus thought he heard the magic name of Kubla Khan. Hopefully he ordered sails set once more and on October 24 and 25 the fleet crossed over to the dangerous rocks and shallows of the Great Bahama Bank.

For the Lucayans in their dugouts this would be the safest route to Cuba, island-hopping from cay to cay with only thirty miles of deep water to cross. With his much larger ships, it needed all of Columbus's sailing skill to carry the fleet safely down the chain of the Ragged Islands, which he christened the Islas de Arena. Finally, on October 27th, he crossed the arm of the Bank now named after him, by way of Lloyd Rock and Cay Santo Domingo, and left Bahamian waters for the last time.

In all, Columbus was only in the Bahamas for fifteen days. His later explorations dwarfed into small perspective this short voyage through the islands. Although he would never be convinced that he had not discovered the westward route to Asia, Columbus by his four great voyages made the vast Spanish Empire possible and opened up a new era in the history of the world. Naturally, it is a proud fact to Bahamians that it was the discovery of one of their own small islands which began such mighty processes. Understandably, the day of the Admiral's landing at Watling's—October 12, 1492—is as well known to Bahamian children as the year 1066 is to English and the date July 4, to Americans.

IV

Spanish Colony

The voyages of Columbus were followed almost immediately by Spanish colonisation. The right of settlement was added to the right of discovery and conquest, and the Papal mandate of 1493 which gave to Spain practically the whole of the western hemisphere. Navidad, the first European colony in the New World, was founded near Cape Haitien in Hispaniola on Columbus's first voyage, and by 1506 when the explorer died there were probably 20,000 Spaniards living in America.

Inevitably the Lucayan Islands, flat, infertile and without mines or any valuable products, aroused little interest among the Spaniards when compared with Hispaniola and Cuba, Mexico and Peru. Despite rumours current at the beginning of the nineteenth century, there is no evidence that the Spaniards ever made a permanent settlement in the Bahamas. The Spanish ruins on Cat Island mentioned by Peter Henry Bruce (1782) have either passed away or were imaginary in the first place.

Until the coming of other nationalities to the Caribbean, when their strategic position gave them a certain importance, the Bahamas occupied a very insignificant place in the Spanish imperial scheme. The one commodity which the islands possessed and the Spaniards desired was their Lucayan population. The Arawak inhabitants of the richer islands were too few, too weak and unwilling to work for their new masters. Moreover, they succumbed in hundreds of thousands to disease, starvation, ill-treatment and even suicide by eating the poisonous juice of the cassava. "I have found many dead in the road", wrote Las Casas, "others gasping under the trees, and others in the pangs of death faintly crying 'Hunger! Hunger!' Many killed themselves in despair, and even mothers overcame the powerful instinct of nature, and destroyed the infants at their breasts, to spare them a life of wretchedness."

Some sort of case can be made out for the Spanish colonists. Especially after the arrival of Nicholas de Ovando as royal governor of Española in 1502, the *encomienda* system of mines and plantations demanded an ever-increasing labour force while at the same time the native population was decreasing alarmingly. Spanish settlers were given large grants of land and authority over a large number of natives who were practically to be used as slaves; but in most cases the natives were just not available to work the land. Enterprising sailors, merchants and planters set out to remedy the deficiency, and in this way the entire archipelago of the Bahamas was both explored and depopulated. As early as 1513 Peter Martyr wrote that "in the waters off the northern coasts of Cuba . . . lie so many islands, great and small, that I scarcely believe what is told of them; although I am kept informed of all the discoveries. Within the twenty years that have elapsed since the Spaniards arrived there they claim to have explored 406 of these islands, and to have carried off forty thousand inhabitants of both sexes as slaves, to satisfy their unquenchable appetite for gold."

Actual details are scanty, but it is certain that between 1500 and 1520 the entire population of the Bahamas, probably about 20,000 Lucayans, was carried off. Las Casas, who with typical exaggeration estimated that half a million Lucayans disappeared this way, recorded that "when some pious persons embarked to visit these isles after the ravage the Spaniards had made in them, they found but eleven people left there". In 1513 Peter Martyr wrote that "there only remains today a very small number of them, either in the Spanish colonies or in the archipelago itself" and in the same year Ponce de León could only find a single old crone in his travels through the islands. Later Spanish writers all refer to the islands as being "destitute of inhabitants".

According to one author, the Spanish slavers preyed upon a Lucayan superstition. Subconsciously recalling their South American origins, the Lucayans believed that when they died their souls migrated to the lands in the south. Thus they were easily persuaded to take ship to visit unknown territories where

39

they could meet the spirits of their departed fathers and ancestors.

Conditions on the slave ships pictured by Peter Martyr and Las Casas foreshadow those described in a later century by the Abolitionists. "It was related to me for certain", wrote the saintly Bishop of Chiapa, "that a ship going from *Hispaniola* to the Island of *Lucayos* sayl'd thither without any compasse, only by the Carkasses that floated up and down the sea." Peter Martyr, with an even more fluent imagination, told of Lucayans exiled in Hispaniola escaping to the northern mountains, "where they might breathe the air wafted from their native country; with extended arms and open mouths they seemed to drink in their native air, and when misery reduced them to exhaustion, they dropped dead upon the ground." He also told of an ingenious Lucayan who fashioned a dugout and with two companions set out for the Bahamas, only to be recaptured 200 miles from the coast of Hispaniola.

Besides the plantations and goldmines, the Lucayans were in great demand as divers in the pearl fisheries of Margarita, near Trinidad. "By this fishing trade the *Spaniards* have destroy'd all the People of the *Lucay* Islands", reads a seventeenth-century translation of Las Casas, "which were the most skilful and experienc'd in this Employment; and the reason why one of those *Indians* was sold for fifty Crowns or more, and sometimes for a hundred, was because they were marvellously dexterous at swimming and diving." At the fisheries the Lucayans were severely maltreated by rapacious Spaniards. Overworked and underfed, many perished by drowning or being devoured by "sea monsters". "Their food is nothing but fish, and the very same that contains the Pearl" wrote the outraged Las Casas, not dreaming that one day oysters would be the delight of epicures and conch the favourite dish of latter-day Bahamians, "with a small portion of the bread which that Countrey affords." The gentle Lucayans were brutalised by their toil. "Their hair also, which is by nature black, is hereby chang'd and made of the same colour as that of the Sea Wolves; their bodies are also so besprinkled with the froth of the sea, that they appear rather like monsters than men."

Vincente Pinzón, captain of the *Niña* on Columbus's first voyage, lost two ships on the Exumas in 1499, but the first explorer of the Bahamas after the discovery of whom we know any details was Juan Ponce de León. Although he was later given a roving commission to subdue and recruit Caribs, his interest in the Bahamas was obviously not the rounding up of slaves but in a quest far more glamorous; the search for "Bimini" and the legendary Fountain of Youth.

Ponce de León, who was probably born in 1460 at San Tervas de Campos in Spain, went to Hispaniola on the second voyage of Columbus in 1493. He was the first coloniser, governor and chief justice of Puerto Rico, then called San Juan de Borinquen; but in the typical *conquistador* pattern, he quickly fell from favour once the island was fully subdued. A protégé of Ovando, he was squeezed out of power by Diego Columbus and his lieutenants in 1511. Returning to Spain, Ponce de León obtained permission to carve out a personal empire in the unknown islands to the north of Hispaniola and Cuba.

Of these islands the Spaniards had heard enticing rumours. The Lucayans spoke of the land of Bimini where there was a fountain with magical properties similar to that reputed to be found in the African domains of Prester John. Eden's translation of Peter Martyr (1612) spoke of "an Islande, about three hundred and XXV leagues from Hispaniola as they say which have searched the same, named Boiuca or Agnaneo, in which is a continual sprynge of runnynge water of such marvelous vertue, that the water thereof being dronk, perhappes with some dyete, maketh owld men yonge ageyne". Hakluyt's version of the same author told of Dean Anglianus of Cuba who had a Lucayan slave christened Andreas Barbatus (unlike most of his compatriots he wore a beard), whose father had been rejuvenated by the spring and had begotten children in his old age. Others spoke of a rich and fertile land, heavily populated and crying out for Spanish exploitation and settlement.

A Capitulation signed by King Ferdinand at Burgos on February 23, 1512, stated that as long as Ponce de León paid for outfitting the expedition, he would be invested with the governorship and administration of justice for life of any lands he discovered, along with a tenth of all profits for the first twelve years. Any forts that were erected could be charged to the royal treasury. Although the King waived his traditional fifth for the first six years, he retained his right to allocate the Indians to the settlers for compulsory labour. No foreigners were to be allowed to settle in the new lands.

Ponce de León set sail from St. German, Puerto Rico, with three ships on March 3, 1513. Although the only detailed account of this important voyage was written by Herrera as late as 1601, that writer had access to contemporary logbooks and

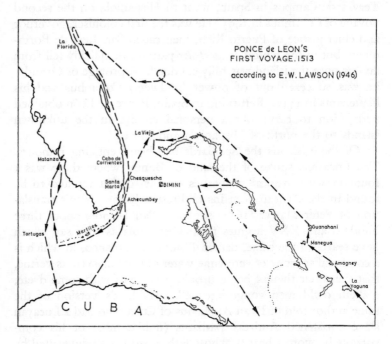

PONCE de LEON'S
FIRST VOYAGE. 1513

according to E.W. LAWSON (1946)

we can follow the itinerary almost exactly. On March 9, the ships reached the Caicos Islands, travelling on during the next five days to three islands called La Yaguna, Amaguayo and Manegua. These were probably Mayaguana, Samana and Rum Cay, all fairly well known to the Spaniards by that time. On March 14 they reached Guanahani, the San Salvador of Columbus, "where they dressed a ship to cross the windward gulf of the islands of the Lucayos". They then sailed steadily to the NW., out of sight of land until Sunday, March 27th, Easter Day, when they sighted a small island some miles to the westward but did not stop. Almost certainly this was Elbow Cay, off the eastern bulge of Abaco.

Two days later, having caught as yet no signs of the hoped-for Bimini, Ponce de León altered course some points to the east, and after weathering a storm he came in sight of land on April 2, 1513. Here he landed and stayed six days, calling the green country La Florida, though the native name was Cautia. It was once thought that this landfall was somewhere in the neighbourhood of Cape Kennedy, but strong arguments have been put forward by E. W. Lawson that it was much farther north, near the present site of St. Augustine, 30° 08′ N. It must be remembered that no European had yet discovered the Florida Channel which flows as fast as $4\frac{1}{2}$ knots in a northerly direction, and Ponce de León's navigator had no way of correcting for the drift. The three ships were therefore carried much farther north than their estimated position. It was only on their voyage down the coast that the Spaniards observed, with amazement, the action of the current, which made a mockery of the winds.

Hugging the coast near the Florida Keys and dealing with the Seminoles sufficiently to discover that they were far less peaceable than the Arawaks, Ponce de León spent April, May and June exploring his new domain, without discovering Bimini and the elusive fountain. On June 24 he came to a huge and mountainous island and was disappointed to find that it was Cuba. Turning back, he sailed once more for the north, touching at Achecumbey (Matacumbe Keys) and Chesquescha (Tequesta Point, Miami) before setting sail NE. into the unexplored Bahamas. "They navigated up to some islands that were in the banks of the Lucayos more to the west", wrote Herrera, "and anchored in them the 18th, of July, where they watered, and they put the name of La Vieja, for an old Indian woman, without any other person, that they found, and they are in 28°." These were probably the small cays, Sand Cay and Memory Rock, at the western edge of the Little Bahama Bank, for "the 25th they went out from the islets, in lookout for Bimini, navigating among some islands he took to be overflowed, and found it to be Bahama". This is a perfect description of the mangrove "swash" and shoals of the Bank, in such contrast to the yawning blue chasms of the channels. It is an interesting fact that *bajamar* means shallow in Spanish; Herrera was probably not quoting a Lucayan name, but the name given to the island by the Spanish between 1513 and 1601.

After gingerly exploring the northern shores of Grand Bahama, Ponce de León returned to La Vieja on August 6. For the next two months he sailed through the Bahamas back to Puerto Rico, losing one of his ships by wreck, though the crew was saved. As far as can be gathered from the somewhat involved description, he seems to have visited Abaco, northern Eleuthera, the Berry Islands and Andros, before returning to his starting point on October 15, 1513.

If Ponce de León actually visited the two small cays the natives called Bimini he did not realise it. He left two navigators, Ortubia and Alaminos, behind in the islands with instructions to continue the search. Some months later they returned with the news that they had found the legendary island, though they seem to have glossed over the paucity of their discovery. Early in 1514 Ponce de León went back to Spain to seek a firmer title to his lands, full of exaggerated tales of their beauty and promise.

Impressed by the explorer's tales, the Crown granted Juan Ponce de León the title of Don and Adelantado of Florida and Bimini, providing he set out to found a colony within three years. Besides this he obtained a *requerimiento* from the Bishop of Burgos allowing him to make war on and subdue the natives in the Catholic cause—in other words, to enslave them for labour on the future plantations. On September 27, 1514, a set of Ordinances for Florida and Bimini was signed by Queen Joanna the Mad. Special favours were granted to the first 500 settlers for ten years, as in the case of Hispaniola. No men condemned by the Inquisition were to be settlers, nor their sons or grandsons. Jews were ineligible even if converted, as were any "Genovese, or Florentines or foreigners from outside our Realms, under the penalty of removal; neither may they send to the said islands any sort of merchandise by their factors or servants or in the company of any Spaniard, under penalty of losing the said merchandise". Each of the first 500 settlers was to enjoy the use of 80 Indians as servants.

Obviously Florida, with its unexplored depths, was a far more profitable prospect than the infertile and depopulated Bahamas.

But Ponce de León was not destined to be the first Spanish coloniser of either the North American mainland or the Bahama Islands. Delayed for years by preoccupations in Puerto Rico, he did not set sail to found his colony until 1521 when he went out with two ships on his final venture, at the age of 61. Landing at Estero Bay, the ageing explorer was mortally wounded in an encounter with the Indians and had to be taken back to Cuba, where he died.

By the time of de León's death, other Spanish explorers such as de Allyon, Grijalva and Cordova had pushed back the curtain of obscurity that still concealed the American coast. Peter Martyr, for instance, gives an excellent account of de Allyon's voyage (1515?) with two ships searching for slaves for Hispaniola. Failing to find any in the Bahamas, he sailed on, reaching the American coast somewhere in the latitude of Virginia and bringing back many fantastic tales of the natives and their customs. Florida was discovered to be a peninsula and not an island and its land crossing was favoured as an easier route from the Gulf of Mexico to the Atlantic than the feared Bahama Channel. The terrible sufferings of the early land explorers such as Narváez and the successful passage of the Channel from the south by Alaminos in 1519, however, made the Florida Strait the invariable route from the Caribbean back to Spain.

The earliest maps which show the Bahamas indicate their early exploration. The first map of the New World, that of Juan de la Cosa (1500), shows vaguely delineated islands north of Cuba and Hispaniola with the names ascribed to them by Columbus; Habacoa (Abaco), Yumey (Exuma), Guanahani (San Salvador), Mamana (Rum Cay), Samana (Long Island), Someto (Crooked Island) and Yucayo (Caicos). The map in the first edition of Peter Martyr's *De Orbe Novo* (1511) does not show the names of individual Bahama islands, which are shown as somewhat indiscriminate blobs, but shows Florida as a huge island, larger than Cuba, called Isla de Beimeni. The Turin Map of 1523 is far more explicit, listing 12 islands. Bimene is shown, as well as Bahama. Habacoa has become Iucayonique and Yumey, Suma. Eleuthera is shown as Ziguateo (later it was to be called Cigateo, Segatoo and Eygatea) and Cat Island as Guanima. Guanahani is shown again and Mamana has become Manigua. Long Island

is called Iucanacan, Someto is Sumete and Inagua and Mayaguana are given their modern spellings. No more accurate map
than that of 1523 was drawn until White and Hood's of 1590
and 1592 and de Laet's of 1630. This fact is significant.

As time went on, Hispaniola lost its supremacy as the Spanish
headquarters in the Caribbean. Cuba, first subdued by Diego
Velasquez in 1511, under its own Governor-General, became a
rival in wealth and importance. Havana, established as early as
1514, became the focal point of trade and bullion on its way back
to Spain; the rendezvous of the *Flota* and the *Galleones*. The
Bahamas, technically a province subordinate to Cuba, lapsed into
obscurity, known only for its rocks and shoals, so fatal to navigation; a place to be feared and shunned. In 1595, for example,
a whole Spanish fleet of 17 ships was wrecked off Abaco. Only
when rival nations, the French first then the English, sought
settlements in Florida and Virginia commanding the Channel,
did this situation change.

V

The Coming of the English

English explorers were not far behind the Spanish, but their activities were inhibited both by the lack of financial support and by an official reluctance to offend the power of Catholic Spain. England was in the Catholic fold until 1534 and the papal Bull *Inter Caetera* of 1493 had specifically forbidden all nations other than Spain "to go for the sake of trade or any other reason whatsoever to the said islands and countries after they have been discovered". Even after the accession of Protestant Elizabeth I in 1558, English navigators could not obtain sanction to claim or settle any regions occupied by "a Christian Prince", though the Bull of Alexander VI was formally repudiated on many occasions and England was actively, if not officially, at war with Spain from 1567 until 1604.

In actual fact, John Cabot, a Venetian sailing in the service of Henry VII, was the first European since the ancient Vikings to reach the mainland of America. His landing at the "New Founde Lande" and "Baccalao" (Nova Scotia) in 1497 ante-dated the South American landfall of Amerigo Vespucci or Christopher Columbus by several months. Cabot sailed south along the eastern shores of North America and the *Matthew* might have become the first English ship in the Bahamas and the Caribbean had not a shortage of supplies forced a return to England. As it was, the discoveries of John Cabot were the basis for all later English claims to the eastern American seaboard north of Florida.

There was an unsupported Spanish report of an English ship off the coast of South America in 1500 and this may possibly have been Sebastian Cabot; but the first English voyage to the Caribbean of which we know any details was that of John Rut in the

Mary Guilford in 1527. Rut sailed down the North American coast and probably through the Bahamas to Puerto Rico and Santo Domingo, Hispaniola, where he traded between November 19 and 26, 1527. The English exchanged cloth for local products, but although the local authorities duly reported to Seville, details of the transactions were obscured for fear that the goods would be confiscated or fines levied. The Spanish settlers, starved of goods from home, were more than willing to trade with any European ship, in spite of the ordinances of the Spanish Government. This attitude of divided loyalties was particularly apparent during the three famous trading voyages of John Hawkins to the Caribbean between 1563 and 1568.

John Hawkins was the first Englishman to trade in African slaves, a commodity for which the demand was almost insatiable. Undoubtedly, Hawkins's aim was to obtain official permission for English trade in the Caribbean and he even went as far as to send two cargoes of sugar and hides to San Lucar in Spain for sale in 1563. It was a hopeless quest, however; the goods were seized and the unprovoked attack by a Spanish fleet upon Hawkins's flotilla at San Juan de Uloa in 1568 was the beginning of a long and bitter struggle in the Caribbean for the right to trade and form colonies.

Hawkins probably knew the Bahamas well and was certainly well versed in the difficulties of the Florida Channel. This vital artery of Spanish trade became a focus of interest among the French and English freebooters to rival the more famous route across the Isthmus of Panama. Indeed, French Huguenot corsairs had already begun to prowl the Old Bahama Channel north of Cuba, to threaten Havana and to show an interest in the mainland of Florida. As early as 1561 a Spanish ordinance forbade any merchant ship to enter the waters around the Bahamas without an escort. In 1583, William Hawkins, brother of Sir John, ranged the waters between Cuba and the Bahamas and caused panic in Havana.

Somewhat belatedly, the English began to show an interest in colonisation as well as trade and plunder. In 1578 Queen Elizabeth I granted to Sir Humphrey Gilbert the right to settle in any land in North America not already colonised by the Spanish or French, and before he set out to form a settlement in

Newfoundland in 1583 he was granted certain proprietary rights over the whole of North America, presumably including the Bahamas. After Gilbert's death by drowning while returning from this disastrous expedition, his half-brother Sir Walter Raleigh took up the cause of English colonisation. In a royal patent dated March 25, 1584, Elizabeth I granted Raleigh—her current favourite—the right to form a colony in North America, with proprietary jurisdiction extending 600 miles north and south of any settlement formed within three years of the grant. Had Raleigh chosen to establish his colony in the present Carolina he would have become the first certain proprietor of the Bahamas, though in fact his Virginia colony on Roanoke Island was a little over 600 miles from the closest Bahamian land.

Forbidden by the Queen to go in person, Sir Walter Raleigh sent out Amadas and Barlow to reconnoitre for a site, and persuaded Richard Hakluyt to write his first book advocating English colonisation. This was the *Discourse of Western Planting* (1584), a pioneer work which put forward many ideas later crystallised as Mercantilism. Among Hakluyt's arguments was the idea that an English American colony should be a base for attacking the Spaniards, and it is unfortunate that the explorers did not know the Bahamas well enough to place their colony there. At least the islands were no less fertile than the sandy islands of Pimlico sound and had many better harbours.

Amadas and Barlow took the usual route to the New World, by the Canaries and Puerto Rico, and then sailed through the Florida Channel to the region of Cape Fear. They were obviously in a hurry; gave a wide berth to the most northerly Spanish settlement, Santa Elena (Port Royal S. Carolina) and carried back exaggerated reports of the suitability of Roanoke. The first colonists, under the command of Sir Richard Grenville, set out from England on April 9, 1585, and actually sailed through the Bahamas. Had they not been misled by Barlow's report, and could they have foretold the unhappy future of the first Virginia colonies, they might well have elected to remain in the islands.

In fact the Spanish feared that this might happen. As the English fleet of seven ships passed Portugal, Don Alvaro de Bazan wrote to the Casa de la Contratación from Lisbon that "of their intentions nothing is known except that they expect more ships and appear to intend to settle. It is presumed that they will go to Florida or to an island 30 leagues long which lies in the Bahama (Channel), by which the fleets must sail."

Grenville kept the Spaniards guessing at his plans. Reaching Dominica via the Canaries in the remarkable space of 29 days from Plymouth, he sailed by St. Croix to Tallaboa Bay in Puerto Rico. Here, where he intended to rendezvous with ships that had been delayed, he built a strong encampment, but set sail again when Spanish reconnaissance parties appeared. Grenville then passed through the Mona Passage, where he took two minor prizes, to Isabella in northern Hispaniola. There he stayed a week, being cordially but warily entertained at a banquet and bullfight by the local governor, while John White recorded the local flora and fauna and the settlers gathered banana cuttings for Virginia.

Still with only three ships, Grenville set sail on June 7, 1585, towards the NW. The admiral was almost drowned while hunting for manatee in a small boat off the Turks Islands, and when the company landed at the Caicos looking for salt they found none. The journey through the Bahamas proper was recorded with tantalizing brevity in the journal of an anonymous crew member of the flagship *Lion*, possibly Arthur Barlow:

" The 12. we ankered at Guanema, and landed.

The 15. and 16. we ankered and landed at Sygateo.

The 20. we fell with the mayne of Florida."

Obviously, the colonists sailed via Cat Island and Eleuthera through the Providence Channels to the Florida Strait, but how much more we would like to know of this eight-day voyage— especially concerning signs of habitation and the depredations of the Spaniards.

In 1586, towards the end of his great West Indian raid, Sir Francis Drake entered the Old Bahama Channel but was not strong enough to attack Havana. His fleet anchored for the night of June 4 off Bucaraneo (Bimini?) before passing on to sack St. Augustine and St. Helena. In the following year, while carrying the settlers for Raleigh's second Virginia colony, John White sailed from Hispaniola to the Caicos Islands, where he again failed to find salt but noticed vast rookeries of "swannes" (flamingoes?). He was careful, however, to steer clear of the

Bahamas and went on direct to Roanoke. In 1590 White, who was a notable artist and cartographer, published a map of Virginia and the Bahamas which showed Bahama, Cigateo, Iani, Iabo, Moyagora and Guinima, as well as many unnamed islands and huge areas of shallow water and rocks. Almost certainly the Englishmen had formed the same opinions of the Bahamas held by the Spaniards at that time: unprofitable islands made all the less attractive by the treacherous shoals which surrounded them.

Although English privateers such as Newport, Middleton, Frost, Wood, King and Roberts swarmed round the approaches to the Florida Straits like wasps round a jam pot throughout the later stages of the Spanish war, English colonial activity was confined to Chesapeake Bay, where a permanent colony was founded in 1607, Bermuda and New England. It was not until 1629 that England laid formal claim to the Bahamas.

On October 30, 1629, Charles I granted to his Attorney-General Sir Robert Heath proprietary rights over the area of the American mainland (as described in a 1632 recapitulation of the grant) "betwixt one & thirety & 36 degrees of northerne latitude inclusively placed (yet hitherto untild, neither inhabited by ours or the subjects of any other Christian king, Prince or state But in some parts of it inhabited by certaine Barbarous men who have not any knowledge of the Divine Deitye) He being about to lead thither a Colonye of men large & plentifull, professing the true religion; sedulously & industriously applying themselves to the culture of the sayd lands & to merchandising to be performed by industry & at his owne charges & others by his example . . . & alsoe all those our islands of beagus [sic] Bahama & all other Isles & Islands lying southerly there . . ."

Sir Robert Heath was an ardent royalist who had distinguished himself by his defence of the royal prerogative in the difficult years of conflict between James I and Charles I and the parliamentary lawyers. Born at Brasted, Kent, in 1575, he was educated at Tonbridge School before entering Clifford's Inn in 1591. Called to the Bar in 1603, he rose quickly through the legal ranks, becoming Solicitor-General in 1621. Knighted in the same year, he became Attorney-General in 1625, the year of Charles I's accession. As Attorney-General Heath spoke ingeniously against the Petition of Right (1628) and was active in prosecutions before the unpopular Court of Star Chamber, including that of Sir John Eliot, one of the parliamentary heroes. By 1629 he was at the climax of his career, rich in the royal favour. Despite his humble origins, he was given privileges in America even greater than those offered to Sir Humphrey Gilbert and Sir Walter Raleigh.

The proprietary rights enjoyed by Sir Robert Heath in Carolina (as Charles I allowed the new province to be called) and the Bahamas were to be similar to those of the Bishops Palatine of County Durham. The land was to be held by Heath and his heirs or assignees as if they were tenants-in-chief under the old feudal system, having subtenants under them liable to knight service. The nominal rent to the king was a chaplet of 20 oz. of pure gold, inscribed with the words *Deos* [sic] *Coronet Opus Suum*; payable, however, only when the king visited the territory.

The rights of the proprietors were to include all Royalties such as whales and sturgeons; the control of all "veines, mines or pits either upon or conceal'd of Gold, Silver Jewells & precious stones & all other things whatsoever"; the patronage and advowson of all churches; the right to build forts and war-ships and to levy musters and declare martial law; the right to confer titles and grant charters.

Heath and his successors were to promulgate under their personal seal "what lawes soever may concerne the publick state of the said province or the private profitt of all according to the wholesome directions of & with the counsell assent & approba-tion of the Freeholders of the same Province or the Major part of them". As Justice, the proprietor had the power of loss of life and limb, the power of pardon and the appointment of all the necessary legal officers. In emergencies he could decree ordinances which had the power of law, though the laws in general were to be "consonant to Reason & not repugnant or contrary but (as conveniently as may be done) consonant to the laws, statutes, customs & rights of our Realme of England".

All subjects of Carolina and the Bahamas were to enjoy the same rights as Englishmen and all English subjects were to be allowed the right of fishing off the coasts, salting their catch and drying their nets without taxation. Otherwise all customs and taxes were the proprietors' to decree and collect. Heath was

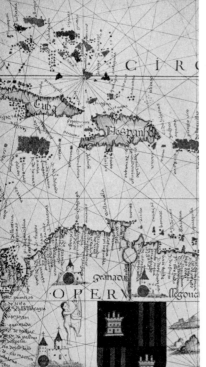

Long Bay, San Salvador, Memorial commemorating the landfall of Columbus (1492)

The first English map (1592) showing the Bahamas. A manuscript chart drawn by Thomas Hood from a Spanish original

promised that all goods coming to England from Carolina would not suffer any taxation additional to the usual royal customs, and he was also pledged a favourable construction in the courts on any disputed points.

The only royal provisos were that the Crown reserved the right to levy one-fifth of the value of all gold and silver and to issue Instructions to Heath and his successors once the colony was established.

Unfortunately, these sweeping proprietary clauses, similar to those granted in the same year to the Earl of Carlisle as "Lord Proprietor of the Caribee Isles" and the Earl of Warwick for the island of Providence, were barely worth the paper they were written on. Between 1629 and 1640, the years of the "Royal Tyranny", Heath was intensely preoccupied with the affairs of the harassed king. In 1642 he fled with Charles I from London and later was Chief Justice of the King's Bench at Oxford. After he tried the radical John Lilburne as a prisoner-of-war, he was impeached by Parliament *in absentia* and his estates sequestered. In 1646, after the collapse of the royal cause, he fled the country, dying in Calais three years later. Thus he was never able to establish the colony overseas of which he had once dreamed. Nevertheless, the formal annexation of the Bahamas on October 30, 1629, is commemorated on a plaque outside the House of Assembly in Nassau, and a fine contemporary portrait of Sir Robert Heath in his Justice's robes is displayed in the nearby Public Library.

The later history of the Heath grant was a complicated one and many disputes had to be ironed out when the area was re-granted in 1663 and 1670. Samuel Vassall (1586-1667), a prominent merchant and M.P., claimed to have been interested in the area between Virginia and Florida since 1628 and had intended to "lead thither a colony of men large and plentifull, professing the true religion". Apparently he had petitioned Heath for a grant without success, but had nonetheless sent one Henry Taverner to the St. Helena River in 1632 to search for a suitable site. In the following year he had entered into a contract with Edward Kingswell to take settlers to Carolina, but Kingswell defaulted and Vassall's venture collapsed. When his claims to the proprietorship were examined in 1663 they were declared null.

Another interested party was the Duke of Norfolk, who declared in 1663 that his father, Henry, Lord Maltravers (a name surprisingly like Vassall's Henry Taverner), had been granted the proprietorship of the "province of Carolana" by Sir Robert Heath in 1632. Unfortunately, no documentation could be produced, though there was no doubt that Maltravers had planned to send settlers, being given a letter by Charles I demanding assistance from the settlers in Virginia. In 1638 Governor Harvey of Virginia had issued a patent for a "semi-independent propriety", and Maltravers commissioned a Captain William Hawley to be his Deputy, with a grant of 10,000 acres. Then the Civil War and the lunacy of Maltravers's eldest son intervened and nothing effective was done.

A further complication was that, at the Restoration in 1660, Heath's eldest son Edward was made a Knight of the Bath and recovered his father's estate and fees. Presumably the grant of 1629 was also included. Over a century later, in 1768, one Daniel Coxe put forward a claim that his ancestor and namesake had purchased the grant from Edward Heath in 1696. Somewhat surprisingly, when this claim was examined by the Privy Council in 1769, it was upheld. Coxe and four relatives were given 100,000 acres in upcountry New York by way of compensation.

None of these disputes seems to have concerned the Bahamas directly. All the interested parties concentrated their covetous gaze on the vast areas of fertile land on the mainland. Through sheer indifference there was a serious danger that the French would forestall the English and become the first European settlers in the Bahamas.

In 1565 Pedro Menéndez de Aviles had to defeat and destroy French Huguenots under Jean Ribaut and René de Laudonnière who had been living in Florida for up to three years, before he could establish the Spanish settlements of St. Augustine, San Mateo and Santa Elena. The chief, and practically sole, function of these isolated posts was to protect Spanish shipping in the Channel. French corsairs such as Dominique de Gourgues were at least as active and numerous as the English between 1568 and the middle of the seventeenth century. A French writer of 1758, M. Bellin, recorded a French attempt to settle the Bahamas in 1625. A company having been formed, a ship was sent with colonists to Lucayoneque (Abaco), an island of good harbours and fresh water, with salt ponds and wild pigs. A relief ship, however, found no trace of the settlers, who have left no other trace to posterity.

More certainly, in 1633 Cardinal Richelieu made a grant to Guillaume de Caen, another Huguenot, of certain specified Bahamian slands, namely Abaco, Inagua, Mariguana, Guanahani and "Gilatur", and along with them Louis XIII gave de Caen the unique title of Baron des Bahames. Unfortunately for him, however, he was not allowed to send his fellow Protestants to form a colony, nor did the grant include the right to levy taxes or customs. Nevertheless, it should have been obvious to far-sighted Englishmen that it was only a matter of time before the French gained a foothold in the Bahamas and thus interposed themselves between the English colonies of the Atlantic seaboard and the Spanish colonies of the Caribbean. In the next chapter we shall see how this danger passed, without being actually averted.

VI

Adventurers
1640-70

It was to be from Bermuda that the first English settlers of the Bahamas were to come, under the leadership of a remarkable man called William Sayle.

By 1640 Bermuda had become a well-established little charter colony run by the Somers Islands Company, subsisting chiefly on the growing of tobacco, fishing and whaling and as the inevitable stopping place for all vessels travelling between England and Virginia. The troubles which racked England during the 1640s, between King Charles I and his Parliament, and between the established Anglican church and militant nonconformists, had their repercussions in tiny Bermuda. There the struggle resolved itself as a painful conflict between the royalist majority, which was true to the Anglican establishment, and a minority of Independent Puritans who tended, with the spirit of the times, towards republicanism. The leaders of the minority were their ministers: Nathaniel White, Patrick Copeland and William Golding, who in 1643 (the year of the "Solemn League and Covenant" between the English Parliament and the Scots) renounced the Church of England and proclaimed themselves "pastors of the Church of Christ".

William Sayle was himself a nominal Independent in religion, though never such an extremist as Golding or Copeland. He was a far more valuable type for a young colony: a practical man, an experienced seaman and a natural leader. He was chosen as Governor of Bermuda no less than three times, his first two terms being between 1641 and 1642 and 1643 and 1644.

By 1645 the religious squabble in Bermuda had reached a crisis. William Raynor, the Sheriff of Bermuda, in a letter to

Governor John Winthrop of Massachusetts mentioned two ships visiting the Bahamas in that year to find a religious sanctuary for the harassed Independents. Unfortunately, one was wrecked with the loss of everyone aboard and the other returned, having found no suitable land. At almost the same time, William Sayle had been chosen to go with William Golding to England to negotiate with Parliament a settlement of the dispute. They returned with a document proclaiming "Liberty of Conscience", that is, freedom of worship, for all in the Bermudas.

But this document seems hardly to have been worth the effort. In the spring of 1647, Sayle was back in England, this time not seeking abstract liberty but the wherewithal to establish a colony where actual freedom could be enjoyed. The result was *A Broadside Advertising Eleutheria and the Bahama Islands* (London, 1647), which led to the formation of the "Company of Eleutherian Adventurers" and the first English colony in the Bahamas in 1648.

The broadsheet, a poster pinned up or circulated by hand, was the most effective advertising medium in the period before daily papers. The Bahamian broadsheet of 1647 was probably passed around the taverns and meeting-houses of London, perhaps even the lobbies of Parliament, and eagerly discussed. Political disputation was the rage of the day and the anonymous author of the broadsheet, in the words of the American historian Fulmer Mood, was a "fresh and powerfully original thinker, not only abreast of the highest aspirations of his age, but, indeed, well to the fore of them". The document advocates republicanism, a single legislature and religious toleration, but not the abolition of property or privilege. It foreshadowed the "aristocratic republicanism" of James Harrington's *Oceana*, published in 1656 and was probably influenced chiefly by the ideas of a Thomas Robinson, whose book *England's Safety in Trade's Encrease* was published in 1641, one of the early arguments for the theory of mercantilism.

The Broadsheet did not venture to make an actual description of the Bahamas. This was probably because most of the contemporary accounts were less than attractive. In 1644, for instance, William Castell in his *A Short Discourse of the Coasts and Continent of America*, derived from the Dutchman de Laet, wrote:

"*Lucaik Ilands*, so near one another, as they make those seas very rough, heady and dangerous: besides this, there is nothing worth noting in them." George Gardyner of Peckham, who later claimed to have advocated a Lucayan colony as early as 1644, and was a rival coloniser to Sayle in 1647, was on hand to give a somewhat rosier account. In his *A Description of the New World* (not published until 1651), he said, "On these Islands are no inhabitants, those that did live there were a harmless simple people, and therefore the easier taken and carried away by the Spaniards that have made them so desolate, many of them seem of a good mould, and the Latitude promiseth much fertility. The aire is certainly good and wholesome, and not so extream hot, as other parts of that height. There is scarcely any beast on them save a Cony, that hath a taile like a Rat, but Pigeons and Birds in great numbers; most of them of a greenish colour.

"There is a Gumme *Benjamin* of the best and worst sort, *Guacom* and *Sasaprila* and *Sasafras*, and on some of them red wood and Amber-greece. The English Seamen are little acquainted with these Islands although they sail round them yearly . . .

"The coasts of most of them are dangerous, and bad to make, and that ship that shall be near, or amongst them must keep the lead always going, but with a wary Pilot, and care in giving the Islands a fair birth, they are easily recovered.

"The Spaniards know this place well and have a yearly trade thither for the aforesaid Commodities, and amongst the Islands are wracks of divers of their ships."

As a result of the interest shown in the Broadsheet, twenty-six signatures were obtained for the famous *Articles and Orders of the Company of Eleutherian Adventurers*, drawn up on July 9, 1647. This document, like so many in Bahamian history, is far more interesting and important for what it set out to do than for its actual results. Had it been effective, the Bahamas would have been an ideal colony, the first example in history of an enlightened constitutional republic formed overseas.

The Articles begin by condemning faction, and proclaim that the Eleutherian colony would be republican and enjoy Freedom of Conscience in religious matters. The very word Eleutheria was chosen because it was the Greek word for freedom.

For an outlay of £100, investors, who were to be limited in

numbers to 100, were styled Adventurers and each entitled to 300 acres in the main settlement, plus 35 acres for each additional person in their household. Besides this, each Adventurer was granted up to 2,000 acres outside the main settlement. Time-expired indentured servants were to be given 25 acres apiece. All land was to be worked in common for the first three years of the colony, or perhaps less by an agreement of the majority.

Of the natural products of the Bahamas (concerning which the farmers appear to have been rather vague), gold, silver, copper, lead or brass [sic] from mines, "wracks, ambergreise, metalles, salts and woods" were to be sold, and after costs had been deducted, one-third of the income was to go to the finder, one-third to the original Adventurers and one-third to the public treasury. Guns from wrecks were to be employed for the common defence.

In fact, defence was to have the first call upon the public treasury. All males between 15 and 50 were to bear arms in common defence, though they were not to be expected to serve beyond the main settlement. What money was left after the expenditure on defence was to be used for works of mercy and charity and for promoting further immigration. Any natives who remained in the islands were to be well treated and an effort was to be made to redeem those who had been transported by the Spaniards.

The government outlined for the colony was the most radical aspect of the Articles. Although the English House of Lords was not abolished by the revolutionaries until 1649, the Bahamian legislature was to be unicameral. It was to be called the Senate and consist of the 100 original Adventurers. When a member died his place was to be filled by co-option, 20 nominees being reduced first to 4 and then to 1 by "scrutiny and ballotines".

The idea of the Sovereignty of Parliament, still radical in 1647 England, was accepted without hesitation. The power of the Eleutherian Senate was to be absolute in the appointment of Justices, the distribution of public lands, in public works and all matters of finance.

The first President, called Governor, was to be chosen in England for three years, but subsequent Governors were to be elected annually by all Freemen in the colony. This revolutionary popular election, which was accompanied by the choosing of an Advisory Council of 12 from among the Senators, was to be held each year on the first Tuesday in December.

The final clause of the 1647 Articles stated that no one was to be allowed to settle in Eleutheria without first agreeing to the conditions contained therein. Among those who signed the document were three who also signed the death warrant of Charles I two years later, one of whom, Gregory Clement, was executed at the Restoration. Apparently few of the signing shareholders, who included Cromwell's Treasurer, John Blackwell, and Peter Chamberlen, later Physician to Charles II, actually went as far as to emigrate to the Bahamas. Indeed, it was the lack of practical support that was the chief reason for the failure of the ambitious colony.

Another reason for the failure of the 1647 venture was that the Eleutherian Adventurers never actually received a charter. A bill in incorporation was debated in the House of Commons on August 22, 1649, and read for the third time on August 31. This specified an area of operations for the Company of between Latitude 24° N. and 29° N., that is, all the northern islands of the Bahamas; but apparently no Act was ever printed nor charter drawn up. After the Restoration of 1660 there was no hope of official authorisation for the Adventurers, and by 1666 even William Sayle had given up the hope of a charter.

In 1647, however, Sayle was full of optimism. Before returning to Bermuda he appeared before the Directors of the Somers Islands Company and thoroughly frightened them with the radical notions he had picked up in London. They wrote urgently to Turner, the acting Governor of Bermuda, warning him against Sayle. But this opposition merely speeded up the process of recruiting dissatisfied Independents in Bermuda for the new colony. Since 1645, Sayle had been part owner with John Trimingham and four others of a ship called the *William* and it was in this and a "shallop" of six tons built specially that he set sail for the Bahamas in the summer of 1648. With him were some seventy settlers, including the 80-year-old Rev. Patrick Copeland. The other two leading Bermudian Independents, William Golding and Nathaniel White, remained behind, Golding dying shortly afterwards.

Sir Robert Heath, the first Proprietor of the Bahamas (1629)

Woodes Rogers Governor (1718-22), his son John and daughter Sarah. From a portrait by William Hogarth

The account of this important voyage has been handed down to us in the pages of Governor Winthrop's Journal. The infant colony seems to have been blighted from the start. The two ships arrived safely at the island of Cigateo or Segatto, which they renamed Eleutheria,* probably landing at Governor's Harbour. But Sayle had a violent argument with one Captain Butler who tended towards anarchy and formed a faction against him. Taking most of the settlers, Sayle set out for another part of Eleutheria, probably Spanish Wells, but "being near the harbour, the ship struck and was cast away". Only one man was drowned but all stores were lost and the hapless Adventurers had to live off the land like Eleutherian Crusoes.

Always a man of resource, Sayle took the little shallop and eight men and sailed to Virginia for aid. Arriving there within nine days, he obtained supplies and the loan of a pinnace of 25 tons. He almost persuaded several of the Virginians to venture their luck in the Bahamas, but they wrote to John Winthrop and were dissuaded. In lending succour, however, the Puritan New Englanders were more forward and within the next year or so they provided corn and necessaries to the amount of between £600 and £800 for their spiritual brothers in Eleutheria. In this way the colony narrowly survived its first disaster.

In January, 1649, Charles I was beheaded at Whitehall in London, but this event merely strengthened the allegiance of the Bermudian loyalists. They proclaimed Prince Charles as Charles II and set about expelling more of the Independents to Eleutheria. In October, 1649, about sixty Puritans, who would not take the oath of allegiance to the new king, set out for the Bahamas under two ministers, Stephen Painter and the notorious Nathaniel White. Within six months the English Parliament ordered Governor Josias Forster to revoke their banishment, and with some trepidation he sent a ship under Captain P. Cradock to bring some of them back. "With what safety we can receive them," his Council wrote to the Directors of the Somers Islands Company, "except they do submit to the government we know not. Yet we do intend to receive such as have any interest, and attend your further pleasure concerning them." White's banish-

* Later abbreviated to Eleuthera.

ment was not quashed until 1652 and he did not dare return to Bermuda until 1656.

A hard core of settlers remained at Eleutheria, eking out a miserable existence based upon the export of braziletto and ambergris, the gleanings from wrecks and the sporadic generosity of other colonies. In return for the timely help of the people of Massachusetts, the colonists sent a cargo of ten tons of braziletto wood to Boston, as the accompanying letter said, "to avoid that foul sin of ingratitude so abhorred of God, so hateful to men", asking that it be sold and the proceeds given to Harvard College. The letter was signed by William Sayle, Nathaniel White, Robert Bidlye and Jonathen Ince, and dated "Eyguatea, May 17, 1650". The sale realised £124, the largest gift to the College up to that time except for the original grant of £400 and Harvard's own legacy of £800.

From time to time the colonists were added to by Bermudians banished for other than religious reasons. The Minutes of the Bermuda Council record, for example, the expulsion of seven Negroes in the *Blessing* of 1656, after the abortive rising of that year, and in 1660 one Neptuna Downham was sent to Eleutheria for having had a child by a "chirugeon", John Morgan, in her husband's absence. Four years before, two colonists, Thomas Wilson and Francis Wood, had successfully petitioned for divorce on the grounds of their wives' misconduct while they were away preparing a home in Eleutheria.

How far from the ideal of the Articles had the colony slipped in the first ten years! We hear nothing of the model commonwealth or even of plantations, but much of exile, disputes and the sufferings of the thin scattering of colonists living on the margin of existence. Braziletto, a valuable dyewood, could command up to £12 a ton, and ambergris, a secretion of the sperm whale used in perfume and cookery, £4 per ounce, but their supply was limited and declining. Nor could wrecks such as the Spanish treasure ship cast ashore at Abaco in July, 1657, which realised £2,600, be relied upon. On December 23, 1656, Oliver Cromwell's Council ordered the acting Governor of Jamaica (which had been captured by Admiral Penn and General Venables the previous year) to take the sixty-odd English in Eleutheria to Jamaica and there to "clothe, feed and house them". But when action was taken, it was found that most of the settlers had already left for Bermuda. Richard Richardson, who disputed with Sayle the share of the spoils of the Abaco wreck described the settlement at "Elethea" when he arrived in July, 1657. At that time all the remaining inhabitants were living at Sayle's own house, using a cave for worship and council meetings.

The political climate in Bermuda had become much more healthy for the Independents. William Sayle, in fact, became Governor for the third time between 1658 and 1662, carrying Bermuda through the difficult transitions of the Restoration of Charles II. Even after he was relieved with a gratuity of £50 he remained a powerful member of the Bermuda General Assembly, advocating shipbuilding and the promotion of discovery, trade and colonisation. Although his activities were concentrated on Bermuda and extended to Barbados and eventually the Carolinas, Sayle continued to take a proprietary interest in the Bahamas.

In June, 1658, while in London, William Sayle commissioned agents to organise a quadrilateral trade between Bermuda, Eleutheria, Barbados and London, using his ship *William* under the command of his son, Thomas Sayle. Carrying supplies to the settlers in the Bahamas, the *William* was to convey seal oil, salt, braziletto, ambergris and salvaged cargo to "Cariba" (Barbados), where they would be sold or carried on to London, presumably with the cargo made up with tobacco and sugar. Besides the *William*, two small ships, the *James* and *Hope*, still sailed periodically between Bermuda and Eleutheria, though about 1662 the *Thomas and Marie* had to be fitted out by one Edward Atwood to relieve the "great distress" of the Eleutherians.

Another activity of the Sayle family, which included Nathaniel and James besides William and Thomas, was whale fishing, which was engaged in from Bermuda and through the Bahamas. It was probably chiefly on account of whaling rights and to forestall competition that Nathaniel Sayle in 1665 petitioned for William Sayle's proprietorship of Eleutheria to be recognised. Nathaniel produced a document with a "brave seal" on it, dated December, 1661, which announced that he had been appointed Governor of Eleutheria by William Sayle, with Thomas Hutt and Thomas Hayes as deputies. The claim was investigated by the Council of Bermuda, but because no royal commission or Act of Parliament could be produced, it fell through.

But William Sayle lived long enough to see his faith in the possibilities of the Bahamas justified. After the Restoration conditions in England became more settled and colonisation was actively fostered, especially after the establishment of the Council of Foreign Plantations in 1660. The stream of colonial settlers to America grew stronger. Bermuda became overcrowded and the Bahamas gained from the surplus, the first tentative plantations being established. Some time around 1666, Sayle's Island was first settled and renamed New Providence, and within five years there were over 900 settlers there. By 1670, the total population of the Bahamas was almost 1,100, including slaves. But these hardy settlers were without government, protection or law. Usually they turned to Bermuda for the settling of disputes and the Bermuda Council often claimed jurisdiction in the Bahamas at this time. But there was no legal basis for this authority. What was vitally needed was some sort of official authority, control and organised development in the Bahamas themselves.

The Adventurers having failed and his own rights as Proprietor being turned down, Sayle looked elsewhere for support. Now approaching 80, he became interested in the Carolinas, granted to eight Lords Proprietor by Charles II in 1663. On September 9, 1670, William Sayle and a man with the unlikely name of Florentius O'Sullivan (he was the Surveyor-General for the Lord Proprietors) wrote to Lord Ashley, begging the Proprietors of the Carolinas to include the Bahamas in their grant. About this time, Sir John Youmans, who was in command of the second colonising expedition to South Carolina, recommended in Bermuda that the aged William Sayle become the Governor and Colonel of the new colony. Apparently he accepted the post but was hardly able to take up the appointment before his death. By the time he died at Albemarle Point, Carolina, on March 3, 1671, "very much lamented by our people", however, the Bahamas had been taken over by the Proprietors and their future looked brighter.

VII

Proprietors
1670-84

If the years 1647-70 in Bahamian history could be called the Bermudian period, for the next forty-eight years the affairs of the Bahamas were as closely enmeshed with those of the Carolinas.

On March 24, 1663, a grant of lands in America between 31° N. and 36° N. was made by Charles II under similar terms to those given by his father to Sir Robert Heath, except that the Bahamas were not included. The area, which had been originally claimed by France a hundred years before and named Carolana after Charles IX, the son of Catherine de Medici, was renamed Carolina in honour of the English Charles. The eight "Lords" who were to share the proprietorship were the Duke of Albemarle, the Earls of Clarendon, Craven and Berkeley and Lord Ashley; Sir George Carteret, Sir John Colleton and Sir William Berkeley, the brother of Lord Berkeley. They were all prominent statesmen or loyalists, the most important at this time, Albemarle, being none other than the General George Monk who made the Restoration of 1660 possible.

Decisions of the Proprietors were always likely to become law very promptly since most of the Proprietors were already members of the king's Privy Council. This close association between Proprietors and the Crown explains why the transition from proprietorship to crown colony was such a gradual one. In one respect this was fortunate for the historian, since the number of Bahamian documents lodged in the Calendar of State Papers (Colonial) for the period of the Proprietors, some 250 for the years 1670-1718, is far greater than it would have been had the Proprietors been private individuals like Penn of Pennsylvania, or had severed their ties with England like the Baltimores of Maryland. There were, however, times, such as the period of Shaftesbury's disgrace, when the Proprietors were in disfavour with the Lords of Trade and Foreign Plantations (at this time an offshoot of the Privy Council) and had to tread warily.

At first it seemed as if the eight Proprietors of 1663 were going to do as little as Sir Robert Heath after 1629 in the actual business of founding a colony. An attempt to found a settlement at the mouth of the Cape Fear River in 1665 was a failure, the only settlers in the area crossing the indefinite southern boundary of Virginia. But in 1669 a more determined effort was made to form a colony from England. In the late summer of 1668 money was collected for a colonising venture and at the same time, on July 11, 1668, a warrant was made out by the Privy Council in London for the Attorney-General to prepare an additional grant to the Duke of Albemarle and his fellow Proprietors of "the islands between 22° and 27° N. Latitude", that is, all the Bahamas between Grand Bahama and the Turks. The archipelago was to be a County Palatine, with the same privileges as granted to Carolina in 1663. It is unlikely that this instruction was actually carried out at this time.

The expedition, which had cost £3,200 to fit out and included the ships *Carolina*, *Port Royal* and *Albemarle*, set sail from Kinsale in late 1669. Arriving at Barbados in November and recruiting settlers there and at Nevis, the fleet set sail through the Bahamas for Carolina. Unfortunately, it never arrived, for on January 12, 1670, both the *Albemarle* and the *Port Royal* were wrecked off Abaco. The survivors sailed on to Bermuda, and it was not until later that South Carolina became settled.

By the time of William Sayle's death, a man called Hugh Wentworth had become most interested in the Bahamas. He was a Yorkshireman distantly related to the most famous Earl of Strafford and had migrated with his family to Bermuda in 1629. In 1663 he became "Husbande in the Islands on the Behalfe of the Adventurers about the Whale Fishery" and between 1663 and 1669 he fished for whales with the Sayles and one John Darrell, using a ship called *Discovery*. By his own account he took two shiploads of settlers to New Providence to relieve the population surplus in Bermuda.

On February 17, 1670, he and John Darrell sent a famous letter to the Lord Proprietors begging them to take out a patent to include New Providence at least. By this time there were no less than 500 settlers on the island, excluding slaves, and they described the place as being "very healthful and pleasant with Gallant Harbour for shipping", producing "as good cotton as ever grew in America and gallant Tobacco". They also mentioned sugar cane and braziletto, ambergris and turtles. "Their greatest need at present", they summed up, "is small Armes and ammunition, a godly minister and a good smith."

In reply, Lord Ashley, shortly to be raised to Earl of Shaftesbury and who seems to have taken over control of the affairs of the Proprietors after the death of the first Lord Albemarle, wrote on October 29, saying that the Bahamas had been officially granted to the Lord Proprietors of the Carolinas and that Hugh Wentworth was appointed Governor. His Commission and Instructions were to follow, and he was asked to send a full description of the islands and the settlers. The official grant of the Bahamas to six of the Lord Proprietors is to be found on the Patent Roll dated November 1, 1670. The Proprietors were to hold the islands in "Free Socage" after the pattern of the King's Manor of East Greenwich, that is, paying merely a nominal quit rent. This, similar to the 20 marks for Carolina and the two Indian arrows for Maryland, was to consist of one pound of fine silver, payable only when the king visited the islands.

Each of the six Lord Proprietors, Ashley, Albemarle, Craven, Carteret, Berkeley and Colleton, had invested £200. Three of the Proprietors appointed personal Deputies to look after their interests in the Bahamas at this time. The Earl of Craven appointed Captain Nicholas David, who was connected with the islands as late as 1702. Shaftesbury chose a certain John Robinson and Carteret one Richard Jones.

Governor Wentworth's Commission, in which he and his Council were given rather vague powers to "lett, sett, convey and assure" lands, was dated in London, April 24, 1671. It was accompanied by a set of Instructions in 16 articles. These are chiefly interesting for the somewhat sophisticated constitution they projected for the backward Bahamas. The Government was to include an elective assembly of twenty chosen by all the freeholders. The Governor's executive council was to consist of five Deputies of the Lord Proprietors, though there was to be an additional "Grand Council", formed by the inclusion of five members chosen from the assembly. In this Council, six were to form a quorum, of whom three had to be Proprietors' Deputies.

The duties of the Grand Council were to settle all controversies among the inhabitants, to act as a court of appeal in civil and criminal cases and to deal with all "Publicke Concernments". They and the Governor had the sole right of drafting Bills, which were then to be presented to the Assembly for passing into Acts. All Acts had to be sent to the Lord Proprietors for ratification, whereupon they became law for sixty years.

Members of the Assembly, Deputies and Councillors were to swear allegiance to the King and "fidelity and submission" to the Proprietors. The Assembly, or Parliament as it was grandly styled, was to be convened in November every second year, unless it were required more often. A curious extra provision was inserted; all visiting ships were to be levied a tax of "one pounde of good gunpowder per ton" for the purpose of defence.

Hugh Wentworth was never able to put his Instructions into effect, since he died in Barbados on his way to the Bahamas in November, 1671. He was succeeded by his brother John, a well-known sea captain who had captured Tortola in 1665 during the Second Dutch War, and who seems to have been the choice of the settlers all along. But Hugh's old associate, John Darrell, was obviously far from pleased and sent a letter full of abuse of Wentworth and suggestions for the colony to London.

"Capt. John Wentworth," wrote Darrell, "debauches himself and has corrupted the people to drink. They have chosen him Governor and neglect their crops." The young settlers loved to "run a-coasting in shallops which is a lazy course of life and leaveth none but old men, women and children to plant . . ." He suggested restrictions in the number of "shallops", which would also help to preserve the turtles, the cutting of braziletto only by licence from the Proprietors, and the granting of land to all settlers who would plant; 40 acres for each man and 30 acres for each woman among the original settlers.

What was needed was strong rule, practical support and financial investment. The best the Lord Proprietors could do was to draw up a document to outline their own powers within the colony. Dated September 4, 1672, those Articles give us a good picture of what proprietary government in the Bahamas should have been.

The Proprietors were to have power to subdivide the colony (which they held of the king somewhat like a feudal *fief*) into counties and baronies. They were to make "any laws and constitutions whatsoever", subject only to the advice and approbation of the freemen of the colony. These freemen were to be assembled periodically as best suited the Proprietors. The Proprietors were to appoint a Governor and his deputy.

The Proprietors had authority to erect courts, appoint judges and grant pardons. They could issue any "reasonable" ordinances-in-council and all published laws were to be obeyed as long as they were consonant with English Law.

Although the Bahamas belonged to the Proprietors, they owed allegiance to the English king and any loyal subject might settle there. The Proprietors were to have the control of trade, licence to establish ports and, with the advice of the freemen, to fix duties. But customs belonged not to the Proprietors but to the Crown.

All land was held directly of the Proprietors, and they had power to confer honours and titles. They could construct forts, raise a levy and make war on sea and land. Finally, they were given the power to grant religious toleration if they so desired.

In drawing up this fine-sounding constitution, Ashley had the expert assistance of his friend and physician, the philosopher John Locke (1632-1704). Locke, who had drafted the Carolina Constitution, seems to have retained an interest in the Bahamas. In 1674 Richard Lilburne sent him a description of Bahamian poison fish which he wrote up for the Royal Society, and in the following year, his health being bad, he was asking Sir Peter Colleton whether the Bahamas were suitable for a plantation. Colleton advised against it and Locke settled instead in France for four years.

The first census for the Bahamas is dated 1671.* The list of names of freemen printed in A. T. Bethell's *Early Settlers of the Bahamas* includes many still common in the islands. Of the 103 different names listed for 1671, no less than 60 are to be found in the 1968 telephone directory. Seventeen of the 24 different surnames found in Eleuthera in 1671 can be found in the Bahamas today. Unfortunately, however, there is no certain proof as to which of these families came with the original adventurers of 1648, if any. The earliest certain settler is one Peter Sands, mentioned in 1671, who in a Bermuda court case gave evidence that he went to the Bahamas as a settler under Nathaniel Sayle, that is, about 1661.

Of the total of 1,097 inhabitants listed in the 1671 census, 913 were resident in New Province, made up of 257 males, 243 females and 413 slaves. Of the 184 living in the settlements of Eleuthera, 77 were males, 77 females and 30 slaves. In all there were some 168 separate households, 127 in New Providence and 41 in Eleuthera. The listed slaves make up 40.4 per cent of the total. John Howell, with 41, was the largest slave owner.

These settlers looked eagerly to the Proprietors to bring them aid. About this time an anonymous writer computed the expense of improving the Bahamas and settling new families to the number of 300 within three years, with costs including "transportation, subsistence, tools, slaves, negroes, goods, wages, fortifications &c. &c." as being £633,000. In fact, there is positive record that the Proprietors spent in the first few years the grand total of £495 : 2s. Their chief activity was to engage in a stream of correspondence and to send a succession of incompetent, corrupt or ineffectual Governors. If somewhat prejudiced, the opinion of the contemporary Governor of Jamaica of the Proprietary Governors of the Bahamas and Bermuda is worth quot-

---

* There is a slight doubt as to the authenticity of these figures. Bethell cited Registry Book C, pp. 166-78 as his source. Sure enough, his list occurs between those pages, but it has no heading and is interleaved among documents of the period 1730-33. Registry Book C, however, is an early recopy and Bethell in 1914 may have had access to the original, in which a heading presumably occurred. Internal evidence points strongly towards the accuracy of the date. No unusual names of a later period occur, nor does the name of any post-1671 Governor. Read Elding (Acting Governor in 1699) is listed as a young married man with a single child. The surnames of three of the four heads of families known to have migrated to Boston between 1684 and 1686 are also found in the list for Eleuthera.

ing: ". . . those small Governors over a few barefooted people", he wrote, "that get into those places to avoid their debts, take on them the title of Excellency and Captain General, which to support they squeeze and prejudice His Majesty's subjects and authority. Whether they have the authority for those characters I know not, but sure I am it's a great diminution to those honourable titles."

It was a losing fight from the beginning. In August, 1672, Governor John Wentworth wrote to Sir Thomas Lynch, the Governor of Jamaica, complaining of the lack of support from England. Although war with Spain seemed imminent, of the 200 able-bodied men in the colony, only 60 had arms. There were no large guns for defence and only 30 pounds of powder and shot. Wentworth begged urgently for 100 small arms, 300 flints, 200 pounds of lead, large guns, two drums, four halberds, and flags. Lynch, although he forwarded Wentworth's letter and a petition from the Bahamian settlers to the Council for Trade and Plantations in London, was unable to help much, sending only a little powder and shot. The war with Spain had not yet materialised, he said, and even if it did, the poor Bahamas had little to attract the Spaniards. The settlers would all be richer, and safer, in Carolina.

Matters did indeed look grim. Ambergris and braziletto were failing. Wrecks could not be relied upon, especially as the islands were off the favoured shipping routes. The climate was not really hot enough, thought Lynch, to produce the crops which were helping Jamaica to thrive; cotton, indigo, ginger, cocoa and sugar. And with its poor soil, the Bahamas could not compete with Virginia in the tobacco trade.

Ashley, now Lord Shaftesbury, hastened to cheer up Wentworth and the settlers. Replying to Lynch, he outlined plans for planting cocoa trees and Jamaican pepper in the Bahamas, asking for seedlings and directions for cultivation. To Wentworth he wrote in late 1672, expressing confidence in his direction of affairs, promising him a tenth share, as large as his own, in the profits of the colony and even hinting tantalizingly at the establishment of an hereditary nobility in the Bahamas. In an intriguing passage he suggested to Wentworth the potential profit to be had through "secret commerce" with the Spaniards. On

71

November 13, 1672, Sir Thomas Chichely, Master of the Ordnance, was given a warrant by the Privy Council to provide four "minions", small guns, and their gear, for use in the Bahamas, and in January, 1673, Shaftesbury's secretary wrote a letter of thanks to Sir Thomas Lynch, stating that vessels with provisions for the Bahamas and the Commission for the Governor, were "now sailing".

Later in 1673, Shaftesbury was instructing Wentworth to control the cutting of braziletto and to ensure that ambergris and other "royalties" were not slipping away unnoticed. As time went on, it seemed that Shaftesbury's confidence in Wentworth evaporated, at least as far as Shaftesbury's private affairs were concerned. He had already appointed one Isaac Rush as his personal Deputy in the islands and on May 17, 1675, he wrote to Wentworth expressing grave suspicions of his connexion with John Darrell and Sir Peter Colleton in Barbados. He had regarded Wentworth as a good friend, he said, but now he must cease correspondence with them and look more closely to the interests of the Proprietors if he wished to remain Governor.

It is probable that Wentworth did not see any profit in the Bahamas and spent too much of his time in outside activities. The next we know of him is that he was succeeded by Charles Chillingworth, who received his Commission from the Lord Proprietors on July 1, 1676. But Wentworth was not entirely out of favour. In May, 1677, he was appointed Shaftesbury's Deputy in place of Isaac Rush. In a spate of correspondence dated May 22, 1677, an account was given of "warlike stores" to the value of £8,695 sent to Barbados and the Bahamas. Rush was dismissed after sundry complaints and Wentworth put in his position with instructions to recover from him certain goods.

Unfortunately, there is a gap in the Bahamian correspondence between the years 1677 and 1682, and we have to rely on the earliest history to mention the Bahamas, John Oldmixon's *History of Providence*, first published in 1708, for our knowledge of the Governorship of Charles Chillingworth and for other details of life in the Bahamas at that time.

By implication, the Assembly of the people carried considerable weight in the colony at that time, though its constitution was on the vaguest of terms and we know little of its deliberations.

In his admonitory letter which preceded the dismissal of John Wentworth as Governor, Shaftesbury warned Wentworth of the dangers of paying too much attention to democracy:

"I desire to know whether you hold your place of Governor as chosen by ye people or us; ffor if you hold it from ye people, we shall quickly try how safe ye Island will be under another . . . your letter expresses that ye Speaker told you in ye name of the country that they had chosen you for their Governor . . . A style for a republique and not persons that live in a government by virtue of His Majesty's Patent granted to ye Proprietors."

According to Oldmixon, the inhabitants, who were "living a lewd licentious Sort of Life", were far from satisfied when Chillingworth supplanted Wentworth. They were "impatient under Government. Mr. Chillingworth could not bring them to Reason. They assembled tumultuously, seized him, shipped him off for Jamaica, and lived every Man as he thought best for his Pleasure and Interest."

During this time, the Governors could expect little practical aid from outside. Sir Peter Colleton, who had at least had an interest in the settlers, retired to Cornwall, most of the Proprietors were aged "sleeping partners" and even the energetic Shaftesbury had, to say the least, more pressing matters in England. He had been bitterly opposed to Charles II's pro-French policy, his "popish" tendencies and the ambitions of the Roman Catholic Duke of York. It was the period of the Secret Treaty of Dover, the Popish Plot, the Exclusion Bill and *Absalom and Achitophel*. Out of this conflict came the terms Whig and Tory, and after the "Tory Reaction" which produced Dryden's poem, Shaftesbury was imprisoned, in 1681. He died in exile two years later.

Charles Chillingworth was succeeded as Governor by Robert Clark some time before 1681. His short period in office was taken up almost entirely by trouble of a new, but soon to be familiar, kind. He was accused of complicity with a notorious pirate called John Coxon, superseded and put under arrest.

England and Spain were at this time at peace, but the ancient animosity between the two countries was always likely to flare up whenever their ships met. Although the Spaniards had given limited acknowledgment of the English right to trade and establish colonies in the Caribbean in the Treaty of Madrid of 1670, the buccaneering raids of Sir Henry Morgan still rankled in Spanish minds. No English ship was safe close to "The Havana" and few Spanish vessels ever risked the perilous passage through the Bahamas.

The Governor of Jamaica, Sir Thomas Lynch, was less lenient towards buccaneers than his Lieutenant, Sir Henry Morgan. Indeed, he had been appointed after the Treaty of Madrid with specific instructions to suppress buccaneers. When he heard that Coxon was raiding Porto Bello and other places on both sides of the Isthmus of Panama with "letters of marque" from Governor Clark, he wrote immediately to the Council of Trade and Plantations in London. This type of commission was valid in time of war, and Clark was probably going on the clause in the Article of the Proprietors which allowed them to wage war at their own discretion. But, in the cause of international peace, Clark should obviously be restrained.

Clark wrote to Lynch on July 6, 1682, defending his action, citing depredations by the Spaniards upon two English ships and the deportation of English planters from the Southern Bahamas to Cuba. It was the Spaniards who were the pirates, wrote Clark, and it was his intention to make war "against those and other pirates who shall invade us which is always justifiable by the laws of nature and nations". Clark also sent to the Council of Trade a copy of his commission to Coxon, but by the time it was read by them, in August, 1682, he had been sacked. In fact, the Proprietors, fearful of offending the Privy Council, had replaced him as Governor by Robert Lilburne within days of first hearing of the letters of marque.

The matter, however, was far from closed. On January 18, 1683, the Council of Trade debated and decided that Clark's commission to Coxon was not justified by the Articles, and even considered whether or not the Patent of the Proprietors should be withdrawn. A week later they decided not to rescind the Patent, but ordered Clark's arrest. On February 17, they wrote to Lynch, informing him that Clark had been summoned home in custody, though since he was still in New Providence in January, 1684, it is unlikely that he actually went.

Governor Lynch was still dissatisfied. Before he received the letter from England he wrote to a William Blathwayt saying that Lilburne was just as bad as Clark in the matter of the buccaneers, only he did not go through the formalities of issuing letters of marque.

Probably warned themselves by the Council of Trade, the Proprietors sent a strong letter of instructions to Governor Lilburne dated October 10, 1683. But this action was ineffectual, or too late. It would have been far more to the point had the Proprietors sent money and "warlike stores". For, in January, 1684, the Spaniards attacked and sacked New Providence.

The immediate cause of Spanish aggression seems to have been a disputed wreck off the coast of Florida. Freebooters from the Bahamas were accustomed to sail there and compete with the Spanish in fishing for silver ingots from the wreck. In March, 1683, one Thomas Paine, who actually carried a Commission from Lynch to suppress pirates, went further. With four other captains he landed in Florida under false colours and sacked settlements around St. Augustine. When he returned to New Providence, Governor Lilburne was either unable or unwilling to have him punished. The Spanish attack followed within six months.

We have at least three contemporary accounts and can piece together a detailed record of what happened. Just before Christmas a Spanish force attacked English shipping off Andros, capturing a William Bell, whom they forced to act as pilot. On January 18, Don Juan de Larco with at least 150 picked men sailed in two *barcolongos* to the southern shore of New Providence. Guided by Bell with a halter round his neck, they sailed round the eastern end and landed half a mile to the east of Charles Town, as the settlement was called. This today would be somewhere near the Eastern Parade in Nassau.

Robert Clark and his son Judah led out some men to investigate, but they were repelled by musketry. Robert Clark was wounded and captured, dying in captivity. There is no certain evidence for the later accusation that he was murdered by the Spaniards by roasting on a spit, though Oldmixon quotes the story from the lips of Governor Trott.

Unresisted, the attackers moved on the town and pillaged it and goods and plate to the value of as much as £20,000. The frigate *Good Intent*, of ten guns, fled ignominiously. Nor did

75

Governor Lilburne distinguish himself by bravery. By his own account, hearing firing at the *Wheel of Fortune* inn, he tried to sound the alarm, but being surrounded by Spaniards, he was forced to flee to the woods with the rest of the inhabitants.

The Spanish raiders left Charles Town before dusk, the settlers creeping back from the "bush" to the plundered town to assess the damage. This was considerable, but a second Spanish raid some time later made it complete. This time, reports reached London that the town was burnt, men stripped and women and children and Negroes carried to Havana. In December, 1684, one Matthew Caldwell estimated his personal losses through the raids as being at least £5,000. Impoverished and insecure, nearly all the settlers left the colony and went to Jamaica. In August, Sir Thomas Lynch recorded the arrival of Isaac Rush and 200 settlers from New Providence, full of tales of woe. A few others went to Massachusetts where in 1686 three refugees from Eleuthera called Davis, Sanders and Albury petitioned Governor Andros for assistance. In November, 1684, a Thomas Lacey petitioned the Privy Council for restitution from the Spaniards for his pillaged ship. To him the most galling experience had been that the Governor had prevented any retaliation or defence against the Spaniards because England and Spain were technically at peace.

The Privy Councillors were in a quandary. Outraged by Spain's warlike action, they were nevertheless reluctant to provoke an outbreak of general war. They took an easy way out. On December 17, 1684, eleven months after the first raid, those who had suffered losses were ordered to "prefer their libel" in the Admiralty Court, and losses being proved, a complaint would be made to the Spanish Ambassador and reparation sought.

Much of the blame was attached to the Governor of Cuba in person. It was said that the profits of the first raid went entirely into his own pockets. Governor Lilburne sent Jonathan Elatson to Havana to inquire as to the reason for the attacks. The Governor's answer was straightforward enough. The raids had been organised as retaliation, since the inhabitants of New Providence were all "pirates proven". Candour compels us to admit that His Excellency was essentially correct.

VIII

Buccaneers
1684-94

No subject in West Indian history has been more thoroughly treated than the story of the buccaneers and pirates, from Esquemeling's famous book of 1678 down to the present day. From this wealth of material it is easy to trace the degeneration of the freebooters from cow-catching buccaneers and wartime privateers to out-and-out pirates; and also to understand how they came to make Nassau their home.

The original *boucaniers*, the forerunners of the "Brethren of the Coast", came from northern Hispaniola. They were wild men in picturesque garb, from France, Holland and England, who hunted the scarcely wilder cattle of the island before drying the meat over open fires called *boucans* and selling the product, along with tallow and hides, to passing ships. As time went on, the decline of the wild herds, overcrowding and the opposition of the Spaniards led the buccaneers to live less off hunting and more off Spanish commerce; first in canoes, then in larger ships and finally in organised flotillas.

For a dozen years after 1629 English buccaneers organised as a Company by the Earl of Warwick used Providence Island off the coast of Nicaragua as a base for attacking Spanish shipping. After the devastation of the island by the Spaniards in May, 1641, most of the survivors shifted to Tortuga, a rocky island off the northern coast of Hispaniola, over which the Providence Company claimed some sort of jurisdiction and even appointed a Governor down to 1650. Tortuga, some 25 miles long and only 55 miles SSE. of Inagua in the Bahamas, was ideal for the buccaneers, being difficult of access but close to the important Windward Passage between Cuba and Hispaniola. From Tortuga the buccaneers sailed out with "commissions" from the "Governor" of the island and articles called *chasseparties* which allocated duties, rewards and compensations. In all things the international brotherhood was expected to observe a rigid, if somewhat peculiar, code of honour called *la coutume de la côte*.

Despite the code and the *chasseparties*, of which Esquemeling, a Dutch physician who spent six years with the buccaneers, gave interesting details, the English and the French were always quarrelling. After the capture of Jamaica in 1655, Port Royal opposite Kingston soon became a notorious headquarters for English buccaneers and remained so for some twenty years. Under Sir Thomas Modyford and Sir Henry Morgan their achievements reached a climax. But the Treaty of Madrid with Spain in 1670, the strict governorship of Sir Thomas Lynch (1670-84), the death of Morgan in 1688 and finally the destruction of Port Royal by earthquake in 1692, first discouraged and then dispersed the Jamaican buccaneers.

The number of English freebooters at Tortuga, now having to rely upon the protection of the French authorities, increased year by year. As progressively severer acts against them were passed in the Jamaica and Carolina legislatures, they became decreasingly scrupulous over their prey. By 1685 even their own people were calling them pirates.

From this time the pirates began to make free with the Bermudian ships which visited the nearby Turks Islands and Inagua for salt, as part of the triangular trade between Bermuda and the mainland colonies. From this it was but a small step to the plundering of the ships of the mainland colonies themselves. Although the English pirates preferred the safety-in-numbers of Tortuga, they made increasing use of the islands of the southern Bahamas. Impressed by the slackness of the proprietary Governors, they began to cast their eyes even on New Providence. In 1689 William of Orange ascended the English Throne as William III and almost immediately war with France broke out, the beginning of an Anglo-French struggle that lasted, with only one long break, for 126 years. No longer were any loyal English welcome in Hispaniola, and when in 1691 the Anglo-French fighting reached the Caribbean, the last of the English pirates left Tortuga and established themselves in the Bahamas.

Here, for a while at least, conditions were ideal. As one captain said, "as surely as spiders abound where there are nooks and crannies, so have pirates sprung up whenever there is a nest of islands offering creeks and shallows, headlands, rocks and reefs—facilities, in short, for lurking, for surprise, for attack, for escape". Around almost all of the islands the pirates could lurk, preying on the passing ships of any nation; safe in their knowledge of the waters from reprisal; safe, too, in knowing that whatever government there was in New Providence was ineffectual if not actually complaisant.

Many grisly tales are told of the cruelty of these Bahamian pirates, who seem to have lacked even the thieves' honour of the original buccaneers. In 1714 when he captured the ship of Samuel Cooper, a Bermudian, Charles Vane hung one of the crew at the yardarm and then cut him down prematurely to slash him to death with a cutlass. When he boarded the sloop of Captain Edward North he tied one of the men to the bowsprit with matches burning down to his eyes and a loaded pistol at his mouth, to force him to disclose the hiding-place of the ship's money. The pirate Spriggs went even further. When the plunder of one ship was disappointing he ordered the captives hoisted aloft to the maintop and from there bounced on the deck. The crippled survivors were allowed to go.

After the Spanish raids of 1684, New Providence was empty of permanent settlers until 1686. In December of that year a sloop-load of colonists ventured back to the island from Jamaica, led by Thomas Bridges, a "conventicle preacher", William Pattison and John Graves. Hearing that the new settlers had elected Bridges "Moderator", the Council of Jamaica feared that they were anti-monarchical, and on February 21, 1687, Lieutenant-Governor Hender Molesworth recalled them all to Jamaica. As Molesworth explained to the Lords of Trade and Plantations, there was a double danger: either the Spaniards might annex New Providence or it would fall completely under the evil spell of the pirates.

The order of recall was disregarded, but instead Bridges asked for the Bahamas to be taken under the protection of Jamaica. The same letter reported a small influx of new settlers from Bermuda and the building of a fort. In April, 1688, the Grand

Jury of Bermuda begged for the annexation of New Providence, since Bermudians were its first discoverers and settlers. But the governments of neither Jamaica nor Bermuda could spare the effort of taking over the Bahamas and the hard-pressed settlers had to make shift for themselves. In July, 1687, a Council of twelve was popularly elected to aid "Moderator" Bridges to decide differences, regulate matters relating to public interest and prevent disorders and factions".

From the outset, pirates caused the Council concern. Bridges reported his vain efforts to prevent obvious pirates like John Thurber, Thomas Wooley and Christopher Goffe from watering in the islands, a task made especially difficult because some of the settlers themselves were not above reproach. In April, 1688, Captains Spragge and Lenham landed in New Province and in a high-handed manner transported suspects back to Jamaica.

Meanwhile, in the southern Bahamas a search for wrecked Spanish plunder was going on worthy of the pages of Robert Louis Stevenson. Some time in 1684 and 1685 one Captain John Smith had reported to the second Duke of Albemarle, one of the Lord Proprietors, the presence of the wreck of a rich Spanish galleon somewhere between Tortuga and the Turks. With some difficulty Albemarle managed to raise £800 and sent out two ships, the *James and Mary* and the *Henry*, under Captain Phipps, on a mixed trading and salvage venture. Their log book can be seen among the Egerton Papers at the British Museum.

Disposing of their cargoes first, the ships arrived at the site of the wreck on January 13, 1687, guided by John Smith. Among the crews were three expert divers, who used a water-cask "diving-bell" invented by a Bermudian. The wreck was discovered within three days of a complete calm and the next day "4 sows, 1 bar, a champ and 2 dow boyds, 2000 and odd dollars" were brought up to the gaping crews. For three months with hardly a break except for Sundays, the diving continued, until the two ships were crammed with bullion. The ships arrived back in the Downs with their sensational cargo on June 6, 1687.

In all, the treasure weighed 26 tons and Albemarle's share alone amounted to £90,000. Each £100 share paid back profits of 10,000 per cent. Phipps was knighted and his wife received a gold cup worth £1,000. Sir Richard Haddock, one of the shareholders, was not so lucky since he had sold his share two months before the ships returned. Nor for a time did it seem that John Smith was to receive any reward, since he had signed no articles. But when he pleaded his cause before the Privy Council he was awarded a two-sixteenths share, less commission of 25 per cent to the rapacious Albemarle.

In London, gold fever broke out unparalleled before the South Sea Bubble of 1720. Innumerable patents were issued to treasure-seekers, none of which came to much. For a short spell, however, the Bahamas became a popular El Dorado. This probably explains why Albemarle, who had become Governor of Jamaica in 1687, wished to take over the lease of the Lord Proprietors for ninety years at this time, a request that was turned down in July, 1688. In the following month King James II even went as far as to order the Attorney-General to rescind the Charter of the Lord Proprietors, an action that was only curtailed by the king's flight and abdication later in the year.

None of the fabulous wealth of the Spanish wreck filtered back to New Providence. The inhabitants remained as poor as before, driven ever closer to the pirates. In July, 1688, the Proprietors had confirmed Bridges as Governor, but he did not last long. Nine months after the accession of William and Mary, he was succeeded by "Colonel" Cadwallader Jones, who arrived in the colony in June, 1690, with orders to proclaim the new sovereigns.

From Oldmixon's account and from the complaints of one Thomas Bulkley, it seems that Jones was an unprincipled ruffian, a sort of Bahamian dictator. Contrary to his commission, he did not proclaim William and Mary but instead added to his own titles of Governor and Commander-in-Chief those of Treasurer, Provost Marshal and Colonial Secretary. Furthermore, "he highly caressed those Pirates that came to Providence", wrote Oldmixon, and "gave Commissions to Pirates without and contrary to the advice of his Council". Bulkley told of sales of powder to known pirates and the refusal to prosecute the theft of "14 great guns".

If his opponents are to be believed, Cadwallader Jones and his agent, John Graves, carried out a reign of terror against the honest citizens. This included imprisonment without trial, a general censorship and oppression against legitimate traders. He delayed the calling of a General Assembly as long as he could and then forced it to make all his previous proclamations law by having his son train the guns of his ship on the Council Chamber from the harbour.

The result of this "abominable slavery" was rebellion. Jones was seized and put in irons and on January 24, 1692, Gilbert Ashley, a member of the Council, was elected in his place. The proclamation was signed by two of the Deputies of the Lord Proprietors and five of the members of the Council. Jones was charged with High Treason and Bulkley appointed Prosecutor in the case.

Jones, however, had his supporters. According to Oldmixon, on February 27, an "ignorant, seditious rabble . . . with force of arms rescued the Governor, proclaimed him again and restored to him the exercise of his despotic power". Bulkley in turn was thrown into jail, where he was kept in irons for 485 days. His wife was literally frightened to death when his house was violently searched for evidence. John Graves went to England, where he gained a Commission from the Proprietors as Secretary of the Bahamas, returning to New Providence to prosecute Bulkley.

By Bulkley's account, the Grand Jury which convicted him and sent him back to jail contained six pirates, two habitual drunks and one man accused of unnatural vice. The foreman, Jackson, was the leader of the mob which had rescued Cadwallader Jones. If this is all true, it is amazing that the lawless Governor ever went through with the formalities of a Grand Jury trial.

The whole era of Bahamian history has an air of farce. Accusations and counter-accusations conceal the truth. Scandal was certainly endemic, and although from what happened later it seems that Bulkley was guilty of exaggeration, Cadwallader Jones was obviously not worthy of his position. In January, 1693, the Lord Proprietors sacked him and appointed Nicholas Trott in his stead, although Trott immediately made Jones a member of his Council. John Graves became Attorney-General. Both Bulkley, once he was released from prison, and Jones returned to England in 1694, where Bulkley besieged the Proprietors and the King himself with complaints and demands for compensation. After innumerable delays his case was referred to the Council of Trade in February, 1697, but that body was forced to admit in April, 1697, that the poor man now appeared to be *non compos mentis*.

IX

Pirates
1695-1717

Nicholas Trott was a Bermudian merchant and landowner who in 1691 had been involved in a complicated legal battle with Governor Isaac Richier over a cargo of tobacco spoiled while impounded for customs. Ruined, he had received the governorship of the Bahamas more or less as compensation, though if he hoped to recoup his fortunes on the right side of the law he was bound for disappointment.

Trott arrived in New Providence in August, 1694, with the usual Commission and optimistic set of instructions from the Proprietors. Nothing less than a new land settlement was attempted. The Governor was to have 100 acres of the best land; the Church 50 acres for its glebe. Each settler arriving in the Bahamas before March, 1695, was to have 25 acres, plus 25 acres for his wife and each child. All land was to be held direct of the Lord Proprietors, who were to have for themselves up to 3,000 acres in each island, along with the "royalties" of braziletto, ambergris and Exuma salt.

In many ways, Trott seems to have been the most energetic of the proprietary Governors. Under an ordinance of the Proprietors dated April 12, 1695, he laid out Charles Town anew and re-named it Nassau after one of the hereditary titles of William III. By 1700 it was a town praised by Oldmixon for its size, with 160 houses and a church. At the same time, Trott began the construction of a fort commanding the harbour, on the site of the present British Colonial Hotel. Completed by February, 1697, and called Fort Nassau, it contained twenty-eight guns. To their credit, the Proprietors ploughed back into the Bahamas the small profit of £800 a year they received from the colony until the Fort was paid for. This action was in contrast to their constant clamouring for the payment of quit rents for land taken up in New Providence and their annulment of a local Act reducing them.

During Trott's term of office, the General Assembly or "Parliament" obviously enjoyed its most active period under the Proprietors, although no direct records have come down to us. We hear of Acts governing the sale and distribution of land, for the control of salt gathering and to encourage new settlement. Once more, it seems, intention outran fulfilment. In April, 1695, the Proprietors summarily declared void four Acts passed by the Bahamas legislature, chiefly because they infringed their own rights. Trott himself vetoed a Bill which cut the king's customs and the tax of a tenth on salt.

During these years, there was a spate of colonial activity in England. As a result of the formation of the Scottish Darien Company in 1695 (England and Scotland were not united until 1707 and there was much commercial rivalry), a more stringent Navigation Act than those of 1650, 1651 and 1660 was passed in 1696. Henceforward all ships trading with the colonies must have crews three-quarters English or colonial. Vice-Admiralty Courts were to be set up in each colony to try offenders against Mercantilism, and the Governors were empowered to impose fines of up to £1,000. In the same year, the Council of Trade and Plantations began to function as an organism independent of the Privy Council.

Although the writ of the new board of trade would not be all-powerful in the proprietary Bahamas, customs there belonged to the Crown and the trying of offenders against the Navigation Acts was clearly out of the competence of the proprietary Governors. A Vice-Admiralty Court was therefore set up in Nassau to which the first officials were appointed on February 25, 1697. The Judge was John Leighton, Registrar Thomas Waldock and Marshal Joseph Harwood.

The many reports sent back to England by Edward Randolph, the Surveyor-General of Customs in America since 1678, help to add much to our knowledge of conditions in the islands at that time. In his report sent to the Board of Trade in July and August, 1696, for example, he estimated that salt would be the most profitable industry to develop in the Bahamas, there being enough in the islands to supply the whole of England. Randolph was not impressed, however, with Trott, and had some rather scathing remarks to make about the Lord Proprietors. "The persons appointed by the Proprietors to be governors of those lands are generally of very indifferent qualifications for parts and estates", he wrote; and later, "Were the Lord Proprietors strictly obliged by bond to make reparation for all the damages they bring upon His Majesty's subjects by their negligent and imprudent choice they make of persons to send over to be Governors of their several Proprieties, they would either make a better choice or submit their countries to His Majesty's immediate government."

Thus speaks the Civil Servant. But Edward Randolph had good reason to criticize the proprietary government of the Bahamas, for in 1696 had occurred the scandalous affair of Captain Avery, which brought renewed notoriety to Nassau and dismissal to Nicholas Trott. Henry Avery was a pirate whose career was glamorized in a play entitled *The Successful Pirate*. In the previous year he had seized a ship called the *Charles* from its drunken skipper off Corunna and re-christening it the *Fancy*, had turned to piracy. By a stroke of fortune he captured the huge ship *Gunsway* belonging to the Great Mogul in the Indian Ocean, carrying booty that included 100,000 pieces of eight, 100,000 Venetian chequeens, many precious stones and the daughter of the Mogul himself. After sailing on to Jiddah with the Indian princess, Avery made a dash for the West Indies, evading several allied sloops sent out to capture him.

On April 1, 1696, the *Fancy*, which carried 46 guns and at least 113 men, dropped anchor off Royal Island to the north of Eleuthera and its captain, "Henry Bridgeman", sent to Trott to ask for provisions and permission to water at Nassau. In fact, Avery wanted somewhere safe to divide up his loot and pay off his men so that they could filter back to England one by one.

Trott conferred with his Council. In Nassau there were only 60 able-bodied men to resist a forced entry. Moreover, if "Bridgeman" were forbidden to enter Nassau, he might choose to sail on and join the French in Tortuga, England and France being still at war. Spurred on by reports that the French had just captured Exuma with three ships and 320 men and were moving on New Providence, Trott gave the pirates permission to stay.

At the inquiry which Trott's successor held in 1698, Joseph Dan, a pirate who turned King's Evidence to save his skin, testified that Trott had received twenty pieces of eight for each pirate who landed in Nassau, forty for Avery and £1,000 in plunder. A Philip Middleton corroborated this, and added that at a party Governor Trott had forced a shipmate to pay eight chequeens compensation for a broken glass. Officially, Trott was exonerated, it being stated that he received only £90 for "refreshments". The *Fancy* and her ordinary cargo which he shared with Richard Taliaferro, was described as being "little better than a wreck".

After the division of the spoils, most of the pirates slipped off to the mainland colonies, leaving behind only those stranded in Nassau by having gambled away their share. Two of Avery's crew, who had originally been "impressed" into service on the *Fancy*, Daniel Smith and William Griffith, went to Bermuda with over £1,000 between them, buying land that had originally belonged to Nicholas Trott. The fate of Avery himself belies the title of the play of which he was the hero. He bought a ship called *Sea Flower* from a Captain Crosskeyes and sailed off to Boston with 19 of his men, carrying as his share only £500, but all of the jewels. From Boston he went to Bristol, settling at Bideford in Devon under an assumed name. Years later he died, miserably in debt, still waiting for dishonest Bristol merchants to dispose of his ill-gotten jewels.

The Avery incident provoked another crisis in the affairs of the Lord Proprietors and cost Nicholas Trott his post. On October 19, 1696, the Board of Trade ordered the Proprietors to produce their charter, with the obvious intention of reviewing the clauses. Egged on by the Board of Trade and Sir Thomas Houblon, M.P. for the City of London and original part-owner of the *Charles*, the Proprietors dismissed Trott on November 9, appointing Nicholas Webb in his place three days later.

Trott's later career shows that if he was a villain he was an enterprising one. In 1698 he married Anne Amy, who inherited 12,000 acres in Carolina, her father being one of the Lord

Proprietors. In fact, when Thomas Amy died Nicholas Trott even petitioned for recognition as a Proprietor himself, but was denied as "an unfit person". His cousin and namesake, Nicholas Trott the Younger, did better in Carolina, becoming Attorney-General, Speaker and Chief Justice of the colony in turn, codifying the laws and wielding "a power in one man not heard of before". Among his unsuccessful legal cases while in London was the defence of Nicholas Trott the Elder in the case of a Dutch ship wrecked in the Bahamas during his term of office. When the *Jufrow Gertrud* had gone aground, Governor Trott had personally appropriated $2,300 worth of cargo. The Dutch Ambassador complained to the Proprietors and they ordered Trott to repay. He was not able to comply and having appealed unsuccessfully to the House of Lords, spent most of 1702 in the Fleet Prison. He was more lucky in litigation over the proprietorship of Hog Island, opposite Nassau, his acquisition of the cay for £50 and a shilling per acre per annum rent, being upheld.

After Nicholas Webb had been chosen Governor by the Proprietors, Edward Randolph suggested that his appointment should be confirmed by the king. After their recent fright, the Proprietors were eager to oblige. Webb's post was confirmed by William III on February 11, 1697, and in the following month he took his oath and kissed hands. Thus, almost imperceptibly, the Crown moved nearer full control of the Bahamas. To consolidate its position the Crown also announced in March, 1697, the appointment of Ellis Lightwood as Judge of the Admiralty Court in the Bahamas, John Leighton as Attorney-General and John Graves as Collector of Customs.

Not that the Bahamas was a rich financial prize for the Proprietors nor the Crown. The Governor's share in the Proprietorship was raised to a fifth, in the hope that his niggardly salary, barely £200 a year, would not force him to accept bribes. It was a vain hope. The Treaty of Ryswick with France (1697) had knocked the bottom out of the Exuma salt trade, in which as many as sixty sail had been engaged at one time. The price dropped from 2s. 9d. per bushel to 4½d., and at the same time the price of braziletto fell from £6 per ton to £2 : 10s. The entire registered trade for the Bahamas for the year 1698-99 consisted of £184 exports to England and imports of £302.

Webb, obviously disillusioned, complained bitterly of the poverty of the islands, describing, for example, the miserable efforts of some settlers from the Channel Islands to grow indigo. He was backed by complaints from the citizens of the excessive dues and quit rents expected by the Proprietors and the exactions of the Admiralty Court. The lot of the honest was a hard one. Wrecking, smuggling and downright piracy were almost inevitable.

In Webb's version, he made a genuine attempt to discourage piracy, since by his own admission the islands had become "a common retreat for pirates and illegal traders" and a "receptacle for all rogues". In his Commission, Webb was empowered to summon an Assembly of twenty-four members elected from the freeholders of New Providence, Eleuthera and Harbour Island and to form a Council consisting of six nominated members and six elected from the Assembly. How exactly this was carried out we do not know, but Acts were definitely passed during his term of office, including one against "ye notorious sin of adultery and fornication", disallowed by the Proprietors "becauce wee conceive your Act will rather encourage that vice than punish it and that you lay a penalty on the person aggrieved when you lay a fine on ye wife which must be paid by ye husband". Webb even went through the motions of passing an anti-piracy Act through the Assembly in 1699, though the pirates themselves were scarcely disturbed.

Edward Randolph, a professional cynic, believed that Webb was no better than Trott or Jones. The Governor of Boston in 1700 also said that Webb "trod in the footsteps of his predecessor Trott, who, if common fame lies not extremely, is the greatest pirate-broker that was ever in America".

Be that as it may, in 1698 a pirate called Kelly from a base in the Bahamas attacked the Jamaica-bound ship *Endeavour*, pillaging her when she went aground in the Florida Keys. Webb gave Read Elding, a mulatto, five ships and a commission to capture Kelly, but he failed and instead seized the *Bahama Merchant*, which he claimed had been "deserted". At first she was declared a prize and Webb began to count his share of the profits. The owner, Edwards, complained to the Governor of Jamaica that Webb was an outright pirate. Then, in February, 1699, the crew

89

turned up in Nassau after a miraculous escape and the Admiralty Court reversed its decision, declaring the ship "flotsam". Since flotsam was a "royalty" of the Crown, the luckless Webb received nothing, and was £80 out of pocket.

Harassed and disappointed on all sides, Webb gave up and "eloped from his government" some time in 1699, going to Newcastle, Delaware. But his troubles were not yet over. His ship, the *Sweepstakes*, of which he was the joint owner with Jeffry Jeffreys, was stolen by pirates with all his worldly possessions, consisting of £7,000 cash and £1,000 worth of "rich goods". £236 belonging to the King also fell into the hands of the pirates who, renaming the ship the *Happy Escape*, sailed off "firing and drinking the governor's confusion several times". Webb is said to have died shortly afterwards, a victim of shock or perhaps his own medicine.

Before leaving Nassau, Webb had appointed Read Elding his Deputy, and, in an access of zeal, the mulatto captured five notorious pirates: Ounca Guicas, Frederic Phillips, John Floyd, John Vantein and Hendrick Van Hoven, alias Hynde, "the grand pirate of the West Indies". Their trial was held on October 23-24, 1699, with Richard Taliaferro judge. John Vantein pleaded Not Guilty and was released for lack of evidence. Indicted for sailing "under a bloody flag, their bloody colours . . . as common pirates and robbers on the high sea" the others were convicted of seizing one sloop and burning another. After a petition to be shot had been rejected and six days granted for saving their souls, the pirates were hanged on October 30. At about the same time Elding made a fine-sounding proclamation forbidding all correspondence with the Scots of the Darien Company, then passing through the Bahamas.

These actions caused satisfaction at Westminster, but any complacency was shortlived. In April, 1700, another optimistic merchant, Captain Elias Haskett, was petitioning the Proprietors to be allowed to take up the vacant governorship. Although the Board of Trade insisted on a well-certified bond of £2,000 as security for Haskett's good behaviour, the Proprietors agreed readily enough. Haskett arrived in the colony some time early in 1701 and within a very short time conditions were as bad as they had ever been.

Haskett found that "disaffection and insecurity" were the rule in Nassau. The fort, so recently erected, was in ruins; the Admiralty Court ineffectual; the pirates rampant. The inhabitants were "of an uneasy and factious temper . . . not scrupling to do all manner of villany to mankind, and will justifie and defend others which have done the like".

Following a precedent set by Governor Trott, Haskett attempted to levy duties upon the Bermudian salt-rakers in the Turks Islands, seizing at least one vessel for non-payment. He had "never hanged a Bermudian", he said, "but would make no more to do it than to hang a dog". The Governor of Bermuda wrote angrily to the Lord Proprietors, challenging their rights to the Turks and Caicos Islands, only to be told, "We have never heard question of our right to Turks and Caicos and we doubt not we may reap what profit we can from them with safety". The reply of Governor Day was to renew the old claim that the Bahamas should come entirely under the jurisdiction of Bermuda and to commission a dozen Bermudian ships with letters of marque for reprisals, ostensibly against pirates, but in reality against seizure by Bahamian customs officials.

In Nassau, Haskett was even less successful. His rule was described by one inhabitant as "arbitrary and tyrannical" and when he attempted to imprison Read Elding and charge him with piracy in October, 1701, he stirred up rebellion. John Warren, Speaker of the Assembly, led a mob that seized the unpopular Judge of the Admiralty Court, Thomas Walker, and then forced its way into the Governor's residence. Warren threatened Haskett with a pistol, there was a scuffle, the gun went off and one of the mob fell wounded. Warren thereupon "broke" Haskett's head with the pistol butt.

The insurgents threw Haskett and Walker into jail, the Governor in irons. A public tribunal was set up, Haskett declared deposed and Ellis Lightwood elected "President". Still manacled, Haskett was expelled to New York in the small ketch *Katherine*. By his own account his family was driven into the woods, and he lost all his "gold, silver, household goods, plate, furniture, merchandise, commissions, instructions, bonds, bills, mortgages and whatever else belonged to him to the value of several thousand pounds, part of which was King's money and the Lords Proprietor's".

Both sides in the dispute engaged in voluminous correspondence with London. From this emerges more clearly the uncouth and unprincipled character of Haskett and the depths to which the government of the Bahamas had sunk. Haskett accused Collector of Customs John Graves and Roger Prideaux, his own servant who had joined the rebels, of High Treason, and James Crawford, Captain of the *Katherine*, of High Treason and Piracy, and had the latter two thrown into prison by John Nanfan, the Lieutenant-Governor of New York. For his own part, Haskett was variously accused of abusing the minister in Nassau, of levying illegal taxes, of monopolising all corn and selling it at a large profit and of appropriating such items as a "parcel of Claret and Brandy".

Lightwood and seven others accused Haskett of charging individuals with Piracy and then offering them their freedom for money. One Tabitha Alfroad testified that she had offered £50 for the release of Read Elding, but Haskett had demanded fifty *pistoles* (that is, £67 : 10s.), as well as "a rich ring and a piece of plate of value", a silver tankard, some items of dry goods, "a set of gold buttons and three Gold Drops".

A Captain Cole, who complained of letters illegally seized by Haskett, described one incredible exchange between the Governor and Lightwood: ". . . our Mr. Lightwood saying it was not just, the Governor presently drew on him, and swore Damn him, he would murder him; but Mr. Lightwood clasping hold of the sword prevented him, but he still swore and damn'd that he would murder somebody or other if they should contradict him in any such thing, for he would do what he pleased". On another occasion Haskett shouted at John Graves, "You pitiful custom-house officer, You Rogue, if ever you go aboard any Vessel before my Boat has been, I'll Roast you alive, you Dog!"

Reaching England, Elias Haskett was immediately in trouble with creditors. In a petition to the Crown, they said that he had absconded to the Bahamas in the first place. Having fixed a rendezvous at the Rummer Tavern, Gracechurch Street, he had gone to Portsmouth instead. A bailiff sent in pursuit had been repelled with firearms. In August, 1702, Queen Anne ordered a Commission of Inquiry, but before it could meet Haskett had fled England from his creditors once more.

The Proprietors allowed Lightwood to remain as Acting Governor, but later in 1702 they appointed Edward Birch as Haskett's successor. Before he could reach Nassau, however, the colony had once more been destroyed.

Renewed war with France had broken out in 1702 over the question of the succession to the Spanish throne. As far as the colonies and trade were concerned, England wanted Spain weak, and went to war to prevent a Bourbon alliance between that country and France. The War rumbled on until the Treaty of Utrecht in 1713 and although attention was centred on Europe, there was much fighting for supremacy in the Caribbean.

The Bahamas could have been an excellent base for privateering activities against the Spanish and French, and many of the pirates could have taken the opportunity of temporary respectability, but the enemy probably had this well in mind and determined to get their blow in first. In October, 1703, Nassau was sacked by a combined Spanish and French expedition from Havana. According to a Colonel Quarry of Philadelphia, besides plundering the town and spiking the guns of the fort, the raiders put many of the men to the sword and, after a stay of two weeks, carried off some eighty persons, including Acting-Governor Lightwood.

Certainly the colony was hard hit, for when Edward Birch arrived with John Graves from Carolina on the first day of 1704, he found the survivors of the 1703 raid not even having "a shift to cover their nakedness". New Providence, which in 1701 had had a population of at least 250 whites, was almost deserted. In despair, Birch left the colony again in June.

Some settlers crept back to their capital, but in the following year and again in October, 1706, the Spanish returned, completing what they had failed to destroy in 1703. In 1706 John Graves estimated that the total population of the Bahamas was between four and five hundred, but the families were scattered and making shift in Cat Island, Exuma, Eleuthera or Harbour Island. Those few hardy souls who did stay in New Providence "lived scatteringly in little hutts, ready upon any assault to secure themselves in the woods".

"I left upon the Island 27 families", wrote Graves, "and amongst all the islands at least 4 or 500 people that are scattered some 200 miles distance, so yt. in a little time they will be worse than the Wild Indians, and at the very best they are ready to succour and trade with Pirates; they have 12 or 14 small sloopes amongst them that escaped the enemy."

That there is a decided scarcity of material for the history of the next ten years is hardly surprising, since all semblance of organised government broke down and by the end of the War of the Spanish Succession the pirates were in undisputed control.

John Graves, who could claim an intimate connexion with the Bahamas since 1686, seems to have kept faith through the bleak years and to have appointed himself spokesman for the long-suffering islanders. In 1708 he addressed a *Memorial* to the Proprietors and the Commissioners of Customs, the only known copy of which is to be seen in the Nassau Public Library.

There was a real danger, Graves considered, that England would lose control of the Bahamas, and thereby, of the Florida Channel. Moreover, he added, "if the Spaniards take Possession, which I heard them say they would, all the Trade from North America to Jamaica will be very Hazardous; and from Carolina to Jamaica, will inevitably, be obstructed, they being forc'd to go between several of those Islands to Jamaica". Only "three days from Havana", the harbour of Nassau was a valuable prize. "New Providence, by reason of a very Commodious Harbour are [*sic*] the greatest Succour for all distressed ships that come through the Gulph of Florida. . . . I have known upward of Fourteen Sail in a year", he added, "come into Providence Harbour for Shelter."

Besides this, the Bahamas could be regarded as rich in resources. "They are", wrote Graves, "the most healthful Islands of all our Settlements; and tho' the Ground be very rocky, it will produce whatever is put into it, the best of Cotton in all the Indies. Dying Wood, Sugar Canes, Indigo, and great Quantities of Salt made by the Sun out of the Sea. Tortoise-Shell, Oyl of Whale, Seal and Nurse, &c Spermacaeti-Whale sometimes. Amber-Greece often washed up on the Bays." The salt of the Bahamas alone, he thought, made their retention worthwhile.

This commodity was vital for provisioning ships and for the fishing industries of Newfoundland and New England.

Nor was it only Spanish acquisition that the Proprietors and Government had to worry about. The French in Hispaniola could move into control very easily and already what dyewoods and cotton the islands produced were being shipped out by the Curaçao Dutch or the Danes of St. Thomas.

Through the lack of visiting English ships, the prices of commodities in Nassau were absurdly high, by the standards of the day. Mutton, veal and pork cost 9d. a pound and beef nearly as much. Butter was 1s. 6d. a pound, milk 6d. a quart and eggs 1½d. each. Only fish were plentiful and cheap.

Without defence, and Graves reckoned that a small garrison and a single sixth-rate frigate would suffice, Nassau was not only extremely vulnerable to foreign attack, but was at the mercy of the Pirates. ". . . One small Pyrat with fifty Men that are acquainted with the Inhabitants (which too many of them are)", he calculated, "shall and will Run that Place."

As boldly as he dared, Graves chided the Proprietors for their short-sightedness and neglect. They had granted Hog Island to the unscrupulous Trott for £50, the whole of Exuma, including the braziletto rights to Mr. Henry Palmer, and the whale and rock-fishing rights to two others. Their Governors, receiving only one-seventh of 10 per cent of the income of the Bahamas, some £30 in an average year, were bound to turn to dishonesty. "I must say that your Governors hitherto have work'd much at such ill Practices for filthy lucre . . ." They would need a salary of at least £400 a year to be enabled to stay on the right side of the law. "We have now been near Twenty Years in war", concluded Graves's modest *Memorial*, "and to my knowledge, Your Lordships tho' often Solicited and Requested, never did send us the least assistance either in Arms, Ammunition, or any Warlike Stores . . ." For this reason alone, Nassau had been "now lately, three times Plunder'd and lay'd in Ashes".

Graves probably realised the futility of petitioning the Lord Proprietors directly, for about the same time he suggested to the Board of Trade that the Crown should take over control of the Bahamas from the Proprietors. The £28,000 compensation probably needed could easily be raised, for example, by renewing the licences of the London hackney coachmen. A hundred troops sent out to the Bahamas would cost about £2,200 extra, and even if all the rents and income from the islands were swallowed up at first, within a few years of the establishment of stable government, profits would begin to build up again.

The immediate response of the Crown to the fervent appeals of John Graves was no more positive than that of the Proprietors. One of the last acts of the Proprietors was to propose as Governor a certain Robert Holden in 1707. In his petition for the office he referred to the islands as rivalling "St. Helena and Bermoodas Islands, ye famed places of ye world for health". Graves was not impressed, however, and suggested that Holden was really more interested in wealth than health, and hankered after wrecks and illegal profits like all the rest. The Crown vetoed the appointment and Holden never sailed.

During the war, delays were inevitable, but even after the Treaty of Utrecht was signed in 1713, action on the Bahamas was torpid in the extreme. In 1715, George I himself proposed the appointment of a Roger Mostyn, but he, too, never reached the Bahamas. Probably he received a reliable report on the condition of the islands and, gaining no promise of support in the shape of troops and warships, dared not face the pirates alone.

For by 1713 there were probably at least a thousand active pirates in the Bahamas, their nefarious actions unbridled by the slightest official control. In April, 1714, Governor Pulleine of Bermuda reported that the two hundred scattered families in the islands were living in a state of anarchy or worse. Three sets of pirates were in control. Cockram operated from Harbour Island, where he had married the daughter of one Thompson, but Barrow and Hornigold had taken over New Providence itself and styled themselves Governors.

By his own account, Thomas Walker had done his best to assert the royal authority. He had been appointed Judge of the Admiralty Court by William III, but his appointment had not been confirmed by Queen Anne. "I have spent my time in takeing upp pirates and routeing them from amongst these islands", he claimed in 1715 and by so doing had averted at least one retaliatory raid from Havana. But the infiltration had become too general and Walker had been forced to take flight to Abaco, or "Habakoe" as it was commonly called then.

Nearly all the notorious pirates to be found in the colourful pages of Captain Johnson or Philip Gosse were lurking at this time in Bahamian waters, including Mary Read and Anne Bonney, the "lady" pirates who sailed with "Calico Jack" Rackham and Stede Bonnet, the Barbadian planter-pirate. But among those who made Nassau their base for attacking the commerce of the Atlantic coast, the leaders seem to have been Benjamin Hornigold, Charles Vane and, of course, Edward Teach, alias "Blackbeard".

In the person of "Blackbeard" has been concentrated the whole disreputable spirit of his age. In the popular mind he is practically a synonym for Bahamian piracy. Like Avery, he was the subject of an eighteenth-century play; in the twentieth century he has had a doggerel "epic" written around his career. In Nassau he is remembered by a Tavern, a well and a lookout tower. Hundreds of tales are still told of his exploits and he is probably the best known of all Bahamian "historical" characters.

The sum total of the stories about Blackbeard is, of course, a caricature, though an instructive one. The Edward Teach of whom we read was a villain of more than vile aspect. The hair of his beard he wore in plaits. Ranting into battle, he wore six brace of pistols in a special belt and fuming slow-matches in his hatband. In a cruel age, his cruelties were legendary. A physical giant, he is said to have had fourteen "wives" and when eventually cornered in 1718 to have gone on fighting after five musket wounds and three sabre-thrusts. His drinking powers were unmatched. One favourite story tells how, at the climax of a drunken spree, he forced his companions to enter the hold of a ship where he had set trays of burning sulphur. Closing the hatches, he shouted, "We have made our own hell. Let us see who is closest kin to the devil by staying longest in it!" One by one his spluttering cronies pushed up the hatches and gasped in the fresh air. Needless to say, the triumphant Blackbeard was last on deck, hardly the worse for his experience.

The real Teach, sometimes called Thatch or Tach, was considerably smaller than the man of legend. A Bristol seaman, he had served on a privateer during Queen Anne's War. After 1713, he joined up with Hornigold, though he did not gain a ship of his own until 1716. This was a captured merchantman, which he loaded with guns and cut-throats and named, ironically, the *Queen Anne's Revenge*. His independent career lasted a bare two years, during which he made himself a thorough nuisance but did not amass a large fortune. There were now so many pirates that pickings were lean and only the most ruthless survived. A much-quoted extract from Teach's log for two days in 1718 gives a pretty true picture: "Rum all out. Our company somewhat sober, a damn'd confusion amongst us! Rogues a plotting, great talk of separation—so I look'd sharp for a prize. . . . Took one with a great deal of liquor aboard, so kept the company hot, then all things went well again!"

In a report on the Bahamas submitted to the Board of Trade in 1717 by Captain Matthew Musson, Teach is merely listed alongside four other pirate captains (Hornigold, Jennings, Burgess and White) who used New Providence as their base, with a total of about 360 men. But in the following year, Governor Robert Johnson of South Carolina regarded Teach as the main cause of an intolerable situation: "The unspeakable Calamity this Poor province Suffers from Pyrates Obliges me to inform Yo^r Lordships of it", he wrote to the Board of Trade, "in Order that his Majestie may know it and be induced to Afford us the Assistance of a Frigate or two to Cruse hereabouts upon them for we are continually Alarmed & our Ships taken to the utter ruin of our Trade; twice since my coming here in 9 Months time they have lain Off of our Barr taking & Plundering all Ships that either goe out or come in to this Port, about 14 days ago 4 Sail of them Appeared in Sight of the Town tooke our Pilot Boats and afterwards 8 or 9 Sail with Severall of the best Inhabitants of this Place on board and then sent me word if I did not immediately Send them a Chest of Medicine they would put every Prisoner to Death which for there Sakes being complied with After plundering them of all they had were sent a Shore Almost Naket.

"This Company is Commanded by One Teach Alias Blackbeard has a Ship of 40 od Guns under him and 3 Sloopes Tenders besides & are in all above 400 men . . ."

In 1716 Richard Beresford had asked why, since the Bahamas were obviously ideal for pirates, they could not also be so for legitimate forces. He was backed by the Governor of Virginia, who wrote in the summer of 1717: "I doubt not Y͏o͏ʳ Lordps will use your Interest that a sufficient Force be speedily dispatched to these Coasts for securing the Trade, and particularly to the Bahamas, to dislodge the Pyrates from thence, where they have settled their Generall Rendezvouse and seem to look upon these islands as their own . . ."

In London, the weight of argument and complaint was, at last, beginning to tell. The fact that the stream of letters came not only from independent citizens and captains but the Governors of every maritime colony, stirred even the indolent Crown to action. The fact that no-one apparently bothered to address the nominal Lord Proprietors any more, shows that their power had faded to a cipher. Fortunately for the Bahamas, their days of control were numbered. The period of complete Crown government was at hand. The long pirate honeymoon was almost over.

X

Woodes Rogers I

1717-21

EXPULSIS PIRATIS RESTITUTA COMMERCIA

The accession of King George I in 1714 should have given fresh impetus to the campaign against the Bahamian pirates, for there was a very real danger that the Bahamas might become a Jacobite stronghold. Around this time, a Captain Cammocke wrote to ex-Queen Mary, the widow of James II, saying that the New Providence pirates "did with one heart and voice proclaim James III for their King", and asking for a Jacobite Captain-General to be sent to organise "resistance" against the Hanoverian "usurper".

Six warships were commissioned by George I in 1715 to patrol the Caribbean but if they ever sailed their effect was negligible. In 1717, believing that prevention would be cheaper than cure, a general amnesty for all pirates was proposed. Governor Benjamin Bennett of Bermuda was instructed to send a responsible person to the Bahamas with a promise of absolute pardon for those who surrendered immediately. He sent his own son, Captain John Bennett, in an armed ship. Although he was fired on at first, Bennett managed to read the Royal Proclamation to about 300 pirates assembled in New Providence. Some seemed enthusiastic but the majority were sceptical. What guarantee was there, they asked, that their personal possessions would not be seized and declared illegal? In that case, they would have "ventured their necks for nothing". Only five pirates took advantage of the pardon and went to Bermuda, though these included the notorious William Jennings. Governor Bennett regarded it as inevitable that even the penitent would relapse, while men like Charles Vane and Edward Teach were beyond redemption.

What the Bahamas really needed was a Royal Governor; a man of character backed up by force. Such a man was not long in coming. His name was Captain Woodes Rogers, and ironically, like Blackbeard he was a Bristol man and an ex-privateer.

Woodes Rogers, the son and grandson of sea captains bearing the same name, was borne in Poole, Dorset, about 1679, the family moving to Bristol when he was a small boy. Following in the family tradition, he was apprenticed as a sailor in 1697, advancing his career substantially by his marriage to Sarah, the daughter of the famous Admiral Sir William Whetstone, in 1705.

Woodes Rogers became famous in his own day for his privateering voyage round the world between 1708 and 1711 during the War of the Spanish Succession, which bears favourable comparison with the exploits of Cavendish, Dampier and Anson. On this voyage, which resulted in the sacking of Guayaquil and the taking of the great Manila Galleon of 1709 as well as about twenty other prizes, Woodes Rogers demonstrated qualities of bravery and leadership which stood him in good stead as colonial Governor. The voyage was also memorable for the rescue of Alexander Selkirk from the island of Juan Fernández, Woodes Rogers' account of which gave Daniel Defoe the inspiration for his immortal *Robinson Crusoe* (1719).

Despite its success, the voyage of circumnavigation did not make Woodes Rogers rich. Within three years he was bankrupt and but for the two fine houses bequeathed by Admiral Whetstone to his daughter would have been homeless as well as penniless. Nevertheless, a life of premature retirement would never have suited the enterprising Rogers. Between 1713 and 1715 he was on a slaving voyage to Batavia and in 1716 he was deep in consultation for further projects with his famous friends Joseph Addison, Sir Richard Steele and Sir Hans Sloane. In May, 1716, for instance, Woodes Rogers wrote to Sloane asking the naturalist for details of Madagascar, since he was "ambitious to promote a settlement" there. The lines of Rogers' thought are obvious, for Madagascar was as notorious as New Providence as a resort for pirates.

It was probably Sir Hans Sloane who turned Rogers' attention to the Bahamas, for he was well-acquainted with the islands, having been in Jamaica some years before. Early in 1717, Rogers persuaded some of "the most considerable merchants of London and Bristol" to form a company to develop the islands, and in June he submitted a "humble memorial and proposal" to the Crown and a petition to the Lord Proprietors.

In his address to the Crown, Rogers stressed many of the arguments already presented by others: the excellence of the Bahamas as a base against the Spaniards; the dangers of them falling into alien hands; their complete lack of government or defence; their infestation by notorious pirates. Rogers was able to claim the use of a 400-ton ship of 34 guns, but suggested the advisability of sending 150 men to form a garrison.

The Board of Trade was impressed by Rogers' proposals and Secretary of State Addison did all he could to further his friend's scheme. On October 14, 1717, Addison wrote to the Secretary of War asking that at least a hundred men be "draughted out of the Guards, or any other regiments now on foot, or out of His Majesty's Hospital at Chelsea". Rogers had suggested 6d. a day for victualling, and the Treasury was asking for £912 : 10s. to keep the men for the first year.

The Lord Proprietors were more difficult. It was not until October 28, 1717, that they replied and then they were obviously under pressure from Addison. The civil and military government of the Bahamas they surrendered to the Crown; the quit rents and royalties they leased to the company and Woodes Rogers for twenty-one years. For the first seven years the lessees were to pay £50 a year, for the second seven, £100 and for the remaining seven, £200 a year; a total of £2,450, or average of £150 a year for the full lease. Along with Rogers, W. Chetwynd, Adam Cardonnel and Thomas Pitt, the grandfather of Lord Chatham, were specifically mentioned as holders of the lease.

Accordingly, on February 6, 1718, Rogers was officially appointed "Captain-General and Governor-in-Chief in and over our Bahama Islands" by King George I as well as receiving a Commission as Captain of the Independent Company of Foot, the King expressing "especial trust" in his "Prudence, Courage and Loyalty". Armed with the Amnesty Declaration of September 5, 1717, and a set of royal instructions, Rogers set sail on

April 11, 1718, in the company ship *Delicia*, accompanied by four warships of the Royal Navy, the frigates *Rose* and *Milford* and the sloops *Buck* and *Shark*. His orders were to publish his Commission, to appoint a Council of twelve, to nominate Justices, Sheriffs and other officers, to report in detail upon the condition of the Bahamas (including the possibility of setting up a General Assembly) and in all things to act similarly to the Governor of Jamaica "as near as the circumstances of the place will admit it".

After a journey of about fourteen weeks, the little fleet reached the Bahamas around July 20, 1718. Some of the inhabitants of Harbour Island came out to greet Rogers with the news that there were over a thousand pirates in New Providence and that Vane at least had no intention of surrendering. The pirates could not easily defend Nassau, however, for the fort was in disrepair and only one nine-pound gun was mounted. It was believed that most of the pirates, including Hornigold, Davis, Burgess and Carter, were prepared to accept the King's Pardon, but there was no certainty.

On the evening of July 26, 1718, Rogers lay off the Bar of Nassau Harbour. In the middle of the night there was a fire and explosion near the town, which optimists believed were made by the pirates celebrating the forthcoming amnesty. In fact, it was Vane firing a French prize as he transferred his plunder to a smaller and swifter ship, in order to sneak out of the shallow East Bay. Captain Whitney of the *Rose* sent a boat ashore to reconnoitre, but its crew was surprised by Vane and the boat captured.

At daybreak, Vane hoisted the skull and crossbones, fired a gun in derision and set full sail for the east. The *Buck* was sent after him but was forced to give up the chase as hopeless. After plundering a merchantman called the *Neptune* off Green Turtle Cay, Vane sailed for Hispaniola and was never seen in the Bahamas again. In 1719, he was shipwrecked in Honduras and was executed in Jamaica in the following year.

The pirates who remained in New Providence were in a mood of penitence that bordered on jubilation. Woodes Rogers landed and walked between two lines of the inhabitants, numbering about three hundred, who fired their muskets continually into the air and shouted convincing "huzzahs" for King George. In front of the dilapidated fort, Rogers was greeted by Thomas Walker and Thomas Taylor, who styled themselves Chief Justice and President of the Council. Opening his scrolls with a flourish, the new Governor read his Commission and the Proclamation of Pardon.

These formalities over, Woodes Rogers went to work with tremendous energy. The following day, martial law was declared and Richard Turnley, the Chief Pilot, and others were commissioned to seize and make an inventory of the cargoes of all ships in the harbour, pending the setting up of an Admiralty Court.

Within a week, Rogers had re-formed the civil government. For his Council he nominated six of those he had brought with him and six of the principal citizens of Nassau "who had not been pirates, and were of good repute". This Council met regularly and most of its minutes are still to be found among the Colonial Office papers. Also in the archives are to be found "Proceedings of an Assembly of Severall of the Principall Inhabitants of the Bahama Islands", dated August 1, 1718, but this does not seem to have been a formal gathering.

At the same time, Governor Rogers appointed an Admiralty Judge, Provost Marshal, Governor's Secretary and Chief Naval Officer, sending to London for official confirmation. As a gesture of conciliation, Thomas Walker and John Graves were continued in the offices of Chief Justice and Collector of Customs which they had claimed for years, though Graves at least proved senile and incompetent. At a lower level, Rogers appointed Justices of the Peace, Constables and "Overseers of the Ways and Roads".

Defence was an immediate problem for the Spanish threat was once more severe. Fort Nassau was repaired and several guns mounted. Its garrison was formed by the Independent Company, which was housed at first within the walls in rough huts thatched with palmetto. The citizens were organised into a militia of three companies to defend the town and some of the ex-pirates were even given privateering commissions and sent after Vane and others.

Rogers' policy was obviously to utilise the current enthusiasm and to put everyone to work. Those not on guard were set to cleaning the roads and clearing the bush in and around Nassau, "so that it began to have the appearance of a civilised place". A new plan of settlement was also put forward. Each new settler was to receive a plot of land 120 feet square with unlimited free timber, provided only that he clear the ground and build a house within a year. Woodes Rogers also proposed the development of the whale industry and the sending of more salt to the cod fisheries of Newfoundland.

Serious troubles, however, lay in store. Hardly had they stepped ashore before Rogers own men were ravaged by an epidemic, which he attributed to the odour of certain rotting hides. By the autumn, 86 were dead and Rogers himself was weak with sickness.

Even those who survived the disease were disappointing. Of those who came with Rogers, 19 deserted or had to be discharged. As for the inhabitants, as Captain Johnson said, "It did not much suit the inclinations of the pirates to be set to work; and though they had provision sufficiently, and also a good allowance of wine and brandy to each man, yet they began to have such a hankering after their old trade that many of them took opportunities of seizing boats in the night, made their escape, so that in a few months there were not many left". Woodes Rogers himself described the remnant in scathing terms: "Then for work they mortally hate it, for when they have cleared a patch that will supply them with potatoes and yams and very little else, fish being so plentiful. . . . They thus live, poorly and indolently with a seeming content, and pray for wrecks or pirates; and few of them have an opinion of a regular orderly life under any sort of government, and would rather spend all they have at a Punch house than pay me one-tenth to save their families and all that's dear to them . . ." This was despite the fact that war with Spain had broken out and the Spaniards were known to have ravaged Cat Island, only 125 miles from Nassau.

Captain Whitney of H.M.S. *Rose* was little help. On one occasion he refused to obey orders until Rogers hit him on the head with a pistol butt. After a very short time he deserted the Bahamas and returned to London to spread malicious stories about Rogers. As to Collector of Customs Graves, the Governor spoke of "that old man's inability to act, wch. he has not been able to do otherwise than in his chamber and bed, but is of so petulent a temper that I have been unwilling to interfere".

Woodes Rogers began to fear that he was not even strong enough to make an example of those pirates he captured. In November, 1718, he sent three to England for trial, but in December he was presented with ten more. This was the crisis of his first regime. A certain John Augur had accepted the amnesty in July but had reverted to piracy, he and his companions pillaging two trading vessels when sent out by Rogers for provisions. Two other ex-pirates, Hornigold and Cockram, were dispatched to bring them to justice and they captured thirteen of them at Exuma, three dying of wounds on the way back to Nassau.

Rogers decided that firm and prompt action was imperative. The trial was held on December 5, 1718, in a Court of Admiralty Sessions before Thomas Walker, William Fairfax, Robert Beauchamps, Wingate Gale, Nathaniel Taylor, Josias Burgess, Peter Courant and Rogers himself. Despite the pirates' plea that all the blame should be attached to Phineas Bunch, one of the dead men, they were declared guilty and sentenced to death. The execution was carried out at 10 a.m. on December 10, after the pirates had been allowed three-quarters of an hour to sing psalms under the gallows. At the very last moment, Rogers reprieved one of them, George Rounsivell, aged 18, as he wrote to the Secretary of State, through a desire to respite him for his future repentance. "He is the son of loyal and good parents at Weymouth in Dorsetshire", he added, doubtless remembering the county of his own parents' birth. "I hope this unhappy young man will deserve his life, and I beg the honour of your intercession with His Majesty on his behalf."

But even this typical act of force and clemency and the surrender at New Providence of "Calico Jack" Rackham in May, 1719, did not cure Rogers' troubles. As many as 2,000 pirates were still at large and the grip of the Spaniards on Nassau was tightening. In February, 1720, Nassau was attacked by a strong Spanish force under Don Francisco Cornego, consisting of an *armadillo* of four warships and eight sloops, with 1,300 men against Rogers' total forces of about 500. Deterred from a frontal assault across the bar by the presence of the armed *Delicia* and the 24-gun frigate H.M.S. *Flamborough*, the Spaniards attempted a landing east of Nassau but were repelled by furious musketry. The Spanish force retreated but its threat remained. As Rogers wrote in one of his letters, reinforcements would be "as good as 500 hangings".

At the best of times letters took six weeks to reach London and replies could never be expected in less than three months. But now, many dispatches fell into enemy hands and Rogers resorted to sending copies by several different ships. There are dozens of his dispatches to be seen at the Public Record Office dated between 1718 and 1720. And yet he waited long frustrating months in vain for replies, let alone supplies. In fact, the Board of Trade and the Secretary of State ignored him while busy with other matters. Even the Company, almost ruined by their expenses and with nothing to show for it, had changed hands without anyone consulting poor absent Woodes Rogers.

From his letters, we can visualise Rogers plunging from optimism to pessimism and from exasperation to despair.

In January, 1719, he had written in fairly good spirits to Sir Richard Steele, the letter being addressed to "Bartram's Coffee House in Church Court, opposite Hungerford Market in the Strand, London. Via Carolina." He complained that no man-of-war had visited Nassau for five months and of the behaviour of Captain Whitney, but his chief concern seems to have been with the nuisance caused by a voluble and snobbish lady called Pritchard, whom Rogers would willingly have ordered placed in a ducking stool "if our carpenters had not otherwise been employed". He ended with a hope that Steele had "thrown away your great cane, and can dance a minuet".

On May 29, 1719, Rogers wrote to the Lord Commissioners of Trade in somewhat more urgent tone. "We have never been free from apprehension of danger from Pirates and Spaniards", he wrote, "and I can only impute these causes to the want of a stationed ship of war till we really can be strong enough to defend ourselves." This promised to be a lengthy task, for the inhabitants gave Woodes Rogers little support. ". . . Though they expect the enemy that has surprised them these fifteen years thirty-four times, yet these wretches can't be kept to watch at night, and when they do they come very seldom sober, and rarely

awake all night, though our officers or soldiers very often surprise their guard and carry off their arms, and I punish, fine, or
confine them almost every day. . . .

"Had I not took another method of eating, drinking and
working with them myself, officers, soldiers, sailors and passengers, and watch at the same time, whilst they were drunk and
drowsy, I could never have got the Fort into any posture of
defence, neither would they willingly [have] kept themselves or
me from the pirates, if the expectation of a war with Spain had
not been perpetually kept up. It was as bad as treason is in
England to declare our design of fortifying was to keep out the
pirates if they were willing to come in and say they would be
honest and live under government as we called it even then . . ."

In November, 1720, the Council was forced to report to the
Secretary of State that the fact that Governor Rogers had received
no letter from him dated since July, 1719, "and none from the
Board of Trade since his arrival, gives him and us great uneasi-
ness least this poor colony should be no more accounted as part
of His Britannick Majesty's dominions".

By February, 1721, despite the ending of hostilities with Spain,
Woodes Rogers was at the end of his tether. Under the constant
strain of indifference, expense and overwork, his health was once
more breaking down. On the 25th, he wrote, "It is Impossible
I can subsist here any longer on the foot I have been left ever
since my Arrivall". He had been stranded, he said, with "a few
Sick men to encounter Five hundred of the Pirates", and had
no support in men, supplies or warships. He had contracted
great debts in having to buy provisions and clothing in North
America at inflated prices. "This place", he added, "so secured
by my Industry, Indefatigable pains and the forfeiture of my
health has since been sold for Fourty Thousand pounds and my
self by a manager at Home, and Co-partners' Factotem here
thought not to Deserve any share of it." Instead, he had been
very badly used and all expenses thrown on him. Expressing
"Intire Relyance on the Honour and Justice of my Lord Londen-
derry, Mr. Wm. Chetwynd, and Mr. Dominicque, the only Surviving of the Copartners worth mentioning", he announced that
he was leaving forthwith for England to save the colony (and,
presumably, to rescue his own health, fortune and reputation).

Appointing William Fairfax Deputy Governor, Woodes Rogers left Nassau in March, 1721, for England, calling at South Carolina on the way to order provisions sent to New Providence to keep the soldiers victualled until Christmas. He reached Bristol in August, carrying with him a testimonial, or "Memorial", from the principal Councillors and citizens of Nassau, dated March 21, 1721. In this, they complained of the ineffectiveness of the Proprietors and Co-partners and begged the power to call an Assembly. They also put in a good word for Rogers, hoping to "do our Governor justice, and prevent any further ungrateful usage being offered him at home, to frustrate his good endeavours when please God he arrives there, for the service of his country, to preserve this settlement; for next to the Divine protection, it is owing to him, who has acted amongst us without the least regard for his private advantage or separate interest, in a scene of continual fatigues and hardships. These motives led us to offer the truth under our hands of the almost insurmountable difficulty, that he and this colony has struggled with for the space of two years and eight months past."

But Rogers had small hope of fair treatment at home. Since by his own account he had spent over £11,000 of his own money in the Bahamas, his presence in London was embarrassing to both the Partners and the Board of Trade. In October he petitioned the Lords of the Treasury, stating his achievements and bewailing his impoverished condition. He had, he claimed, saved the islands "from destruction by the Spaniards, or from again being possessed by the pirates, he had disbursed his whole fortune, and credit, and stood engaged for large sums. He prayed that he might be granted an allowance for victualling for the last three years." The appeal apparently fell on deaf ears, for Woodes Rogers spent some time later in prison for debt. Thus were the services of Nassau's saviour rewarded.

XI

Woodes Rogers II
1721-32

Clearly it was impossible for Woodes Rogers to return to govern the Bahamas in 1721 and George Phenney was appointed in his place, filling the post until Rogers returned for his second term in 1729. Phenney was obviously a man of lesser calibre than his predecessor, but his term as Governor has always been somewhat unfairly overshadowed. He seems to have made persistent efforts to increase the efficiency of the administration, and it was during his term that the plans for forming a legislative assembly were worked out. His chief misfortune was that he was burdened by an overbearing wife.

A study of the Board of Trade "Original Correspondence" for the period 1721-29 gives us a fairly complete picture of Phenney's work as Governor. These documents alone are worthy of editing and publication as a separate volume. Besides the Minutes of the Council from 1721 to 1723, the public accounts of the colony are given for each year without exception. There are interesting reports of Admiralty Court cases and a discussion of the legal jurisdiction still claimed by the Lord Proprietors. The confused state of land tenure at the time is also obvious from many entries; land disposal being divided between Proprietors, Company and Crown. Besides these items, Phenney's own routine reports and replies give invaluable details of the islands; their produce, currency, fees and fines, with lists of christenings, marriages and burials, and other population statistics. From these we learn that in 1726 the population of the Bahamas was only about 1,140, consisting of 500 whites and 250 Negroes in New Providence, 200 whites and 40 Negroes in Eleuthera and 130 whites and 20 Negroes in Harbour Island. Of these, Phenney reckoned that only 116 were capable of bearing arms, of whom "seldom above seventy are at home at a time". This was hardly encouraging considering the permanent likelihood of a resumption of fighting with Spain. In this last respect, Phenney's correspondence with the Governor of Havana in 1722 and 1726 and his frequent references to Spanish movements and plans must have been of great use to the authorities at home.

Optimistically, Phenney praised the fertility of the islands with their white, reddish and black soils, which could produce . . "very large sugar canes, the finest cotton in the world, fine Madera, Mahogany, Cedar and Pine fit for building of vessels; Manchineel, Prince Wood, Lignum Vitae, brown Ebony, great quantities of Brazeletto, Fustick and other dying woods, Senna, Gum-Elmi, Guiacum, Mastick and several other Gums and Medicinal Drugs.

"The Palmetto Trees afford as good Platt as on Bermuda with which I have invited some people hither to make an Essay thereon. The land produces most sorts of Provisions for Familys, various sorts of fine Fruits, the Pine Apples here being of the best kind in America.

"On the shores of these Islands are often found Quantities of Ambergreece, one piece taken up last Year weighed 166 lbs. and some Amber. The Sperma Ceti come yearly about the Winter, at what time the Seils likewise come upon the shores to breed, and are caught, each of which affords about 20 Gallons of Oyl. . . .

"Our present inhabitants are mostly sea-faring men.

"The Trade chiefly consists in cutting the Dye Woods, which with the salt, Oyl, Turtle and Turtle Shell and Fruits in their Seasons are exported to the neighbouring Colonys for which sometimes the Vessels belonging to No. America bring in Barter several Comoditys . . ."

The earliest surviving drawing of Nassau, by one Gascoigne, is dated "1729/30". From it we can picture the "city" that George Phenney and Woodes Rogers knew. Despite the obvious intention of the artist to magnify the place, it appears a straggling collection of about thirty wooden houses gathered around the Fort like a brood of chicks around a hen. The "prominent landmarks" shown include the tiny steepled church at the eastern fringes, somewhere in the present location of Rawson Square, the Courthouse-and-Gaol building on the waterfront, the house of Thomas Walker on the hill where Government House is today, Fort Nassau with its guardhouse, and Governor Phenney's residence on the far extreme of the western ridge. This unimposing group of buildings, obliterated by the erection of Fort Charlotte in 1787, at least enjoyed the finest site in Nassau, overlooking the town and harbour. How often must Phenney and Rogers have looked out to sea from its porch; hopefully for British ships bringing supplies and news from home, and fearfully for the return of the pirates or Spaniards.

One of Governor Phenney's most notable achievements was to bring the troublesome inhabitants of Eleuthera more firmly under government. During the recent war with Spain they had failed to come to the aid of Nassau and now they were carrying on a clandestine trade with all manner of foreign vessels. Moreover, their morals and general slackness seemed to hark back to the anarchy of pirate days.

On January 13, 1724, the Governor issued an Order-in-Council directed to the people of "Islathera" and Harbour Island, containing nine rules. The services of the Church of England were to be regularly performed by the Magistrates and attended by everyone except nine French, Swiss and Palatine Calvinists specifically excused. Swearing, drunkenness and "other scandalous Actions in derogation of God's Honor" were to be severely punished. Returns of population, slave and free, and of ships entering and clearing harbour were to be sent annually. Wrecks were to be registered, and no-one was allowed to leave the islands without the written permission of the Governor. A general muster of the Militia was to be held four times a year and the approach of any pirate or enemy ship was to be speedily reported to Nassau. Finally, no lands were to be held without patent; these holding deeds for less than two hundred acres would never be allowed to sit in the Assembly and no-one with title to less than fifty acres would be allowed to vote.

Concerning the formation of an Assembly, foreshadowed in Woodes Rogers' Commission in February, 1718, and pleaded for in the *Memorial* of March, 1721, George Phenney was extremely active, although he received little more attention in Whitehall than had Woodes Rogers. Shortly after his arrival in November,

Fort Montagu (1742), guarding the eastern approaches to Nassau

1721, Governor Phenney submitted a list of 27 "fit persons to be recommended to his Majesty to be elected by the Publick to make an Assembly or execute other Publick offices under the Government", 15 being from New Providence, 6 from Eleuthera and 6 from Harbour Island. This petition was not received by the Lords Commissioners of Trade until April 26, 1722, being read on May 1 and promptly shelved. By this time Phenney had forwarded a second petition dated March, 1722. This received a suave but unsatisfactory reply in mid-1723, in which Phenney was told that the question was "being considered". Another letter in 1725 less graciously rebuked Phenney for being remiss in his regular returns, but made no mention of the Assembly. Phenney, concealing what irritation he must have felt, complied with the request for more detailed statistics in 1726, but pointed out that although the Fort had been rebuilt, it was unarmed, since requests for gunpowder and gun carriage wheels had gone unanswered. In fact, the heavy guns had remained unmounted for no less than five years. He also repeated, almost parrot-wise, the plea for an Assembly, without which the raising of revenue was almost impossible.

Phenney's heroic persistence paid off, but he was not destined to preside over the first elective Assembly, which was authorised in Woodes Rogers' second Commission on December 26, 1728. For George Phenney had fallen into general disfavour, chiefly on account of his wife. Apparently, this formidable lady had forced a lucrative monopoly in salt, planking, bark, palmetto and "platt",* and compelled the masters of trading ships to sell direct to her so that she could control the retail market. In August, 1728, a certain Townshend stated that "The Governor ingrosses all the Trade. Mrs. Phenney sells Rum by the pint and Biscuits by the Half Ryal." Mrs. Martha Vere went even further. "She had the Opportunity", she wrote about the same time, "of keeping the very Life of everybody there in her Mercy, who could not have any Provisions or Subsistence whatsoever without paying her own exorbitant prices. . . . The Ld. Governor's wife has frequently Brow beated Jurys and insulted even the Justice on the Bench."

Although Phenney's personal character was championed by

* Thin strips of palm leaf used for weaving into hats, mats and baskets.

John Mulcaster, agent to the Company, and by Cuthbert Jackson, his attorney, the Lord Commissioners petitioned the King to send a more responsible Governor to the Bahamas, so that more settlers might be attracted there. By lucky chance, Woodes Rogers was also petitioning the Crown at the same time to be reinstated as Governor. This document, which was sent to the Prime Minister, Sir Robert Walpole, was supported by twenty-nine influential persons, including Sir Hans Sloane, Samuel Shute, ex-Governor of Massachusetts, Alexander Spotswood, Deputy Governor of Virginia, ex-Governor Bennet of Bermuda and Lord Montagu, who stated, "We never heard any complaint against his conduct in his duty there, nor that he behaved otherwise in that employ, than with the utmost resolution and fidelity becoming a good subject, though to the ruin of his own fortune".

Accordingly, George Phenney was dismissed and Woodes Rogers reappointed. Phenney was not disgraced, however, the Board of Trade merely criticising him for "conniving at or indulging his wife in so extravagant and oppressive a conduct, altho' in other respects Mr. Phenney bears a fair character". In 1731, he was appointed Surveyor-General of Customs in the Southern Colonies, becoming in 1733 an extraordinary member of the Council of the Bahamas and the other colonies under his jurisdiction.

In an interesting coda to his career in the Bahamas, we learn that George Phenney tried to leave his wife behind in the islands preparatory to getting a divorce. In a letter to the Hon. Charles Delafaye, Woodes Rogers explained how he had ordered them to leave Nassau together, though he feared proceedings in Doctors' Commons were pending nonetheless.

The terms of Woodes Rogers' second Commission were more generous than those of the first. Besides being empowered to call an elective Assembly of twenty-four members, he was granted a salary of £400 a year. This must have been a relief, for his fortune had been swallowed up during his first term and he had been forced to live for some years on the niggardly half-pay of a Captain of Independent Troops, Besides this, he had acted as unofficial adviser to the Government on maritime matters and may have been employed by the Dutch in Madagascar in 1724, though details are lacking. Certainly, his re-employment in 1728 at the age of 50 gave him a fresh spurt of energy and optimism.

Woodes Rogers reached the Bahamas on August 25, 1729, accompanied by his son William and daughter, Sarah. His wife remained in London. Among Rogers' effects were "two little flagons, one chalice, one paten and a receiver to take the offerings for the Use of His Majesty's Chapel there", a strict contrast to the soldiers and cannon he had taken to Nassau in 1718.

The first duty was to convene the Assembly. Writs were prepared and a proclamation issued on September 8, 1729. The elections for the five districts were staggered and spread over the week September 15-20. The Assembly first met on Michaelmas Day, September 29, at the house of Mr. Samuel Lawford. The eight members for Nassau were John Colebrooke, Edward Elding, Peter Goudet, Benjamin Hall, Samuel Lawford, William Pinder, Roger Reading and Moses Simms. John Bennett, Thomas Downham, Samuel Frith and Thomas Saunders represented the East and Jacob Jarroed, Cane Belou, Florentine Cox and Thomas Lory, the West. The four from Eleuthera were John Bethell, Joseph Ingraham, Paul Newbold and John Carey. The four from Harbour Island were John Thompson Senior, John Thompson Junior, John Roberts and Seabom Pinder. Of the 24 elected, only 6 had been listed among Phenney's 27 "suitable persons" of 1721.

John Colebrooke was chosen Speaker and committees were formed to inquire into the state of the islands. During the first session, no less than twelve Acts were passed; for the encouragement of new settlers, to settle the thorny problem of the quit rents, to aid the building of roads, to prevent the destruction of standing timber by fire, to govern the slaves, to control the export of ships' planking, to levy the public revenue; to lay out the town of Nassau, to discourage stray cattle and fruit stealing, to encourage the planting of cotton and the stocking of the Out Islands with cattle.

But the longed-for Assembly was far from the panacea some had hoped. Difficulties soon crowded in upon the luckless Governor. There had been a disastrous hurricane only three weeks before Rogers' arrival and he found the Fort in disrepair, trade at a low ebb and the revenue non-existent. Moreover, there was still a danger from piratical and Spanish attacks. In November, 1729, he pleaded for the Independent Company of Troops in Bermuda to be sent to Nassau, which was done forthwith, despite the forebodings and opposition of Governor Pitt.

By October, 1730, Woodes Rogers was forced to write to the Board of Trade in very despondent tones. Despite his attempts to promote sugar and cotton planting, shipbuilding and the production of salt, progress was painfully slow. Seven ships were on the stocks, two plantations had been established for sugar production and one for rum and an expedition to Exuma under guard had netted 18,000 bushels of salt. But the entire revenue for the first six months of 1730 was a paltry 418 pieces of eight. Except for a few Palatinate Germans, few settlers had been attracted to the poverty-stricken colony. The population in 1731 consisted of only 925 whites and 453 slaves. "I found the place so very poor and thin of inhabitants", wrote Rogers, "that I never mentioned any salary to them for myself or anyone else, and the fees annexed to all offices here being the lowest of any part of America, no one can support himself thereon without some other employment." He also begged for "an orthodox divine" to be sent as chaplain for the colony's spiritual needs.

Rogers' chief burden, however, was not spiritual but opposition and lack of support within the Assembly itself. This was led by the Speaker, John Colebrooke, who seems to have become the Governor's implacable enemy. Colebrooke had been a partner in trade with William Whetstone Rogers, son of the Governor, and the antagonism between Colebrooke and Woodes Rogers seems to have been connected with a break-up of this partnership in 1730 upon the appointment of William Rogers as Colonial Secretary. Clearly Colebrooke resented the implication that a business connexion was incompatible with the proper exercise of an administrative post, but the origins of the conflict can be traced back much further, to 1721, or even 1717.

The *Memoirs* of John Ker of Kersland relate that even before Woodes Rogers was first appointed to the Bahamas Ker had been negotiating with the Ostend Company to set up a Caribbean free port on New Providence under Imperial protection. In 1721 John Colebrooke, "a cunning man and perfect Master of the

Art of Stock-jobbing", entered the scene, intriguing privately
with the highest Imperial authorities in Vienna and stealing all
the credit for the free port scheme from its true author, John
Ker of Kersland, With the successful establishment of a Crown
Colony in the Bahamas the project fell into abeyance, but in
1729, Colebrooke wormed his way into Woodes Rogers' confidence and appeared in Nassau itself, to test the practicality of
his far-reaching plot.

As Bryan Little so aptly puts it, "Colebrooke's chosen
weapon was the control of the newly convened Assembly. His
chief ally was John White, unknown to the innocent Rogers as
one of Colebrooke's cronies. So White was made second senior
member of the Council, also Treasurer and Chief Justice. As
Rogers' staunch ally, Lewis Bonnet wrote later to Delafaye, the
Duke of Newcastle's Secretary, the two merchants were neatly
combined to make poor Rogers 'uneasy', the more so as many
Assemblymen were soon the 'creatures' of Colebrooke. Another
of Colebrooke's allies, named Jarrold or Jenner, went out as
Governor's secretary to complete the spider's web being woven
to imprison Woodes Rogers."

"During the sessions of the last Assembly", wrote Rogers
in February, 1731, "I endeavoured (pursuant to His Majesty's
instructions) to recommend to them the state and condition of
the Fortifications, which much wanted all the assistance possible
for their repair . . . to which I did not find the major part of the
Assembly averse at first, but since, they have been diverted
from their good intentions by the insinuations of one Mr. Colebrooke, their Speaker, who imposed so long on their ignorance,
that I was obliged to dissolve them, lest his behaviour might
influence them to fall into schemes yet more contrary to the
good of the Colony and their own safety. Another Assembly is
lately elected, and (I) still find the effects of the above Mr. Colebrooke's influence on the most ignorant of them, who are the
majority."

When the House was dissolved, Colebrooke refused to give
up certain papers demanded by the Governor. He was promptly
arrested and charged with sedition. His trial occurred in May,
1731, before Chief Justice Knowland, Attorney-General Bacon
prosecuting. The Petty Jury found Colebrooke guilty and he

was fined a crippling £750, being ordered detained during the King's pleasure until he could post a sufficient bond for his future good behaviour.

"How great an enemy Mr. Colebrooke hath been to this Government", wrote Woodes Rogers in June, 1731, "and what vile means he used to make the Garrison mutiny and stir up a spirit of discontent and opposition in the inhabitants, by the great influence which he had artfully gained over the most ignorant of them, while he was Speaker of the Assembly, from all which I humbly hope that the method taken to prevent his proceeding in his seditious and wicked designs will meet with his Majesty's and your Lordships' approbation." The Lords of Trade probably supported Rogers' harsh action, for a letter from them crossed his, in which they upheld his earlier dissolution of the Assembly. This letter, dated June 29, 1731, contained the following important general statement: "It would be proper that the proceedings of the Assembly should also resemble those of the Parliament of Great Britain as far as the circumstances of the Colony and Your Instructions permit . . . the constitution of England owes its preservation very much to the maintaining of an equal balance between the branches of the legislature, and that the more distinct they are kept from each other, the likelier they will be to agree, and the longer they will be likely to last."

But there seemed no hope now of agreement between Governor Rogers and the group of Colebrooke's supporters. Faction reigned in Nassau. In August, 1731, Rogers reported: "I can yet procure no assistance from the inhabitants towards the fortifications, though I have without any help from them built a new Barrack for the Garrison in the Fort, and have made upwards of twenty new carriages for guns of this country timber, and shall continue to do all I can towards the Fortifications as soon as the heat of the summer is over, that I can put the garrison to work again, without endangering their healths. And as soon as possible will try in a new Assembly what I can do, though I fear little public good is to be expected from them if Mr. Colebrooke and his accomplices here can have any influence to prevent the peoples working, they being too poor to contribute anything worth contributing in money."

John Colebrooke even stirred up trouble at home and Woodes

Rogers dispatched his son to England with a further letter of explanation, in October, 1731. "As I am at a loss what complaints Mr. Colebrooke may make, I entreat your Lordships will please to allow me to refer you to my son who will have the honour to wait on your Lordships with this, and is instructed to give you such particular information, as you may desire to be apprised of, either with regard to Mr. Colebrooke, or anything else relating to this colony, I have also transmitted herewith transcripts of the Council and Assembly proceedings, and answers to your Lordships' queries, together with an account of every family on this island in as particular a manner as possible. . . . I hope soon to visit Columba alias Cat Island, which being esteemed the most fertile of any in this government, I shall transmit to your Lordships a particular account thereof."

Some of the difficulties of the colony, thought Rogers, could be resolved by the Crown buying out the Proprietors, who still held on to their title to land in the Bahamas. In April, 1730, the Proprietors had offered to sell their rights for "one thousand guineas each, clear of all fees". In October, 1731, Rogers recommended that this offer be accepted to "end the discouraging contests on titles to land". The six Lord Proprietors were actually paid £1,000 each in 1733 and the Company £2,000 at the same time for the unexpired portion of their twenty-one-year lease. By this time, however, Woodes Rogers, the only real asset the Company had ever had, had himself expired.

The first Royal Governor probably never made his promised visit to Cat Island, for he died in Nassau on July 15, 1732, doubtless worn out by his difficulties and the opposition he faced. On July 20, Richard Thompson, President of the Council, wrote laconically to the Secretary of State: "Whereas it pleased Almighty God to take unto himself the soul of Woodes Rogers, Esq., our late Governor on 15th day of the inst. We acquaint Yr. Lordship therewith."

The exact cause of Woodes Rogers' death will never be known, nor the place of his burial. His will, bequeathing his goods to his two surviving children, was proved in London on November 24, 1732. His family did not long survive him. Sarah Rogers, his wife, from whom he had evidently been estranged for some years, died in London later in 1732. William

Whetstone Rogers, who continued to serve as Secretary of the Bahamas until 1734, died at Whydah in West Africa in 1735, presumably while on a voyage to obtain slaves for the Bahamas. Sarah Rogers, the Governor's daughter, died in 1743. Since neither William nor Sarah were married, Woodes Rogers has no direct descendants.

Woodes Rogers was the first really honest and effective Governor of the Bahamas and the first fully appointed by the Crown. We must, however, beware of oversimplification. Too often the date 1718 (or 1729) is taken as an absolute break; the end of a "bad" and the beginning of a "good" period in Bahamian history. History, alas, is rarely so simple.

We have already seen that the assumption of Crown control was a gradual process. The Proprietors had never controlled Customs and the Crown had confirmed Governors and approved officials since 1697. Moreover, the surrender of proprietary interest was even more gradual and was not completed until 1787. Woodes Rogers was not a complete civil servant. Through the Company formed in 1718 he himself held a proprietary interest in the Bahamas, and the troops he commanded in Nassau were an "independent company" not under the direct control of the War Office.

Even the common assumption that the House of Assembly, with its records almost continuous from September 29, 1729, was a creation of the first Royal Governor, is untrue. As we have seen, there are indications of an elective legislature as early as the first settlement in 1648, and frequent mention of a law-passing Assembly, complete with Speaker, during the period of the proprietary Governors. Only in 1703, with the revolt of Speaker Warren against Governor Lightwood does this seem to have broken down.

In his first term, Woodes Rogers ruled by ordinance of Governor-in-Council and he seems to have preferred this form of government, for his relations with the Assembly after 1729 were hardly untroubled.

Woodes Rogers is too often pictured as an unmitigated hero. In his personal character he seems to have inspired obedience and respect, but not much love. It is probable that he was inclined to be harsh and humourless, especially in his second term. One ex-pirate even called him a tyrant. He was a great believer in the efficacy of hard work, always an unpopular attitude in the Bahamas, and his remedy for discord was discipline. It was the attitude of the quarterdeck, and Woodes Rogers always remained a sea captain at heart. Nonetheless, he guided the Bahamas through stormy seas and into the comparatively calm waters of Crown control.

XII

Eighteenth-Century Government
1732-38

Despite Rogers' undoubted work in expelling the pirates and restoring commerce, commemorated in the Great Seal granted him by George I in 1722, it must have been a disappointing colony to which his successor, Richard Fitzwilliam, came early in 1734. Ignorant of the piratical anarchy that had preceded Rogers, his personal disillusionment rings loud in his actions. Like so many of the proprietary Governors, he resorted to cynicism and greed, until complaints, the corollary of his own disenchantment, reached London and he was replaced.

Unnoticed by Fitzwilliam, processes had begun, however, which shaped the colony towards its present form. As the eighteenth century unrolled, the individual Governors meant less and public opinion, or the feelings of prominent local interests, much more. Except for the separation of the executive and legislative functions of the Governor's Council in 1841, the constitution of the Bahamas as it evolved during the four governorships following the death of Rogers remained essentially the same until the achievement of responsible and internal self government in 1964.

The Bahamas, as we have seen, had been a Crown Colony since 1718. Royal Instruction implied that the Crown, in the person of the Governor, controlled the administration, finance and judicial business; while the popular Assembly occupied an inferior position rather like that of a municipal council, its job being the passage of by-laws and ordinances for meeting the immediate needs of the colony. The islanders, however, never regarded themselves as completely subject to the royal prerogative and in their fight for greater autonomy they were aided

by two factors; the inefficiency and indifference of the departments of state and the opposition within England itself to the
royal prerogative.

The king's Privy Council regarded itself as omnicompetent
in colonial affairs, but throughout the eighteenth century it
lacked a formal composition and was fighting a long and losing
battle with Parliament over the extent of its powers, which
eventually turned it into the modern Cabinet, responsible to the
House of Commons. Although it could fix boundaries and settle
disputes, the Privy Council's most important power was the
appointment of colonial officials. Through it the Crown appointed the Governor, Secretary, Attorney-General, Treasurer
or Receiver-General, Chief Justice, Provost Marshal and Collector
of Customs. These posts were always to be held at the royal
pleasure and to be responsible to the King alone.

The Privy Council could veto colonial laws but it could not
pass them. Parliament was too jealous of the Privy Council to
allow this, but ironically, although Parliament itself reserved the
right to legislate for the colonies, as Harcourt Malcolm observed,
there has never been a single British Act aimed exclusively at the
Bahamas. This may have been the result of the insignificance
of the islands, but it is a fact that if a domestic British Act is
operative in the Bahamas, it has been re-enacted in the House of
Assembly. The Bahamian Act of 1799 which determined "How
much the Laws of England are practicable within the Bahama
Islands" cited the Common Law in general, the prerogative Acts,
the Acts governing oaths and tests for officers, those guarding
the rights and liberties of individuals and 192 specific Acts,
dating back to the Middle Ages and including 29 passed since
1729. The fact that applicable Acts were specified, postulated
independence to colonial legislatures, though at the same time
the Imperial Parliament insisted that colonial laws should never
conflict with English Statutes, a principle laid down in the
Bahamas as early as Heath's grant in 1629 or Bridges' Commission in 1688.

Although the Privy Council could act in colonial matters as
a committee consisting of all members, calling witnesses and
legal counsel and issuing decisions as Orders-in-Council, it almost
invariably referred colonial matters to the Board of Trade, the

Treasury, the Admiralty or the War Office. Of these by far the most important was the Board of Trade, originating in 1696; but it was always too small and ill-defined and, as far as the colonies were concerned, too dedicated to the principles of mercantilism. It was only as it expanded to become the Colonial Office under its own Secretary of State assuming the colonial functions of the Treasury, Admiralty and War Office, that this body became paramount in non-legislative colonial administration. As it was, during the eighteenth century the ordinances of the Board of Trade were usually regarded as a meddlesome nuisance, the fact that the Treasury disbursed all colonial money was taken as the chief reason that the Bahamas were always poor, and because the Admiralty and War Office were technically responsible for defence they were held responsible for the fact that the islands were never defended adequately.

Much, almost everything, depended upon the character of the Colonial Governors, and it must be admitted that the Crown did its best to appoint men of substance and ability to these posts. Of the 321 Governors appointed within the Empire down to the end of the eighteenth century, 37 were noblemen and 47 baronets or knights. These naturally took the "plums" and the Bahamas, as Sir Alan Burns has said of a later period, suffered as a consequence of their poverty and insignificance. All in all, the islands were lucky during the eighteenth century to receive such men as Woodes Rogers, John Tinker and William Shirley, though with the approach of the nineteenth century the Governors lapsed into mediocrity and we shall treat them with the prominence they deserve.

The arrival of Governor Rogers in 1718, which set the pattern for later Governors, has already been described. The Governor represented the royal prerogative in the colony. As the king had his Privy Council, the chief instrument of the Governor's power was his Council, which he nominated himself. According to one colonial Instruction, the Council should consist of leading men "of good life, well affected to the government, of good estates and abilities and not necessitous people or much in debt". In the Bahamas the Governor's Council consisted traditionally of ten members, any six making a quorum. Almost inevitably they were men susceptible to the Governor's views, and consequently were almost bound to be at variance with the majority of the people.

The Council acted as an advisory body for the Governor, as a Court of Chancery and Appeals and as the upper house of the legislature. Thus in the Bahamas the Council could initiate legislation despite the fact that until 1841 it combined legislative with executive functions. In 1706 the Board of Trade declared and in 1718 the royal Instructions repeated that the Governor's Council had "as much to do in framing bills for the raising and granting of money as the Assembly has", but this claim was disputed from the very beginning. Nor did colonial legislatures ever accept without a struggle the validity of colonial Orders-in-Council. The Bahamas House of Assembly in 1729 inherited these attitudes ready-made, just as it adopted as a matter of course all procedures and privileges made customary in the English and colonial parliaments up to that time.

The best indication of the Governor's influence was shown not in his dealings with the Council but in the skill with which he was able to preserve friendly relations with his Assembly. The balance of power was a delicate one and quite beyond the attainment of a clumsy man. The Governor had the sole right of convening the Assembly. He signed the writs of election and handed them to the Provost Marshal, who carried out the election just as the Sheriffs did in England. Once the members were chosen, their names were written on the back of the writs and these given to the Secretary. The Governor then gave his *dedimus potestatem* and the Assembly met.

Disqualification, resignation and death made by-elections a frequent occurrence. There was seldom a session during the eighteenth century when the Governor was not petitioned for writs for new members. In June, 1753, for instance, no less than six seats were vacant and there were not enough members present to constitute a quorum.

Only the Governor could prorogue or dissolve the Assembly and as in England this was used as a gambit of the prerogative power. Woodes Rogers dissolved the Assembly during the Colebrooke crisis of April, 1731, and again in December, 1743, Governor Tinker dissolved the House after a month because it would not pass defence legislation he deemed necessary. He did not bother to convene it for nearly five years, the colony being ruled by martial law for the remainder of the War of the Austrian Succession. In 1772, the House held back a Bill that had been passed in both Assembly and Council and Governor Thomas Shirley dissolved them for their delay. A peak in this political gamesmanship was reached in 1833 when Governor Balfour prorogued the House for a single hour to force the members to "cool off", passing the time by playing a game of chess with the President in the Council Chamber. Bills became void upon prorogation and had to be reintroduced in the following session.

For most of the eighteenth century the term of the Assembly was not fixed and tended to be long to avoid the nuisance and expense of general elections. One "Long Parliament" in fact lasted nine years, between 1785 and 1794. The term of seven years, which lasted until the Quinquennial Act of 1962, was a compromise instituted by an Act of 1795. By this time, however, the House of Assembly's control of the Estimates meant that the Governor was bound to convene the legislature at least once a year.

The question of adjournment was always one that caused friction between Governor and Assembly in the colonies and the Bahamas was no exception. By the middle of the nineteenth century, the House was able to force a dissolution upon Governor Rawson by adjourning the House week after week, but as late as December, 1797, the House was humbly begging Governor Dunmore for an adjournment. By tradition the House of Assembly now adjourns automatically on the death of a Member and does not sit on Sundays or holidays. It sat on "holydays", however, in 1773 and 1774 and in 1779 it even met on Christmas Day.

The Governor had the right of approving or vetoing the Speaker chosen by the Assembly. One of Governor Fitzwilliam's first official acts in 1734 was to reject the House's choice of John Yerworth, whereupon James Scott was chosen in his place. Coincidentally, in 1753, when Scott was Acting Governor he was moved to reject the House's choice of Thomas Petty as Speaker.

Traditionally the Governor appointed the Clerk, Messenger, Sergeant-at-Arms and even the Doorkeeper to the Assembly, but towards the end of the eighteenth century the House of Assembly won the right to choose its own officers. This probably followed from the fact that the officers' pay was voted by the House itself and not drawn from the royal revenues. Sums of money to pay the officers, varying according to the length of the session, can be found entered in the minutes for most of the early sittings of the Assembly. Between 1795 and 1846, the Assembly also appointed and paid an official Chaplain.

The Crown, through the Governor, had the prerogative of choosing the number of Members in the House, the place and frequency of meetings. Qualifications for voting and membership were fixed by Acts passed in 1762, 1784, 1794 and 1799. There were 24 Members of the House of Assembly from 5 districts down to 1784, when this was changed to 25 Members from 10 districts; Abaco, Andros, Exuma, Cat Island and Long Island having been added. In 1799, additional Members from the Turks Islands, Caicos Islands, Long Cay and Watling's brought membership up to 29, which was not surpassed until 1960. In November, 1730, the quorum was fixed at 14 of the 24 Members, reduced to 12 in 1768. It always remained low, since regular attendance from the Out Islands was a problem.

Although among the lowest in America, the property and other qualifications for voting and membership always ensured that only the most prominent citizens sat in the House of Assembly and only a minority of the inhabitants voted. Woodes Rogers' Commission of 1728 was not explicit over qualifications other than that Members and electors were to be freeholders. Since superseded Acts were not printed in the earliest copy of *The Acts of the Bahamas* (1803), the details of the 1799 Act are the earliest we have.

By the lengthy Act of 1799, electors were to be male, free, white and 21 years of age. They should have been residents of the Bahamas for at least a year and freeholders in their voting district for six months. Additionally, they had to have paid £50 Duties in the previous year and to have taken an oath before the J.P. as to their qualification. No manager or plantation officer was to have a vote unless he possessed property to the value of £500. Each elector was to have only one vote and no property was to be transferred for the purpose of obtaining a vote. A fine of £100 was to be levied for bribery by a candidate. No arrests for civil causes were to be made within forty-eight hours of an election.

Members of the House of Assembly after 1799 were to be free male whites at least 21 years of age, residents of the Bahamas at least one year and "of the Protestant Religion". They were to hold no less than 200 acres of land or to possess property to the value of £2,000. Although this was reduced to 50 acres or £1,000 in 1804, it was a stringent qualification. In addition, Members had to take oaths as to their qualifications and the Oaths of Allegiance and Supremacy before they could vote in the House.

Free Negroes did not vote until 1807, and it was several more years before a coloured man sat in the House of Assembly. In 1834, however, at the time of the Emancipation Act, four men of colour sat in the Assembly. The Members during the eighteenth century could always be relied upon to put and defend the planter and merchant point of view, so often at loggerheads with the official policy of the Board of Trade. In 1788, for instance, the Members included four Planters, five Merchants and six licensed Wreckers. The custom that all Members, including those representing Out Island constituencies, come from Nassau is a modern anomaly. In the earlier eighteenth century the Members for Harbour Island and Eleuthera almost invariably lived there, and this accounted for many delays and absences.

Down to 1815 when the present chamber was completed, the House of Assembly first met in private houses and then in the Court House over the Gaol, at the corner of what are now Market and Bay Streets in Nassau. For the first century of its existence the House met daily while in session, except for frequent adjournments. Until 1800, the time of meeting was 9.30 a.m. Weekly or twice-weekly meetings, in the afternoon and evening, were later developments.

Although the Governor could not directly initiate legislation, he could, and always did, suggest it in his Speech from the Throne at the official opening of each session of the Assembly. Strong Governors used the right of initiation enjoyed by their Council and their personal powers of adjournment, prorogation and dissolution to see their pet measures put into law. All Bahamian laws, which are usually styled Acts, not Statutes, had

Lord Dunmore Governor (1786-97), from a portrait painted by
Sir Joshua Reynolds in 1756

to have the royal assent, which the Governor was empowered to give by writing "I assent" on Bills that had passed three readings in both Assembly and Council. The Governor could also veto any Bill which he thought unfit or which conflicted with an English Statute, though in practice, he rarely, if ever, did so. No royal Governor had to go to the length of ordering a Bill thrown from the Board, as did Elias Haskett in 1701.

The imperial authorities retained the right of disallowance, and in cases of difficulty the Governor was instructed to refer Bills to the Privy Council, though frequently this was not done. In any case it would have been a certain way of consigning an unwelcome Bill into obscurity.

There were three fields of prerogative jurisdiction in which no colonial legislature was able to trespass during the eighteenth century; trade, defence and foreign policy. Additionally, legislatures could never infringe the rights of the Crown specifically reserved in Acts, nor pass any Act without the ultimate royal assent. Colonial Assemblies in 1729, however, had very real powers which steadily expanded throughout the century. It is a significant fact that as early as 1741, P. H. Bruce chose to sit in the Bahamian Assembly rather than take the seat offered him on the Governor's Council.

At the opening of each session the Speaker demanded, and invariably received, the traditional parliamentary privileges fought for in England over the centuries; free speech in the House, freedom from arrest except for treason, felony or breach of the peace, free access to the Governor and a favourable construction by the Governor on all actions. In addition, Members were paid expenses of 3s. a day, provided by their constituencies, a practice that was discontinued in the nineteenth century*. Although neither insanity or bankruptcy automatically debarred a Member, all Members could beg the Speaker leave to resign and need not even inform the Governor of their reasons. This principle was finally established in 1791 during the Governorship of Lord Dunmore, when it was declared an "undoubted and inalienable Priviledge of this House". Finally, any Member could initiate Bills, except those dealing with financial matters or pertaining to his private interest.

* Payment of Members was reintroduced in 1967.

The authority of the House of Assembly over its own Members was conceded from the beginning and the earliest Rules of Procedure date from August 26, 1734. The Speaker could suspend Members for breaking rules and fine them for un-authorised absence, for refusing to carry a Message or for using indecent language. Some Speakers went further. In 1741, a Member was committed to prison for disobedience and in 1804, Freeman Johnson, M.H.A., was fined £200 for abusing the Speaker and in the following year was imprisoned ten days for non-payment. After January, 1764, the expulsion of a Member meant automatic disqualification. By a coincidence this was resolved in Nassau just four days after a similar resolution passed by the English Parliament in the case of John Wilkes. Members were also disqualified for prolonged absence without permission and for leaving the colony at any time during a session of the legis-lature. So jealous were some Speakers of the dignity of the House of Assembly that even outsiders were summoned to the Bar. In 1768, the Rev. George Tizard was asked to explain some slighting references he had made in a sermon. Later, he was reprimanded by the Governor and offered an apology. The case of Attorney-General Wylly (1817) will be dealt with later.

As with most British legislatures, it was over the question of the control of finance that the House of Assembly in the Bahamas levered itself into a stronger position in relation to the executive. From the time of Rogers onwards, the Governors had to rely upon the Assembly to vote them their salary. In 1741, John Tinker was voted £300 a year, to be raised by a levy of a hundred-weight on each ton of braziletto cut and a tax of a *ryal* on every thousand limes and oranges and 6s. for each house in the colony. Bruce attributed the dissolution of the Assembly by Tinker in 1744 not to its failure to pass defence measures, but in its refusal to grant him his salary.

In such a small colony as the Bahamas the assent of the people to any tax was essential to its success. In 1753, Governor Tinker's request for money to finish the new church sounded much like a plea. He promised the Members that he would make no other demands on them "in your present Circum-stances". Although the Governor's Council claimed the right, money Bills invariably originated in the Assembly from the beginning, through a Committee of the Whole House.

The first Bahamian revenue Bills were introduced on December 4, 1734 and passed two days later. These levied a head tax of four *ryals* on "all White Man Indian Mullatoe and Negroe Men and Women from the Age of Sixteen to Sixty", a tax of 6s. on waterfront lots in Nassau and 2s. 3d. on others, a duty of 6s. a head on imported slaves, a levy of 1s. 6d. a ton on all foreign ships, duties on imports of wine, cider, beer and rum and exports of salt, boards, timber and turtles.

The House of Assembly could demand that the Treasurer, later the Receiver-General, lay before them the details of revenue and expenditure and did so, for instance, in 1741 before voting the Governor's salary. In such cases a committee of seven was usually appointed, as in 1753, when it was reported that the public account contained the grand balance of £860 : 14 : 11½d. in the fund for officers' salaries, and £87 : 14 : 4½d. in that for providing a schoolmaster. From this, it followed that no Receiver-General could be dismissed without presenting his terminal accounts. In 1795, Philip Dumaresq was committed to prison for refusing to present his accounts on leaving office, and he stayed there until he complied and apologised to the House.

As we shall see later, during the governorship of Lord Dunmore (1787-96), the House of Assembly further entrenched itself in its control of finances. In several other ways the Assembly extended its powers at the expense of the Council, even as far as to infringe the spheres of the executive and judiciary. Early on, the House gained the right to sit as a court to judge election disputes and cases of alleged irregularities in elections. This system, suitable perhaps for the sophisticated Mother of Parliaments, offered certain chances of bribery and corruption in a colony like the Bahamas, where the legislature represented a class. A corrupt body does not readily reform itself.

During the building of Fort Montagu in 1741 and the rebuilding of Fort Nassau in 1744, the House made direct orders to various civilians to help in the work. At other times during the eighteenth century the House acted on presentments made to it by the Grand Jury, formed committees to sit during prorogations, collected, through the Clerk, claims from Government debtors and even issued advice to the Secretary in 1789 and the Receiver-General in 1790.

Perhaps the most significant measure of this kind made during the eighteenth century was the selection by the House of Assembly in November, 1785, of Commissioners for several matters, most notably accounts, correspondence, schools and public works, with a request to Acting Governor Powell for their official appointment. Thus can be traced the first faint beginnings of the Board System which was a unique feature of Bahamian government until the creation of responsible ministries in 1964.

One matter very much the concern of the Members of the House of Assembly was the appointment of an Agent for the Bahamas in London. The jealous divisions between the various offices in Whitehall, their inefficiency in general and the over-worked personnel and dilatoriness of the Board of Trade in particular, made it essential that such a small colony as the Bahamas should have someone in London to watch over its interests. During his second term, Woodes Rogers employed a man called John Eden as his personal agent and Richard Fitz-william seems to have used Henry Popple for the same purpose. The first true colonial Agent of whom we hear, however, was Richard Cumberland, appointed in 1760 during the governorship of William Shirley at a salary of £100 a year. A committee con-sisting of the Speaker and members of both the Assembly and the Council was formed to correspond with him regularly. Agents, five in all, were appointed continuously down to 1833. In 1850, the Agency Act of 1785 was repealed, since an Agent was regarded as an extravagance the Bahamas could no longer afford.

Although commissioned in January, 1733, Richard Fitzwilliam did not arrive in Nassau until June, 1734. As Woodes Rogers had begun his first term with an epidemic and his second in the aftermath of a hurricane, Fitzwilliam was confronted almost immediately with the prospect of a Negro insurrection. On August 30, he told the Assembly that "having been informed of a Combination among Your Slaves, to rise on Sunday morning next and destroy the White Inhabitants, thereby to possess themselves of this Island, I ordered several of these wicked wretches to be seized and examined, and from their own Confession and Behaviour I am too well convinced of their bloody intentions". The House immediately introduced a "Bill for the Governing of Negroes" and drafted an enthusiastic vote of thanks to the new Governor. Fitzwilliam's refusal to accept a salary "untill you are in some Measure relieved from your present difficultys" also met with general approval.

The popularity of the Governor, as so often, was short-lived. The reason is not difficult to find. It was not so much Fitzwilliam's actions which antagonised the people as his unfortunate manner. Richard Fitzwilliam had been one of the boundary commissioners in the dispute between Virginia and North Carolina in 1730. In Byrd's *Secret History of the Dividing Line* his petty self-importance is parodied in the character of "Mr. Meanwell". In the Bahamas, Governor Fitzwilliam in lieu of salary tried to gain exemption from customs for all ships with cargoes addressed to himself. To the Assembly this seemed too much like Mrs. Phenney's attempt to force a corner in supplies. Less reasonably, they opposed Fitzwilliam's demand for a tax of 10 per cent on all salt raked, especially when he appointed measurers to prevent any cheating. Fitzwilliam also claimed 20 per cent of all ambergris found and forcibly seized a huge piece weighing 32 lb. 5 oz. as his share.

The Governor's appointments were no more popular than his haughty demeanour, and the rift between the executive and the legislature deepened. In the forefront of the dissent were Collector Chaloner Jackson and John White, though in the background can be detected the sinister shadow of John Colebrooke the perennial trouble-maker. Although the word of his opponents is to be judged with discretion, Governor Fitzwilliam is said to have called the Bahamians "beasts of burthen" to their face, fit only to be "ruled with a rod of iron", and to have employed "one Archibald his servant, who used to knock down anyone who dared to refuse to enter into the governor's measures". Fitzwilliam was accused of tacking a notice on the church door announcing a census and threatening those who did not send in returns with imprisonment and whipping. We are also given the amusing picture of the Governor prowling up and down outside the Courthouse during cases in which he had an interest, scowling and sending in messengers until judge and jurymen quaked in their shoes. In cases which went against the Crown, Fitzwilliam ordered the Attorney-General to appeal to him in Chancery, where he invariably reversed the judgement.

One accusation went even further. "He obliged one Captain Smith at his departure from Providence", alleged his enemies, "to take an oath that if he met any of the inhabitants of Providence at sea in boats or saw them upon any of the small Cays or Islands he would either bring them back to him in Providence or put them on some desert place or remote or uninhabited Island and there leave them." No evidence was offered to support this wild charge.

It is obvious that Fitzwilliam's tactlessness merely aggravated an already almost impossible situation. His own letters home have a note of desperation. In September, 1734, he described his difficulties in raising money and said that "such a sett of headstrong, simple, ungovernable Wretches were never convened in legislative capacity". On March 27, 1736, his troops "dying for want of medicines, and starving on account of the prices of provisions" mutinied and some went off with the pirates. Twelve were captured and executed. By this time Fitzwilliam was ready to throw in the sponge. Beset by enemies and almost without home support, he wrote, "It will be impossible for me to answer the Ends of my being sent hither without Your Lordships' Interposition in Favour of this miserable Place".

Concurrently matters were coming to a head in the Assembly. Despite an avowal by the Speaker that the House dissociated itself from John Colebrooke, Jackson and White made bitter attacks upon the Governor. Even the sale of a plot of ten acres by Speaker Scott to Governor Fitzwilliam to build a new residence—the site of the present Government House—was seen as a subtle plot of another kind. Both Jackson and White were expelled from the Assembly and went straight to London with their complaints. The House itself did not last much longer, being prorogued early in 1737. It did not meet again until 1741.

By 1737, the Spanish threat made salt-raking in the windward islands a hazardous operation and none was collected. As a result, the mainland colonies would not send their customary provisions and Fitzwilliam reported that the people were forced to subsist "on crabs, fish and wild fruit".

It is difficult to know who wished Fitzwilliam to leave the Bahamas most; the people of the Bahamas or the Governor himself. It must have been a considerable relief when he was recalled early in 1738 to answer the charges laid before the Privy Council by Jackson, White and Colebrooke. His replies were evidently satisfactory, though he did not return to the Bahamas. In 1741 he received from the Treasury back pay amounting to £1,816 : 17 : 4¾d.

XIII

Tinker and William Shirley
1738-67

The regime of Richard Fitzwilliam proved once more how difficult it was to be a popular Governor when times were hard. His successor, John Tinker, was successful for two reasons unrelated to his personal character. Firstly, he governed the Bahamas for no less than twenty years, from 1738 until his death in 1758, a period unmatched in Bahamian history. Secondly, for no less than eleven of those years England was at war and, paradoxically, the islands enjoyed one of their intervals of brief and somewhat dubious prosperity. It is always remarkable to the historian how still is the voice of criticism, how smooth the path of government, when times are good.

John Tinker was unambitious. The Governorship of the Bahamas was the crown of a career which had included the post of agent at Panama for the South Sea Company and Governor of Cape Coast Castle for the Royal African Company. He was well acquainted with the "Spanish threat" which broke into open war in 1739, ostensibly over the question of Captain Jenkins' Ear but in reality over the far more important problem of the control of commerce with the Spanish colonies of the Caribbean. During the War, the Bahamas became a privateering base, to which the captains could return for their prizes to be adjudicated in the local Admiralty Court. Besides this, Nassau became a stopping place in a flourishing illicit trade between the mainland colonies and the French islands, the goods being transhipped to the beleaguered Spanish by the French. This trade, which became directly traitorous in 1743 with the entry of France into the War, did not stop then and was revived again during the

136

Seven Years' War (1756-63). The privateers spent freely, fees from the Court cases enriched officials, lawyers and agents and the wharves were filled with goods, both condemned prize and illicit. Individual merchants and privateers became prosperous by steering a dangerous course between contraband and seizure, and the Vice Admiralty Court was at the same time popular for the speedy condemnation of enemy prizes and execrated when it penalised the Bahamian merchant or privateer for illicit trade.

We have an invaluable, if one-sided, account of the first period of Tinker's governorship in the *Memoirs* of Peter Henry Bruce, privately published in 1782. This book gives an admirable description of Nassau life between 1741 and 1745; a life of boredom and disappointment enlivened by occasional danger and frequent petty feuds.

Bruce was an irascible Prussian of Scots ancestry, born in Westphalia in 1692. As a boy he served under Marlborough at Ramillies and Malplaquet. Between 1711 and 1724 he was an engineer in the service of Peter the Great of Russia, before settling on a small estate in Scotland, where he remained for sixteen years. On the outbreak of war with Spain in 1739 he was appointed Engineer through the patronage of the Duke of Argyll and was ordered by Lord Montagu, Master of the Ordnance, to accompany Governor Tinker to the Bahamas and restore the fortifications there. His pay was a generous twenty shillings a day.

Tinker and Bruce left London on November 11, 1740, aboard H.M.S. *Rose* in a convoy of seven ships. Off Torbay they captured a small Spanish privateer, Tinker having a narrow escape when a musket ball pierced his clothing. In appalling winter weather they sailed to Carolina via Madeira, arriving at Charleston early in February, 1741. Bruce went on to the Bahamas in the sloop *Tartar*, was nearly wrecked off Abaco but reached Nassau on April 21. Governor Tinker followed on shortly afterwards.

Bruce was soon installed in a large furnished house at a rent of £20 a year. In his methodical way he describes the strategic situation and products of the islands in great detail, listing many kinds of timber, dyewoods, bark trees, fruits, wild animals and 57 species of fish. He was the first writer to mention the conch as a native delicacy. The population of the Bahamas he listed in the following way:

Heads of Families	310
Women and Children	689
Negro Male Slaves	426
Black Women and Children	538
Independent Company	100
Harbour Island and Islathera	240
	2,303

None of the other Out Islands had any permanent settlers.

Bruce found Nassau a petty place still smarting from the tyrannical rule of Richard Fitzwilliam. The situation had not improved much under the presidency of John Howell, who had once been "surgeon to the pirates". The defences were in a shocking state. In the Fort there were 16 serviceable guns, many others having been spiked, buried in the sand or used for ballast. The eastern entrance to the harbour, "the back door through which the place had often been surprised", was totally unguarded.

Word reached Nassau from Havana through a Mr. Bullock that the Spaniards were preparing a small Armada to attack the Bahamas, consisting of 2 warships of 80 guns each and 3 galleys. Immediately there was a bustle of belated preparation in Nassau, the House of Assembly granting Bruce any assistance he required. First he collected all the discarded guns, drilled them out, tested them by firing and fitted them to the carriages brought for the purpose from England. In no time at all, Fort Nassau could boast 54 pieces, ranging in size from 6- to 18-pounders. Then Bruce started work on Fort Montagu, sited where the eastern bay narrowed to form the harbour, where the roadstead was less than a cannon shot wide. The foundation stone was laid on June 10, 1741, and the little fort, just as it is today, completed by the end of July, 1742.

As in the whole of the Bahamas there was not a single mason, Bruce employed 2 bricklayers from Philadelphia and taught them masonry. The local limestone he found excellent; easily cut like cheese, but hardening like flint. Cannonballs fired at this stone lodged where they hit, but did not splinter nor crumble the wall. In the absence of any wheeled vehicles in the island, the blocks of stone were carried from the quarry on the heads of Negro slaves.

When completed, Fort Montagu mounted 17 guns, including eight 18-pounders. On the landward side was a palisade of 8-foot mastic stakes, 8 inches square with 3 inches between each stake. Within the total area of the Fort were a barracks and a guard-room, a cistern to hold 7,000 gallons of fresh water and a magazine large enough to contain 95 barrels of powder. At the same time, Bruce constructed Bladen's Battery, a powerful array of 8 large guns guarding the western approaches to Nassau.

The expected Spanish attack did not materialise and Nassau soon sank again into its familiar torpor. Bruce turned his attention to local politics and was soon embroiled in the current feuds. After a fight in a tavern with William Stuart, one of the officers of the Independent Company and close to the Governor, Bruce was confined to his own house for a fortnight. Later, after a more serious verbal bout with James Irving he went round town expecting sudden attack or even assassination. Concerning this last fear, he mentioned that the sudden death of the hale and hearty Chaplain Hodges "gave rise to a variety of speculations".

Governor Tinker refused to take sides, though the self-righteous Bruce took this very indifference as a sign of antagonism. His enthusiasm for the Governor, never high, waned to vanishing point and he had nothing but hatred and contempt for the faction that clustered round the Executive. Tinker's two chief agents seem to have been William Stuart and James Scott. When Scott was dropped as Speaker by the Assembly in 1744, Bruce recounted that Tinker thereupon appointed him "one of his council, and made him chief justice, treasurer, naval officer, storekeeper &c. thereby to enable him to revenge himself upon the inhabitants". Tinker, Stuart and Scott were popularly known as "The Triumvirate" and even went as far as to give this name to a boat which they jointly owned.

The Spanish War provided relief from the local squabbles. In 1742, H.M.S. *Rose* brought in to Nassau no less a person than Vandeño, the captain who was alleged to have cut off Jenkins' ear in 1736. It is not clear what happened to him or even if he were tried for the offence. In September the same year two rich Spanish prizes were brought into Nassau by two privateers from Philadelphia, the *George* and the *Joseph and Mary* under the command of Captains Sibbald and Dowall. The value of the seized goods was no less than 188,000 pieces of eight, of which the majority belonged to the Spanish Crown. Governor Tinker assessed the ransom value of the royal cargo at 90,000 pieces of eight, which his opponents considered too low. Besides, it was his obvious policy to delay the payment as long as possible so that the privateers would spread their newly gained wealth around the town.

In February, 1743, Pedro Ferón arrived in Nassau under flag of truce with thirty chests, each containing 3,000 pieces of eight. A little later, John Snow, the Governor's secretary, came from Havana with four more chests to pay for the private cargo, along with some important exchange prisoners and presents for the Governor. These included "a purse with one thousand quadruple *pistoles*, a gold-hilted sword, a gold-headed cane, gold buckles and buttons, besides many other valuable presents".

Despite the privateers' Articles, which declared that all prize money was to be shared out in Philadelphia, Tinker refused to disburse any money until all debts had been paid. By this time, most of the sailors had wasted their share of $450 each in drinking and gambling, and "they soon found to their cost, now all their money was spent, that instead of being courted as formerly, they were thrown into jail, and very exorbitant fees extracted from them".

Bruce asserted that because of Tinker's treatment of the Philadelphians, all privateers steered clear of Nassau from then on, and even Langland, the captain of the stationed warship, took his prizes elsewhere for assessment. This is not borne out by the facts. In 1746, for instance, a Spanish prize was brought to Nassau for which the colossal ransom of 100,000 pieces of eight was received. Bruce's bitterness was probably caused by the fact that he was cheated of all but 8 of 42 cwt. of quicksilver which he had wangled from the prize, by James Irving and other Nassauvians. In all, more than a dozen privateering cases were settled in the Nassau Vice-Admiralty Court during the War.

Meanwhile, money to complete the fortifications showed no sign of arriving from England and relations between Bruce and the Governor grew almost impossible. With the mainland colonies clamouring for his engineering skill, Bruce was more than ready to quit Nassau. Tinker refused to grant permission, reminding Bruce that war with France had just begun and that Fort Nassau was still little but a well-armed ruin. According to the biassed Bruce, Tinker once stated "with great warmth and earnestness, that he was king in this government; and if he gave orders to kill any man whatsoever, his officers were to obey him, without enquiry into the cause thereof". He did agree, however, that Bruce might go as soon as the fortifications were complete.

Bruce accordingly set to work once more with a will, supported again by the House of Assembly. Within a very short time Fort Nassau was transformed. By December, 1744, a new bastion, casemates and a sally-port had been constructed, there were barracks for 600 men and accommodation in an emergency for the Governor, Chaplain, Surgeon, Gunner and Armourer. Within the walls or the surrounding palisade were 3 wells, a kitchen and bakehouse, a magazine and gunner's store for 600 barrels of powder. Besides the 54 cannon there were 26 brass mortars mounted.

The entire cost of the work done by Bruce in Nassau was £4,000, though this sum probably did not include supplies sent out in 1741 by the Ordnance. It compared very favourably with an estimate presented by Thomas More in 1734 (worked out with the quaint exactitude of those times) of £12,254 : 9 : 10¾d. Given a garrison of 300 to augment the 100 of the Independent Company, Bruce reckoned that Nassau would be the strongest place in British North America. Although armed men had not sprung up magically, Bruce could at least claim to have sown dragons' teeth in the undefended soil of the Bahamas.

P. H. Bruce left Nassau on January 5, 1745, in the *Pelham* sloop belonging to Speaker Florentine Cox. He carried with him "a quantity of quick-silver, dyeing wood and cotton", half of which was seized by the French between Charleston and England. He reached London in July, to be greeted by the news of the rising in support of Bonny Prince Charlie. With the campaign in the North of England against the Jacobites, the *Memoirs* end.

Back in Nassau Governor Tinker must have sighed with relief at the departure of the troublesome Teuton. The remainder of his governorship was tranquil and much of it was prosperous. In April, 1748, at the end of the War of the Austrian Succession, Tinker was able to write that "the island of Providence has indeed since the Commencement of the War increased most Surprisingly in Strength and Wealth, and the Town of Nassau Grown Populous, and many Edifices in it that may be called Sumptuous in the Indies, its Station is so Commodious for the Privateering Trade, that it invites almost all the Adventurers, especially in the Winter Season who send their prizes here to be Adjudicated".

With so much money flowing in, it was easy to forget concommitant evils. Prices in Nassau soared as the privateers gambled and caroused. Letters were still delayed and answers and supplies seldom arrived. One letter from London dated August 8, 1744, did not arrive until May 25, 1745, and in April, 1747, Tinker was complaining that he had received only one letter in two years. For his own part he was writing his communications in triplicate to ensure delivery at home.

The Treaty of Aix-la-Chapelle pricked the bubble of prosperity and for eight years of uneasy peace Nassau suffered the inevitable depression. Tinker foresaw the dangers and admonished the people in a memorable speech to the House of Assembly when it re-convened in 1749. "The War now at an end we must have recourse to Industry and Frugality, Nature has been sufficiently liberal in furnishing these Islands with the Means of amply rewarding the laborious but I am afraid the War has introduced and left us two formidable Enemies, I mean Luxury and Sloth, the Country is almost drained of its Currency, the extravagant Wages given to all Tradesmen and the Excessive dearness of every Necessary of Life would make a stranger at first sight imagine we had golden Mines no further off than the blue Hills."

The decline in wealth and activity was reflected in the sparse records of the period. The Legislature levied no taxes, save to finish the new church in George Street, and even that reluctantly. No important Acts were passed and the Assembly faded almost away for lack of business. There are in fact no "Votes", or minutes, at all for the years 1753-60, and we must interpolate much for the later period of Tinker's office.

Letters from Governor Tinker to the Board of Trade concentrate on the decline of Nassau's fortifications and the hints of renewed war. In 1752 he complained of illegal seizures of vessels by the Spaniards and in 1754 described French designs upon the Turks Islands, far to the windward but guarding the passage between Cuba and Hispaniola to Jamaica. "What right the French may have to claim these Turk's Islands your Lordships must know best", wrote Tinker. "I should as soon have expected the Grand Signor to have planted Mahomet's Standard there." Tinker also feared for Inagua, where the French had briefly landed in 1749, and Exuma, the harbour of which was in some ways preferable to Nassau.

War broke out again between England and France in 1756 and continued officially for seven years. At first the struggle was concentrated in Europe and North America, but soon Nassau became a privateering base again. Technically, Spain was neutral until 1761 and the activities of the privateers were directed against the French. But seizure of Spanish ships and counter measures were a common occurrence and eventually provoked war with Spain.

By this time John Tinker was an old man tired out by his long governorship, despite three trips back to England. On February 25, 1758, he wrote despondently what turned out to be his epitaph, of "having to sacrifice so many years of my life upon a barren rock, in the Atlantic, struggling under many and great difficulties, in very bad company . . . the sphere I act in, is so narrow, the events so few, & insignificant in this place, that they are seldom worth recounting . . . at present the spirit of privateering has taken possession of these people, & extinguished every other industrious or commercial application in times of war". Five months later, Tinker was dead.

As far as the wider history of the British Empire was concerned, William Shirley, who received his Commission to succeed John Tinker in November, 1758, was the most notable of Bahamian Governors. Born in England in 1694, he emigrated as a young lawyer to Massachusetts, where he rapidly ascended the ladder of official government. In 1731 he occupied the lowly post of Surveyor of the King's Woods, but by 1734 he was Advocate-General and in 1741 was appointed Governor. This position he occupied with considerable distinction for no less than fifteen years.

It was Governor Shirley who planned the capture of Louisbourg at the mouth of the St. Lawrence in 1745, the most brilliant exploit of the Austrian Succession War, the return of which in 1748 was so unpopular with the New Englanders. Shirley, with Benjamin Franklin, was also the architect of a plan for military co-operation against the French and Indians by the northern colonies, which was discussed at Albany, New York, in 1754. It was the failure of this plan through the jealousy of the various member colonies that incidentally brought the downfall of Shirley, by this time designated Governor of New England and Commander-in-Chief in North America. In 1756, he was unfairly held responsible for the capture of Fort Oswego on Lake Ontario, which was, according to the inaccurate Horace Walpole, "of ten times more importance than Minorca". Accordingly, the hapless Shirley was demoted, not as he hoped to Jamaica, but all the way down the scale, to Nassau. He was 64 years old.

It speaks much for the character of William Shirley that his unkind treatment did not sour him. New England's loss was Nassau's gain. Shirley's management of the Bahamas during the difficult period of the Seven Years' War was efficient and popular. His dispatches were a model of their kind and his relations with the House of Assembly firm but almost uniformly harmonious.

Shirley did not arrive to take up his duties until early in 1760, having been delayed in England by lack of supplies and transportation and then having been, as he explained to his first session of the Legislature, "cast away in his Majesty's ship *Mermaid* on one of the Bahama Keys". Immediately he was in the thick of affairs concerning the indefatigable privateers. In an Address dated October, 1760, "sundry merchants of New Providence and Others, Commander of or interested in Privateers" claimed that "the Business of Privateering is the most beneficial and almost the only profitable Trade carried on in these Islands".

The privateers thrived on the capture of French ships, and

Spanish ships carrying goods to and from the French colonies. Since the victories of Cape Lagos and Quiberon Bay in 1759, the Royal Navy commanded the Atlantic, and the French West Indian islands had largely to rely on the Spanish for succour. In March, 1760, for instance, eight Spanish merchant ships were brought into Nassau and declared lawful prizes in the Admiralty Court, a circumstance that brought forth a delightfully explosive letter from the Governor of Havana referring to William Shirley. "This Bastard should be made to know the Nullity of what he hath done because in the minds of these same Englishmen they are secure by being Pirate untuched by those who should take care."

The situation was complicated by the fact that many ships from the northern colonial ports, especially Philadelphia, were carrying on an indirect trade with the French through the Spanish port of Monte Christi in northern Hispaniola. Shirley estimated that between 80 and 90 vessels were permanently engaged in this illicit trade, carrying as many as 500 cargoes a year and thus prolonging the war.

Doubtless many Bahamians were profiting from the illegal trade which inevitably passed through the islands on its way to Monte Christi, and the privateering interests singled out no less a person than Samuel Gambier, Admiralty Court Judge and brother of John Gambier who had acted as Governor between 1758 and 1760. In their petition they claimed that "the said Samuel Gambier was lately sent here from Philadelphia, fee'd, hired and employ'd by the Philadelphians concerned in holding Correspondence and Communication with, aiding, supplying, supporting, relieving, comforting and assisting the said French . . . having openly and avowedly both in Court & Out of Court declared the same Flag of Truce a fair, honest and legal Trade".

The focus of trouble was the case of the sloop *Polly*, which had been declared a prize by Gambier's predecessor Gersholm Williams. Gambier had reversed the decision "in direct Opposition to the Statute in that Case made & provided, & likewise suspended the Execution of that Decree'. In addition, Gambier was accused of releasing several consignments of condemned sugars and ordering that the wages of seamen on condemned ships should be paid out of the confiscations.

Had he been weak or venal, Shirley would have been in a dilemma. Complaints by the Philadelphians of high-handed seizures, such as that of the *Ranger* privateer captured after clearing from Monte Christi in suspicious circumstances, were already reaching London and Shirley could ill afford another mistake. But he was a man to whom Duty was its own reward, as a man called George Barry who tried to bribe him with 60 *Johannes*, found to his cost. In October, 1760, Gambier was sacked from the Judgeship, being dismissed from the Council at the same time.

In his explanation to the Board of Trade, Shirley explained that the unfortunate Admiralty Judge had "had a direct Tendency to Support and Encourage the Owners of English Trading Vessels concern'd in carrying on a General Illicit Commerce with the French Island of St. Dominique". Gambier had actually gone as far as to say in court that the king had no right to prevent trade by his subjects and that since Parliament had not specifically forbidden the Monte Christi trade in an Act, it should be deemed legal and beneficial. Furthermore, Gambier had been insolent to Shirley "upon a point of His Majesty's prerogative" (always a good scoring point with Whitehall, and was alleged to have entered into a contract with one Don Gregorio Joseph to provide "considerable quantities of Baccalao [dry' Codfish and Maycril] wch. he the Spaniard was to carry to the French Islands".

Shirley's treatment of the Legislature was equally firm. This was well illustrated by the case of John Green in 1762. Green was accused of "publishing a gross libel on the Court of Chancery", over which the Governor presided. When imprisoned for contempt, Green, a Member of the House of Assembly, pleaded parliamentary privilege. Shirley demurred, saying that Green was lucky not to be sentenced for life, to have his ears cut off and to be exhibited in the pillory as provided for in English law. Furthermore, Shirley added that "the levity of the Government in not presenting him according to Rigour by the Law" had only resulted in "a great aggravation of the contempt". Green hastened to purge himself with a humble apology and the entire House of Assembly was obviously chastened.

William Shirley was more fortunate than earlier Governors in that Nassau was prospering and was in no great danger from enemy attack. For this was the period of victories which followed the appointment of William Pitt the Elder to the Secretaryship of State in 1757. French power in North America had disappeared with the capitulation of Montreal in 1760 and between 1761 and 1762, the French islands of the Caribbean fell one by one. When in 1761, the Spaniards were foolish enough to complain of the infringement of their trade in the West Indies and the multiple seizures of their ships, the invincible British promptly declared war. In 1762, a vast fleet sailed through the Bahamas and captured Havana, including booty worth over a million pounds and a quarter of the remaining Spanish fleet.

By the Treaty of Paris, signed in March, 1763, the position of the Bahamas was made more secure. In fact, although the weak diplomacy of Bute had surrendered much that the vigorous war policy of Pitt had gained, this Treaty marked the zenith of British colonial power down to the middle of the nineteenth century. With the loss of Dominica, Grenada, St. Vincent and Tobago, French power declined in the Caribbean, though she retained Martinique, Guadeloupe and St. Lucia. Although Britain gave back Havana, along with Manila, to Spain, she received in return the peninsula of Florida, which remained British until 1783. Thus, for twenty years, Britain controlled both sides of the Florida Channel, and the stronghold of St. Augustine could no longer threaten Georgia or the Bahamas.

The Treaty of Paris did not, however, quite terminate the French threat and a small crisis was reached in 1764 over the possession of the Turks Islands. These poor but strategic salt islands had long been a bone of contention between Bermuda and the Bahamas, but now the French seemed likely to resolve the dispute by seizing them for themselves. Contrary to the clauses of the Treaty, the French commander, the Comte d'Estaing, had not withdrawn from the West Indies. He simply withdrew from the Caribbean and set up the *Fleur-de-Lis* on Grand Turk. The question was finally settled by the Privy Council after some very useful information had been supplied by Governor Shirley. In November, 1764, the Privy Council was able to inform Shirley that d'Estaing had been persuaded to withdraw, suggesting that the Turks Islands should be taken more firmly under the government of the Bahamas. Unfortunately, the Agent who was appointed, William Symmer, was an ambitious man who hankered for autonomy and contested the authority of Nassau right down to 1772.

Peace once more brought depression to Nassau. At the end of the war, Shirley had recommended the disbanding of the largish force of troops then in Nassau. By 1767, he himself was feeling the pinch of economy and successfully petitioned Lord Shelburne for additional salary of £300 a year following the loss of his pay as commander of the Independent Company.

With the end of privateering and the Monte Christi trade, the whole colony began to suffer. In 1766, John Bishop was tried and convicted of piracy for seizing the Spanish ship *Nuestra Señora de la Soledad*. To relieve the economic distress and attract legitimate trade, Shirley in 1767 put forward sound arguments for making Nassau a free port. This suggestion was, of course, anathema to the strict mercantilists at the Board of Trade and Shirley's suggestion was shelved; though Nassau did become a limited free port in 1787.

At this unpropitious moment occurred the attempt by the British Government to levy the Stamp Duties, intended to help pay the cost of the late war. With good reason they were no more successful in the Bahamas than in the other colonies, though details of any active opposition have been lost.

By this time William Shirley considered that his active life was finished. Citing an "inveterate scurvy these last twenty months", he resigned from the governorship and left Nassau for Massachusetts in mid-1768. He died at Roxbury, near Boston, only three years later at the age of 77. Perhaps the most lasting of his actions was to initiate a re-survey of Nassau and the reclamation of swampy land without which the town could not expand towards the east. It is fitting that one of the chief streets of the modern city should bear his name.

XIV

American Independence
1767-83

The governorship of Thomas Shirley, who succeeded his older brother in 1768, reminds us once more that, however interesting their history, the Bahamas were insignificant in the grand panorama of the eighteenth century. As in most periods of international peace, it was a time of domestic discord and discontent. But Governor Shirley's squabbles and problems were paltry when compared with the constitutional struggle rising to a climax on the near-by continent.

For these were the years of incipient revolt, which led downhill from the Stamp Act in 1765 to the Battle of Lexington ten years later. Thomas Shirley arrived in Nassau as the Townshend Duties were being levied in the Thirteen Colonies; he left in 1774 at the time of the first American Congress at Philadelphia; William Shirley, his brother, died at the time of the Boston Massacre. Few echoes of these deathless events were heard in distant Nassau; only when the War broke out did the Bahamas take sides, and even then the chief question was not one of principle but of profit. And yet, despite this typically opportunist attitude, the War did result in great changes in Bahamian history. The period 1767 to 1783 was the end of an era.

Early in 1767 when William Shirley had informed the Members of the House of Assembly of the repeal of the Stamp Act, they drafted an Address to the King in which they referred ingratiatingly to their "warmest sentiments of Gratitude for his paternal tenderness to his American Colonies so conspicuously shown in the Repeal". Their loyalty was obviously not disinterested, however, for at the same time they petitioned for the improvement of Bahamian trade by the relaxing of the restrictions on free commerce with the French and the Spanish. They obviously had in mind the example of the Turks Islands which, as the Board of Trade well knew from their correspondence with the Shirleys and William Symmer, were flourishing as a base for the contraband trade between the northern colonies and the foreign settlements at Monte Christi and Cape Nicholas. Thomas Shirley backed up the arguments in favour of making Nassau a free port with a long letter in December, 1768. But when nothing was done, the Assembly held him to be responsible and began to cause trouble on the least pretext. The mantle of John Colebrooke seems to have fallen on John Green, one of the Members for the East, who was almost continuously in trouble with the Governor from 1764 until 1776. The Public Treasury, an accurate index of Bahamian discontent, contained in December 1768 the lordly total of £144 : 7 : 7½.

Over the question of the Turks Islands discord reached the point of rebellion. In April, 1769, Shirley ordered Symmer the Agent in the Turks Islands to observe all Bahamian laws. Symmer was reluctant, telling the Commissioners of Trade that "the settlers here are alarmed to the greatest degree for fear they must . . . be subject to the Legislative Authority of Providence, in which case they are unanimously determined to leave the islands".

The British Government was unsympathetic. It frowned upon any trade slipping through the mercantilist net and in 1770 Lord Hillsborough told Shirley to legislate for the Turks and tax them, even though the islands were not represented in the Assembly at Nassau. He declared that "as the whole body of People belonging to the British Empire are represented by the Commons of Great Britain, so are the inhabitants of the Bahamas in general represented in the Assembly of that Government".

This attitude the Bahamians resisted, not necessarily because it implied legislation and taxation without representation. Almost certainly some of them were engaged in the Turks Islands trade and clung to their fingerhold on prosperity. On January 25, 1770, Shirley asked the Legislature to pass laws controlling trade, salt-raking and the protection of property in the Turks Islands. The House declined, denying that the Turks were ever "before certainly known to belong to the Bahamas". Even when informed by Shirley of the orders of the Privy Council and the Secretary of State, the Assembly procrastinated. Explosion point was reached in October. In reply to an angry message from the Governor on October 3, the House, on October 10, refused to legislate, forwarding seven firm resolutions. These repudiated their right to legislate for the Turks, suggested that the islands apply for membership and expressed anger at Shirley's "threats and disrespect". Counter-attacking, Shirley dissolved the Assembly the following day. "As I found by the Minutes of your House", he informed them, "that you are carrying on the Business of this Session in an unconstitutional manner, and in open defiance of the King's Instructions to me, it is my Duty to suffer such proceedings no longer."

Although a new session of the legislature passed the salt-raking laws and taxes were levied with partial success after 1771, the Turks Islands remained troublesome; a colourful rendezvous of lawless New Englanders, Bermudian salt-rakers and French and Spanish *contrebandiers*. Shirley accused Symmer of complicity in the illegal trade, especially in liquor, and hinted that "while the Nights are dark and the Bar is smooth, you will not want your usual Night Cap". The outbreak of war stilled trouble for a time, but only because Nassau gave up all attempts at control. The Turks Islands always remained a safe place for smugglers. Members for the Turks and Caicos Islands sat in the Bahamian House of Assembly after 1799, but their interests were purely sectional and their attendance sporadic. In 1848 the attempt to integrate the islands within the Bahamas was finally given up.

Although no-one dared mention yet the quarter from which attack might come, the problem of defence was as severe as ever. Thomas Shirley found a garrison of a gunner and eight men guarding Fort Nassau and four men stationed at Fort Montagu. Only 13 guns were serviceable and those rusted, and the store of 300 barrels of gunpowder had been spoiled by the climate. The pitiful remnant of the 9th Regiment, consisting of two officers, two sergeants, two corporals, a drummer and sixteen men, had been posted to St. Augustine, thus opening up a connexion which was to be remembered later.

Shirley made the usual plea for reinforcements, asking for

150 men and help for the fortifications. For once, something was done. In August 1769 the Secretary of State wrote to mention that he had ordered General Gage, the Commander in North America, to send an engineer with stores up to the value of £1,000. Captain Montresor arrived in 1770 and proceeded, with little of Bruce's energy, to repair the defences. It was a heart-breaking task. There were no suitable tools and labour was scarce and costly. The islands were so poor that even the £20 a month upkeep of the fortifications was beyond their means.

With poverty went apathy. In 1771 when Shirley tried to introduce Bills for reforming the militia and instituting a night watch, the Assembly refused to comply. Once more it was dissolved. "I am obliged to tell you", said Governor Shirley, "that your treatment of His Majesty's Council of the Bahamas is so indecent, illiberal and unjust, and shows such an intemperate spirit to prevail in your House that I despair of any business being carried on this session with any moderation or to any salutary purpose."

By 1773, distress was acute. Shirley wrote that the revenues were "almost annihilated, the Treasury exhausted, the Contingent charge of the Government will be unprovided for, the salaries to the officers unpaid, for want of which the Courts of Justice have long been shut up". Because the dead hand of the Proprietors still discouraged settled farming, turtling, wrecking and woodcutting were the only activities from which the islanders could scrape a living. Shirley pleaded that the British Government help out, citing the example of Georgia, where prosperity followed the revocation of the royal charter. At least the Crown could assume the responsibility for paying some of the chief officers. The reply was as unsatisfactory as ever, and although some reinforcements in the shape of Captain Blackett's Company of the 14th Regiment arrived in July 1773, it must have been a relief for Thomas Shirley when he heard early in 1774 that he had been appointed to the Governorship of Dominica "as a reward for merit". It was only a small promotion, but one which took him away from troublesome Nassau and that much further from the events brewing in the north.

Montfort Browne, his successor, seems to have been a weak vessel more or less at the mercy of the tides of events. His

Instructions of May 5, 1774, included an order to enforce the laws of trade, but this was difficult where the trade was practically nil. His first letter home described the dismal hopelessness of the islanders, to whom wrecks were a gift from providence and even illicit trade would have been a relief. But things were about to change. This letter was dated May 6, 1775; only two weeks before, the Massachusetts militia had fired at General Gage's troops on their way to and from Concord and already the British in Boston were in a state of siege.

As early as August, 1775, Gage wrote to Browne warning him that American ships were fitting out to attack New Providence and seize the military stores there. He therefore proposed to send two merchant ships and a man-of-war to carry off the guns and powder to a place of safety. Governor Browne demurred, reminding Gage that the defence of the Bahamas was his responsibility and he, and not Gage, was the Commander-in-Chief there. In a footnote, Browne added that "the inhabitants of these Islands have upon all Occasions given every possible proof of their inviolable attachment and loyalty to H.M. Person & Govt."—an exaggeration that was to prove somewhat ironic later.

On February 25, 1776, Captain Andrew Shaw arrived in Nassau with news that a fleet of eight small warships was gathering off Cape Delaware with the intention of attacking New Providence. This was the very first American fleet on its initial operation, under the command of Commodore Ezekiel Hopkins.

Hopkins had received his orders from the Naval Committee of Congress on January 5 to gather his fleet and sweep Chesapeake Bay. He had managed to recruit the *Alfred* (24 guns), *Columbus* (20 guns), *Andrea Doria* (14 guns), *Cabot* (14 guns), *Providence* (12 guns), *Hornet* (10 guns), *Wasp* (8 guns) and the *Fly*, a dispatch vessel. Among his varied band of officers with only privateering experience of naval warfare was John Paul Jones. Later in his career, Jones, the American Drake, claimed to have been the master-mind of this expedition—a wild exaggeration in keeping with the braggart side of his character. In fact, Jones was a mere lieutenant in the *Alfred* and, unlike Hopkins and Saltonstall, the second-in-command, was totally ignorant of the Bahamas.

As soon as Philadelphia was free of ice, Hopkins slipped down the Delaware. The decision to attack the Bahamas was apparently his own, having decided that Governor Dunmore's squadron in the Chesapeake was too formidable a foe. On March 1, 1776, the American fleet reached Hole-in-the-Wall, Abaco, where two local sailors were impressed as pilots. Later the same day a Captain Dorsett sailed into Nassau with the news. For some reason Browne asked Dorsett to keep the information secret. Perhaps he hoped that if he ignored trouble it would go away. At daybreak on March 3, however, seven of the American ships appeared off the bar of Nassau.

The best contemporary account of the American "invasion" interpreted the events in a manner unfavourable to Browne. In his own version Browne accused many Nassauvians of entertaining the rebels. One thing is certain: neither the Americans nor the Bahamians were very eager to come to actual blows. At this distance of time the whole affair has an air of comedy.

Governor Browne was awakened and came to the door of Government House in his nightshirt. The Council was hastily summoned to Fort Nassau, the militia drum sounded and three cannon shot off as a general alarm. Apparently these were the only guns fired throughout, but they were enough to deter the Americans, who began to sail for the eastern end of the island.

At 7 a.m. John Gambier, "who was so lame with the Gout he could not walk", rode into the Fort to find the Governor all of a dither. What should he do? Gambier asked what had been done. Nothing—should he send Captain Chambers away with the powder in his fast ship? Gambier suggested that the powder might be useful for defence. The Governor agreed. Chambers was sent out to reconnoitre but he soon returned, saying that he could not beat up to windward. A detachment of militia was sent forward to Fort Montagu.

The situation did not look very hopeful for the defence. The roll of the militia was called and it was found that many were absent and most of the others unarmed. In the Fort two of the cannons fired as an alarm had been blown off their mountings; the others were embedded to their axle-trees in drifted sand and required a dozen men to traverse them. One buttress of the Fort was crumbling and there was a pitiful shortage of equipment such as rammers, sponge-staves, powder-horns, priming wires and wadding.

At this critical juncture, Browne deserted the Fort, "saying that he would just go home and make himself a little decent". While he was absent a report came in that an enemy ship had landed between three and four hundred men two miles east of Fort Montagu. This fort was in an even worse state than Fort Nassau, not having a single barrel of gunpowder usable and no guns properly mounted.

Once he returned, presumably now dressed out in his full uniform, Browne ordered Lieutenant Burke and then Captain Walker forward from Fort Montagu to engage the rebels. But Walker's men advancing tangled with Burke's men retreating, who, having found that the news of the landing was no rumour, were now thinking of the defence of their own property in Nassau. Within minutes the militia had melted away without the exchange of a shot. Ordering two men to stay behind to spike the guns on the sight of the enemy, Browne also returned to Nassau.

During the afternoon about 150 men bustled around Fort Nassau trying to prepare it for a siege. They saw little of the Governor, who spent most of the time getting his effects together at Government House. He did not call another roll, make a plan of defence nor even order the gates shut, thus making it possible for "Spies and disaffected persons to come in and discover the Condition and State of the Fort and to Carry an account whereof to the Enemy". When he returned after an absence of three hours he complained "that he had had a violent fit of Cholick, which had detained him so long".

At 4 p.m. Lieutenant Burke went forward again to reconnoitre and apparently spoke with the rebels. He reported that they consisted of 250-300 marines "completely Armed" and ready to attack Nassau. At 8 p.m. the Council, militia officers and chief inhabitants decided that the position was untenable and that the Fort should be disarmed. At midnight the powder was loaded on board Chambers' sloop and at 2 a.m. he sailed for St. Augustine.

In the morning the Americans distributed leaflets promising security of life and property. The inhabitants needed no further assurance and gave up all pretence of defence. Montfort Browne was seized at Government House and the two forts formally occupied. The unfamiliar Grand Union flag, with its horizontal stripes and Union Jack in the corner, fluttered bravely over Nassau.

The rebels stayed in Nassau two weeks (not as is often stated for a single day), According to Browne, Hopkins and his officers were "contenanced by many of the principal inhabitants, and elegantly entertained at the Houses of some of the officers of the Government". The men caroused on captured, or surrendered, wine to such an extent that over 200 were seriously ill on the voyage home. But the chief business was the dismantling of the forts. When they sailed away on March 17, Hopkins carried with him no less than 88 cannon, ranging from 9- to 36-pounders, 15 mortars, about 5,500 shells and over 11,000 cannon balls. With all this booty he was scarcely disappointed to find only 24 barrels of gunpowder. Montfort Browne and Thomas Arwin, Inspector-General of Customs for North America who happened to be in Nassau, were carried off as hostages, much to the delight of John Green, whom Hopkins released from one of his periodic spells in gaol.

The taste of their bloodless victory in Nassau went sour on the Americans, for off Block Island on their voyage home they were worsted in an encounter with a single British man-of-war, the *Glasgow*. Congress was torn between jubilation and shame and Hopkins was praised and censured in the same vote.

Montfort Browne was soon exchanged for the rebel Lord Stirling, but did not return to Nassau until 1778. He raised troops and fought in the siege of Rhode Island, bringing back four companies of "invalids" with him to the Bahamas. He found the situation in Nassau almost out of hand. Another party of American marines under Captain Rathburn had invaded in January, 1778, and had been admitted by John Gambier, the Acting Governor, after threatening to burn Nassau to the ground. After two days they had spiked the remaining guns and left, but since that time many Nassauvians had deserted the island to join the rebel cause.

Browne found that the worst aspects of the revolution had infected the inhabitants. John Gould, the Speaker of the Assembly, had gone over to the enemy with eighty of the militia and the remainder he found "licentious, poor, haughty and insolent". In a telling echo of the American Declaration of Independence, Browne bewailed that "neither life, liberty or property was safe among them". John Gambier, like his brother in the Seven Years' War, had been guilty of issuing illegal letters of marque and now formed a "juncto" to oppose the Governor. In January he asked Browne "to continue a Licence he had thought proper to grant to the merchants of this place to carry on an open and free intercourse with the Rebells, under the pretext of procuring Provisions". Browne refused but "five rich cargoes of rebel property" were landed nevertheless only one month later.

On March 30, 1779, Browne dissolved his Council, an unprecedented step. A little later he dismissed Collector Hunt and Attorney-General Sterling. Although war with France and Spain had broken out and an attack was impending from Cape François, Browne complained that he was "totally deserted as well by the civil as the military power". The Council members for their part complained to the Board of Trade that they were "now in a state of absolute Anarchy".

Despite the seizure of the *Young Cezar*, "a remarkable fast sailing Schooner" which, Browne claimed, was "Employed by the disaffected Inhabitants of the Government for the purpose of supplying the wants of the Rebels", the authorities in London listened to the complaints against the harassed Governor. A Governor without the support of his Assembly was taken as a matter of course: a Governor out of tune with his Council must be in the wrong. In 1779, the Board of Trade recommended to the Privy Council that Browne be recalled "considering the animosities between parties" in the Bahamas. They stated that the "charges appear to be well founded" and that Browne's proclamations were "well-meant but ill-judged". Somewhat unfairly the Governor was sacked in April, 1780, though he was still in Nassau when his successor, John Maxwell, arrived later in the year.

Material for the last three years of the War is tantalisingly meagre. One thing is certain: the Bahamas enjoyed one of their most prosperous periods as a privateering base. On June 30, 1780, Governor Maxwell sent to London a list of 37 American vessels

"Captured and Libelled in the Court of Vice-Admiralty in New Providence". In April, 1782, an account brought up to date included the startling total of 127 rebel ships. So many American prisoners were brought into Nassau that Maxwell was unable to "keep or Victual them" and was forced to send them to the nearest American port and turn them loose.

Obviously Nassau was a base highly damaging to the trade between the rebel States and their allies in the Caribbean. Throughout the War the strong Spanish base of Havana fumed and threatened. Considering its defenceless state it is remarkable that Nassau survived so long. The pitiful ineffectiveness of the American fleet was one reason, but the seizure of naval supremacy by the French Admiral de Grasse in 1781, which was largely responsible for the surrender of Cornwallis at Yorktown and the practical end of the land fighting, meant that Nassau's days were numbered.

Warnings had been sounded ever since Governor Maxwell arrived in the Bahamas. In his first meeting with the House of Assembly in April, 1780, he had to warn the Members of an impending invasion from Havana. He proposed calling out the local militia and sending to Sir Henry Clinton and Admiral Arbuthnot at New York for help. The aid was slow in coming, but luckily so were the Spaniards. There were further alarums in September, 1781, which persuaded the Assembly at last to pass the long-awaited Militia and Night Watch Acts. In April, 1782, Maxwell was able to report to Clinton the arrival of two transports with stores, 170 men, 10 sergeants and 2 drummers, bringing the garrison up to 346 men. Unfortunately, 25 of the new arrivals were wounded veterans and Maxwell reported that "to detain them here is Burying them".

None of the troops, however, were destined to stay long in Nassau. On May 6, 1782, the Governor wrote urgently that he was "attacked by two American Frigates (large ones) some Galleys and 40 sail of Transports from Havana with Troops on board". This was a force of several thousand men under the command of the Governor of Cuba himself, Don Juan de Cargigal. Optimistically Maxwell added that three British frigates might deter the invaders. He might as well have asked for an earthquake.

On May 7, Commodore Gillon, the commander of the American ships, sent Governor Maxwell a message of "gallant respect" urging the wisdom of surrender. Bowing to the inevitable, Maxwell hastened to agree and articles of capitulation were signed the same afternoon. In these savage days it is pleasant to read of the generosity of the terms granted by the Spaniards, which were remarkably similar to those dictated by George Washington to Lord Cornwallis five months later. The garrison was allowed to march out with all the honours of war, with arms shouldered, drums beating and flags flying. Officers were to be permitted to keep their side arms. All troops were to be embarked for the nearest British port at Spanish expense. All officers and other inhabitants who wished to leave were allowed to take their families and Negro slaves with them and were given eighteen months in which to settle their affairs. Those who chose to stay were guaranteed protection of goods and property and freedom of worship. Finally, Governor Maxwell was to regard himself as a prisoner only as long as it took to land with the troops at the nearest British port.

The Spanish occupation lasted a little over a year, during which Don Antonio Claraco acted as Governor. Unfortunately details are lacking, but from Governor Maxwell's references to "the insults and Calamities inseparable from Despotic power" on his return in 1784 it seems likely that the Spaniards did not stay closely to the spirit of the capitulation. In any case, subjection to a foreign power, however mild, is never congenial. It is likely that those Bahamians who could deserted the islands and those who were forced by circumstances to remain envied their departure. After Rodney's brilliant victory at the Battle of the Saints in 1782 the British once more commanded the Caribbean and the Spaniards in Nassau became practically a beleaguered force. Supplies dwindled and only the recapture of Providence and the signing of peace in 1783 averted the threat of starvation.

One more interesting event occurred before the end of the War. Early in 1783 a French force seized the Turks Islands and defended itself successfully against an amphibious attack led by young Captain Horatio Nelson of H.M.S. *Albemarle*, then serving in Admiral Hood's West India Squadron. This petty setback was to be forgotten in the glory of Aboukir Bay, Copenhagen and Trafalgar.

Article V of the preliminaries of peace signed at Versailles between England, France and Spain on January 20, 1783, stated that "His Catholic Majesty shall restore to Great Britain the islands of Providence and the Bahamas without exception in the same condition in which they were conquered by the arms of the King of Spain". The return of the Bahamas and six small islands in the Caribbean was small compensation for the loss of the thirteen American colonies, and generally the peace terms were badly received in the British Parliament. In Nassau, however, there must have been rejoicing when rumours began to trickle in.

In Eastern Florida also there was interest. Loyalists who were no longer safe in the American States and heard that Florida was to be returned to Spain turned their eyes with desperate hope towards the almost unoccupied Bahamas. Among these was a certain Andrew Deveaux, Lieutenant-Colonel of the South Carolina militia, then in exile at St. Augustine. The islands were not to be restored until the definitive treaties were signed and there was no telling how long that would be. In fact, the formal Peace was signed on September 3, 1783, but by that time Deveaux and several other adventurers had seized the initiative. In April, "a handful of ragged militia" set out for the Bahamas in two armed brigantines. Recruiting a few settlers and Negro slaves at Harbour Island they sneaked towards Nassau by night and landed just east of Fort Montagu.

Although the garrison of New Providence numbered over 700 men, the impending peace had rendered them supine. The single guard at Fort Montagu was easily disarmed and the sleeping garrison captured without a shot being fired. Before morning, Deveaux had seized the highest points of the ridge overlooking Nassau.

An almost contemporary account gives an amusing description of the events that followed. "Every artifice was used to deceive the Spaniards, both as to the number and description of the enemy they had to contend with. A show of boats was made continually rowing from the vessels, filled with men, who apparently landed, but in fact concealed themselves by lying down as they returned to the vessels, and afterwards made their appearance as a fresh supply of troops proceeding to disembark. Men of straw, it is said, were drest out to increase the apparent number on the heights; and some of the troops, to intimidate the Spaniards, were painted and disguised as their inveterate foes the Indians. One or two galleys in the harbour had been captured; and trusting to the circumstances in his favour, Colonel Deveaux summoned the Governor to surrender, with a pompous description of his formidable force. Some hesitation being at first discovered, the Colonel seconded his overtures with a well-directed shot at the Governor's House from a field-piece, during his deliberation, which produced an immediate capitulation. The Spanish troops, in laying down their arms, it is said, could not refrain from expressing their mortification and confusion as they surveyed their conquerors, not only so inferior in point of numbers, but ludicrous in their dress and military appearance."

The terms of capitulation offered to Claraco were similar to those dictated to Maxwell in 1782. Government House and all stores were to be given up but the garrison was allowed to retire with the customary honours, including "a piece of cannon and two shot per day, in order to hoist the flag of his Catholic Majesty". The enemy troops were to keep their baggage and effects and to be conveyed to Havana and the Governor to Europe at British expense. All Spanish naval vessels in the harbour were to be surrendered but private property was to be returned, Spanish merchants having two months' grace to settle their affairs in Nassau.

Naturally enough, no-one gained more from this brilliant exploit than Andrew Deveaux himself. Carving out an estate of 250 acres in eastern New Providence and another 1,000 acres in Cat Island, he became a prominent Member of the reconstituted House of Assembly. The first of the Loyalists to settle in the Bahamas, he gained immensely from his status as an already established landowner when the other Loyalists began to flock to the islands in 1784 and 1785.

XV

Loyalists
1783-88

The influx of Loyalists after the Treaty of Versailles is often pictured as a Bahamian revolution. In fact, it was a quantitative rather than a qualitative change. On the constitutional scene we have already noticed that the period after 1783 merely accelerated and strengthened processes that were latent already. Except for the developments made possible by the vastly increased population, very little that was actually new was introduced into the colony; but these changes were real enough.

In less than five years the population of the Bahamas was trebled and the proportion of slaves increased from a half to three-quarters of the whole. Many Loyalists had owned plantations in the southern colonies and their arrival meant a great expansion of the plantation system in the Bahamas. New Providence was too small and infertile and several of the Out Islands were permanently settled for the first time. This brought about an extension of the government, so long concentrated on Nassau and Eleuthera, and the redistribution of seats in the Assembly.

The Loyalists had opted to remain under British colonial power and had chosen the unsophisticated Bahamas. That did not mean, however, that they were patient of royal control in excess of that to which they were accustomed, or willing to accept a standard of living much below that which they had left behind on the mainland.

Perhaps the new spirit of independence and responsibility was symbolised, as Harcourt Malcolm suggested, by the acquisition of the present Speaker's Mace in 1799. The improvement in standards was similarly expressed in the laying out of fresh settlements, the creation of new parishes and the building of new churches, schools and handsome private houses, and by the publication of the first newspaper, the *Bahama Gazette* in August, 1784. The arrival of the Loyalists did not revolutionise Bahamian life, but it infused the inert colony with fresh blood and energy. The death of the Old Empire was the beginning of modern times in Bahamian history.

The vast majority of those who found it uncongenial or inexpedient to remain under the government of the United States flocked northwards to Nova Scotia and Upper Canada where, as the United Empire Loyalists, they made a profound impact upon Canadian history. Guy Carleton, Lord Dorchester, for the second time Governor of Canada and British Commander-in-Chief in North America, feared the effects of this great flood of immigration and recommended to the British Government that unescheated lands in the Bahamas might be offered to Loyalists from the southern colonies who were reluctant to migrate to a colder climate.

Accordingly, Lieutenant John Wilson of the Engineers was sent in 1783 to make a survey. In his report he stated that the islands were grossly underpopulated and underdeveloped. The soil, though rocky, was fertile and particularly suitable for the growing of cotton. The primitive people, government and economy of the Bahamas, Wilson implied, could not but gain from a wave of Loyalist southerners.

In a royal proclamation signed by George III in September, 1783, it was definitely stated that the Crown intended to purchase the Bahamas from the Proprietors. The Governor of the Islands was instructed to allocate unoccupied lands, "to every head of a family, forty acres; and to every white or black man, woman or child in a family, twenty acres, at an annual ground rent of 2s. per hundred acres. But in the case of the Loyalist refugees from the Continent, such lands are to be delivered free of charges, and are to be exempted from the burdens of the quit rents for ten years from the making of the grant."

On February 7, 1784, the royal terms were quoted in a proclamation by Governor Patrick Tonyn of East Florida, in which he announced eighteen months' grace for those who wished to accept. Brigadier-General Alexander McArthur, the military commander of East Florida, was given orders to convey refugees at British expense to their new homes in the Bahamas. The first group of about 650, originally from New York, had sailed from St. Augustine to Abaco in September, 1783. They called their settlement Carleton. From there, one of their leaders wrote to their patron, Lord Dorchester, begging hopefully for "a small Military Force, for the present to Protect them against the Depredations of Evilminded Persons, a few Canon, Ammunition, etc., for their best defence, that a surveyor be appointed to lay out the town and survey the Lands . . . a vessell to carry a few Horses, and Horned cattle;—and as Saw Mills cannot be erected on the Island, request that Cross-cut and Whip Saws may be furnished for the purpose of clearing the lands—also two Setts of Tools for Black Smiths, and some coals. . . ."

Carleton (probably the present Hope Town) was obviously a poor place, very similar to a frontier town or the earliest settlements in Eleuthera. Like the original Adventurers, the Carletonians were soon squabbling and in March, 1784, General McArthur wrote almost in terms of civil war. Troops were brought in from St. Augustine to restore order and a court of inquiry was set up. As a result, certain militia officers were sacked and a Captain Stephens of Philadelphia placed in command. The chief dissentients left the settlement and formed a rival township at Marsh Harbour.

Throughout 1784 and the early part of 1785 an uncontrolled torrent of refugees poured into the islands just as fast as transports could be found for them. There was little organisation and no-one will ever know exactly how many went. The best guess is about 8,000, including slaves. Some idea of the details can be had from the *Bahama Gazette*, which listed the frequent sailings between St. Augustine and Nassau. But the newspaper did not begin until August, 1784, and the file for the first year is incomplete. Governor Tonyn listed seven typical refugee ships which reached Nassau in 1784, bringing lumber, shingles and other building materials, as well as 300 Loyalists and 1,700 slaves. The last official sailing was announced by Acting Governor Powell in February, 1785, and thereafter the flow became a trickle which dried up completely by 1789.

Governor Maxwell arrived back in the spring of 1784 to find the immigration in full flood. In his first speech to the House of

Assembly on April 4, 1784, he generously hoped that the Members would "have a tender respect to the unfortunate situation of your fellow subjects whom their Loyalty and sufferings have forced to seek an asylum among these islands". The House, which included Andrew Deveaux as one of the Members for the West, promised support and the new Act for Governing the Slaves was obviously framed with the new settlers and their thousands of slaves in mind. Besides this, a real effort was made to settle the newcomers in the Out Islands, and by the end of 1784, provision had been made for the admission of Members from five new Out Island constituencies.

The land grants recorded in the Registry at Nassau would amply repay a systematic study, though the confusion over tenure down to 1787 and the fact that records before 1790 are patchy in the extreme would make it a life's work. A. T. Bethell in the first and third editions of his badly organised book (1914 and 1937) listed 114 grants of land in 16 islands, totalling 42,829 acres for an average of 382 acres. The grants varied from a smallholding of 13½ acres in New Providence to a large estate of 1,460 acres in Abaco.

	New Providence	Long Island	Exuma	Abaco	Cat Island	Eleuthera	Crooked Island	Watlings Island	Others, including Acklins, Andros, Rum Cay, Bills Cay, High Cay, North Cay, Hog Cay, Royal Island	TOTALS
Grants	32	25	16	14	7	5	3	3	9/7	114
Acreage	7186	12,203	7710	3580	4720	1460	2200	400	3370	42,829
Average	224	488	482	256	674	292	733	133	481	382

TABLE A: LAND GRANTS TO LOYALISTS, 1784-89

The table of land grants to Loyalists (Table A), incomplete as it is, should be compared with the figures for the population in 1783 and 1786 (Table B), which show both the great increase and its distribution.

	1783			1786		
	Whites	Negroes	Totals	Whites	Negroes	Totals
New Providence	755	1739	2494	1572	4019	5591
Eleuthera	476	310	786	486	315	801
Harbour Island	360	144	504	365	149	514
Exuma	17	15	32	66	638	704
Long Island	33	78	111	41	99	140
Cat Island	6	9	15	59	305	364
Turks Islands	75	41	116	75	41	116
Abaco	—	—	—	282	384	666
Andros	—	—	—	2	59	61
TOTALS	1722	2336	4058	2948	6009	8957

TABLE B: BAHAMIAN POPULATION BY ISLANDS

By 1789 the total population had risen to 11,300, of whom about 8,000 were Negroes. A very pertinent fact is that the families of the original landowners are still very prominent, and indeed dominant, in Bahamian affairs. Bethell's full list of about 630 Loyalists contains almost every modern Bahamian surname. Of the 114 landowners listed, practically all of their names could be found in a 1966 list of Bay Street merchants and members of the government.

The newcomers did not gain a foothold as easily as Andrew Deveaux. It is evident that the original inhabitants resented them and discriminated where they could. Not even half the Loyalists were willing to be shipped off to the Out Islands and serious friction developed in Nassau. In a perceptive letter to Lord Sidney in mid-1784, Governor Maxwell distinguished between two types of Loyalist: " (a) Farmers who have set themselves down on the out Islands with large families and from 10 to 100 slaves each. These merit particular attention. (b) Officers, merchants and people who hope to return to the continent after peace there—nothing can satisfy this lot. They demand everything immediately—land, stores and employment, in fact they almost wish to take over the government. Flour is very scarce. The Americans are supplying it for the time being, but some loyalists consider it a monstrous offence and try to tear down the American colours." A little later, he called these "the most tormenting, Dissatisfied people on earth".

About this time a Loyalist wit circulated a broadsheet which teaches us much of the current bad feeling:

TO BE SOLD

Any day when Loyalists are out of town looking for lands. A quantity of beef and pork (not a word of this to any of the committee) for the very plausible purpose of paying expences—Entre-nous—that I may touch a Commission and the Old Inhabitants of this Town (who I commonly call damned villains behind their backs) may come in for snacks.

Governor Maxwell issued a proclamation concerning the tearing down of the Stars and Stripes from American ships in the harbour. He also ordered American sailors buying supplies to stay aboard their vessels on Sundays to prevent the occurrence of brawls on the Sabbath.

By June, 1784, rioting had reached serious proportions. Maxwell wrote General McArthur that he almost expected the Loyalists to force a *coup d'état*. In the following month he wrote to Lord Sidney asking for a regiment and three sloops to preserve the Government. He enclosed a printed handbill calling "a General Meeting of the Loyalists from the Continent of North America, at Mr. Johnston's House" on July 29. This was signed by fourteen prominent Loyalists, including James Hepburn who had been Attorney-General of East Florida and now styled himself "President of the Board of Loyalists".

The "Board" met with the Governor on September 3 and almost accused him to his face of partiality and incompetence. Maxwell must have regretted his earlier generosity to the Loyalists, who seemed to be loyal only to their own interests. Once more he wrote home for aid. When none materialised he weakly deserted his post, leaving for England in February, 1785.

James Edward Powell was left as Deputy Governor to face the orchestra of discontent.

The Legislature drafted an expression of thanks to Maxwell, which aroused the anger of most of the Loyalists. On March 5, the *Bahama Gazette* published a dissenting message signed by 136 prominent Loyalists "who happened to be in and near the town of Nassau at the time", in which they stated that "We the subscribers . . . deem it necessary publickly to disavow all knowledge or approbation of the same; having every cause to deprecate Mr. Maxwell's return to this Country, as the greatest evil that can possibly befal these Islands . . ."

One of Governor Maxwell's last official actions had been to convene the reconstituted Assembly, in which Members for Exuma, Abaco, Long Island, Andros and Cat Island sat for the first time. Of these 11 new Members, at least 9 were virulent Loyalists. Although the number of Members from New Providence, Harbour Island and Eleuthera had been reduced from 24 to 14, all of these were established settlers, 8 of whom had sat in the House after the General Election of 1784.

Immediately, the Loyalist faction challenged the means by which they had been deprived of their majority in the new House. Petitions were presented to the Assembly alleging that John Baker the Provost Marshal had arbitrarily declared six established settlers elected for Nassau and the Western District of New Providence, despite the fact that the Loyalist candidates had received a majority in the poll. As a counterblast, the unsuccessful candidates in the Andros election claimed that the Loyalists had validated the votes of their supporters by the last-minute conveyance of 70 or 80 lots of land. When it was proposed and seconded that consideration of the petitions be deferred, seven of the Loyalist Members withdrew from the House without waiting to gain the Speaker's permission, led by James Hepburn, the Member for Cat Island.

Acting Governor Powell prorogued the Assembly for a fortnight, hoping, as he said at the reopening on April 20, 1785, that he had thereby "allayed those Heats and animosities that seemed ready to burst into a Flame". It was a vain hope. None of the Loyalists was present. When the Messenger was sent out to summon them he reported "Mr. James Hepburn gone to Cat

Island, Peter Dean not to be found, James Moss gone to S.W. Cay, George Miller gone to Andros Island, James Ridley and Hugh Dean gone to Abaco. John Petty being summoned returned for answer that he did not *chuse* to attend the House while there were persons in it *illegally* chosen."

John Petty and Peter Dean went further than this, circulating a *Protest* that incensed those sitting in the House. On April 25, the Speaker ordered a copy burnt publicly by the Common Hangman outside the Courthouse door and severely censured John Wells, the printer. A motion was passed that the election petitions be disregarded since they had not been renewed at the opening of the new session.

On May 9, a meeting of Loyalists was held which sounded like a revolutionary tribunal. It was "resolved, that the Members of which that meeting was composed were not represented in the present Assembly, and of course not bound by any laws the Assembly might pass". Governor Powell was petitioned to dissolve the House and prepare writs for a new General Election. Instead, he prorogued the Assembly once more, this time for four months.

In July Powell received explicit instructions from England on how to deal with malcontents. He was advised to suspend James Hepburn, Robert Johnson and John Wells from any offices they might hold and to resist further appeals for a new General Election. When the House of Assembly was reconvened on September 20, 1785, the thirteen Members present felt strong enough to pass measures against the recalcitrant Loyalists. On September 26, Peter Dean, John Petty and James Moss were expelled for their part in the petitions and protest against the House, which were regarded as Contempt. Three days later the other five radicals were expelled for their persistent non-attendance.

The victory of the "Old Guard" seemed complete, and since the Assembly was not dissolved between 1785 and 1794, it would be easy to say that the Loyalists were excluded from the government for the whole of that period. It was not so. With one exception, the new Members chosen at the by-elections, although far less vocal and troublesome than their predecessors, were newcomers themselves. It was merely the extremists who had been neutralised; such men as Hepburn, who, re-elected for Cat Island, was declared ineligible on account of his previous expulsion.

As the years passed and took their toll of the Members by death or resignation, the "Long Parliament" of the Bahamas took more truly the appearance of a body representing all the people of the Islands. Far from being controlled by a government party and split by dissension, it became united in increasing its powers at the expense of the Governor.

1786 and 1787 saw a diminuendo of discord. Much of the credit for this was due to Deputy Governor Powell. His wit and charm, which shine through the dull clichés of the official dispatches, won back many elements antagonised by Maxwell. When he died suddenly in February, 1786, he was generally mourned. His temporary successor, John Brown, President of the Council, was also well liked, being, as a contemporary eulogist stated "an old inhabitant and a man of most respectable character . . . and as he convened the Assembly but seldom, and only for the purpose of continuing the laws that were about to expire, he was troubled by no applications upon the subject of dissolution; party dissension died away, and his government was the easiest, and most prosperous that ever was experienced by the people in the Bahamas".

As so often, economic prosperity went hand in hand with goodwill. 1786 and 1787 were the most prosperous peace-time years in the eighteenth century. Before the appearance of the *chenille* bug and other pests in 1788, the prospects of the Loyalist cotton planters were optimistic. The black loam soils noticed by Lieutenant Wilson proved excellent for growing the long staple "sea island" cotton. By the end of 1785, 2,476 acres had been planted and 124 tons were exported. In 1786 this increased to 150 tons from 3,050 acres and in 1787, 219 tons were produced from 4,500 acres, for a total value of £27,393 : 1 : 3d. Other trade figures were even more impressive. Whereas between 1773 and 1774 exports had only totalled £5,216 and imports £3,592, between 1786 and 1787 these had leaped to £58,707 exports and £136,359 imports. This increase was largely the result of the Free Port Act of 1787, which opened New Providence, like Jamaica, Dominica and Grenada, to trade in certain enumerated

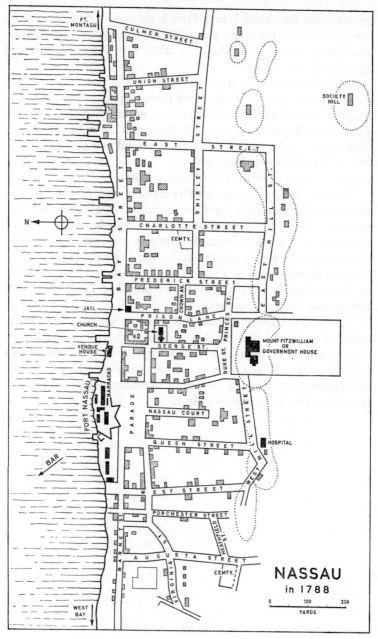

FT. MONTAGU

CULMER STREET

UNION STREET

SOCIETY HILL

EAST STREET

SHIRLEY STREET

EAST HILL ST.

N

CHARLOTTE STREET

CEMTY.

BAY STREET

FREDERICK STREET

CROWN AV.

JAIL

PRISON LANE

DUKE ST.

PRINCES ST.

MOUNT FITZWILLIAM OR GOVERNMENT HOUSE

CHURCH

GEORGE ST.

VENDUE HOUSE

FORT NASSAU

BARRACKS

PARADE

NASSAU COURT

QUEEN STREET

WEST HILL STREET

HOSPITAL

BAR

WEST STREET

BARNES ST.

PORCHESTER STREET

HEATHFIELD ST.

AUGUSTA STREET

VIRGINIA ST.

CEMTY.

NASSAU

in 1788

0   100   200

YARDS

WEST BAY

171

goods with the Spanish and French colonies. France did not reciprocate, but for some years Nassau became an important—and now quite legal—entrepot in trade with Cuba, Mexico and Spanish Central America.

Inflation was of course inevitable. The proximity of the infant United States with its paper money problems did not help matters. Food prices* in Nassau, for instance, doubled between 1784 and 1786, when at the peak flour cost $8 a barrel; butter cheese and soap as much as 1s. 3d. a pound and sugar from the nearby West Indies an incredible 1s. 2d. to 1s. 5d. a pound. Even rum could cost as much as 10½ *ryals* a gallon!

Nevertheless, one source of confusion and discontent was removed when in 1787 the Crown finally bought out the Proprietors. In a mammoth conveyance dated March 19, each of the heirs of the six original Proprietors was given £2,000 to surrender their rights absolutely to the Crown. This was in addition to two sums of £7,850 and £6,356 voted by the House of Commons in 1784 and 1786 to purchase lands from the Proprietors for the Loyalists.

All in all the Loyalists had little to complain of in their treatment. By the end of 1787 they seemed to have become almost integrated and content. Unfortunately, their contentment was to be short-lived. Within a single year came a pernicious insect to blight their crops and a Governor to remind them of the worst tyrannies of their continental days.

---

* See Appendix for the values of the different currencies.

XVI

Lord Dunmore
1788-1815

In April, 1789, a writer in the *Bahama Gazette* bemoaned the slump in cotton production. Because of the voracious appetite of the *chenille* bug, and perhaps also already the overworking of the thin soils, the yield in 1788 had been 112 tons instead of the expected 394 tons. Output had been halved instead of doubled. It was thus an air of deflated optimism that shrouded the governorship of Lord Dunmore from the start. Nor was the Scottish Earl a character likely to lighten the gloom. By most accounts he was a hot-headed and licentious boor.

The fourth holder of a title granted by Charles II, John Murray, Earl of Dunmore, had the dubious distinction of having been the last royal Governor of Virginia. Born in 1732, he was appointed to New York in 1770 and Virginia two years later. His rule had been outstandingly inept. Haughty and dissolute, his intellect had been no match for such brilliant patriots as Patrick Henry. His treaty with the Ohio Indians was as unpopular in Virginia as Lord North's Quebec Act was in Massachusetts, for much the same reasons. His attempt to seize the militia men's gunpowder in Williamsburg in 1775 was a hasty echo of Gage's march on Concord and united Virginia and Massachusetts in revolt. Dunmore fled his capital at the first sign of rebellion and, to the disgust of Loyalists and derision of republicans, proclaimed a warship anchored safely off Yorktown the seat of the government. After some sporadic service at sea during 1776, he was unemployed until he arrived in Nassau in October, 1787, at the age of 55.

It was in opposition to Dunmore that William Wylly made his debut in Bahamian history. Born in 1757 and called to the

English Bar, he had fought as a Loyalist in the War of Independence and migrated to the Bahamas in 1787. From then till his death in 1828 he was a potent force in Bahamian affairs.

Solicitor-General in 1787 and 1788, Wylly was soon antagonised by Dunmore's conduct and appointments. Writing under the pseudonym "A Barrister of Gray's Inn", he called the Governor "obstinate and violent by nature", with a "capacity below mediocrity, little cultivated by education, ignorant of the constitution of England . . . the lordly Despot of a petty Clan". Nor was "the immorality of his private life any less reprehensible than the defects of his public character".

The obvious animus in Wylly's account would be discounted entirely if it were not corroborated by others. Another writer characterised Dunmore's appointments as being "bankrupts, beggars, blackguards and the husbands of his whores". The Chief Justice was a "quack doctor" and the Searcher of Customs the unfortunate husband of a woman by whom Dunmore had fathered a child.

According to Wylly's version, Chief Justice Matson visited him stealthily and warned him that he should "take a party"; that is, should support the government more loyally. When he refused, he was arrested on a trumped-up charge of having called the Chief Justice "a damn'd liar". The trial was an uproarious farce. Wylly's counsel, Robert Johnson, recommended the two Justices by all means to consult. "Perhaps what one has not in his wig the other may have in his tail. You would probably consult better over a bottle of brandy." Wylly was discharged on the grounds of conflict of evidence, to continue his running fight against the Governor.

Dunmore provided plentiful fuel for the opposition. In February, 1789, he persuaded his son, the Hon. Alexander Murray, to stand in the Nassau by-election against Thomas Brown, one of the men who had testified for William Wylly at his trial. In an acrimonious fight on the party issue, Murray lost by 54 votes to 41, but was promptly returned for Eleuthera the following month. Another son was appointed Colonial Agent for the Turks Islands and Dunmore moved closer to open nepotism when he recalled him from the Turks Islands in 1793 and appointed him Lieutenant-Governor, without bothering to consult

London. This action drew a stinging admonition from the Secretary of State and Dunmore might have been faced by open revolt for his favouritism had not the sons been much more popular than their father.

Another source of grievance was the allocation of Crown Lands, which Dunmore treated very much as a means of patronage, much as Newcastle had used official appointments and sinecures in England as rewards for government supporters. The situation became much more serious after 1790 when the automatic grants to the Loyalists finally ceased. Besides this, it is obvious from the innumerable land transactions in the Registry under his name that Lord Dunmore was the first of the long line of Bahamian land speculators.

The rift between the Governor and people assumed its most serious proportions, naturally enough, in the Assembly. In 1791 Dunmore questioned the right of two Members to resign without showing him cause. Over this he was politely but firmly snubbed by the Speaker. Shortly afterwards, the question of the control of expenditure provoked a more important crisis. In October, 1791, while discussing the Appropriations Bill, the House resolved that it should oversee the expenditure of the taxes which it levied. This right was challenged by the Council, and Lord Dunmore prorogued the Assembly for a year before the Bill could become law.

In July, 1792, although the need for revenue was becoming urgent, Dunmore sent down to the House a letter from Secretary of State Dundas which stated that supervision of expenditure by the Legislature would amount to an encroachment on the royal prerogative. "If on the production of the public accounts", the letter suggested, "it shall appear that abuses have been committed in the Expenditure the remedy by an address to the King in Council is always in the power of the House." This was far from satisfactory to the Assembly and the Members refused to concede. On August 3, 1792, Dunmore was forced to sign the Appropriations Bill despite several provisions he deemed unconstitutional, because money was so short.

In 1793, the controversy reached its climax. On August 26, the House of Assembly passed the important Resolution "that as all Bills for granting supplies for support of Government or whereby money may be directed to be levied on the subject must constitutionally originate in this House, so it is also the undoubted and sole right of this House as the Representatives of the people, sanctioned by Parliamentary usage, to direct, limit and appoint in such Bills the purposes, considerations, limitations and qualifications of such grants and sums of money which might not be changed or otherwise altered by the Council". The House also refused point blank to allow either the Governor or his Council to see the accounts and vouchers which had been the basis for the Appropriations Bill.

Although Lord Dunmore tried once more the gambit of proroguing the House, he had lost the battle. War with France had broken out again and the Treasury contained the grand total of £4,500. On September 10, 1793, Dunmore reconvened the Assembly and five days later signed the controversial Bill. Since that date, although the Governor did not formally concede the fact until 1828, the House of Assembly has controlled the Bahamian budget.

To consolidate the ground won, the House clamoured for a dissolution and a general election. A Bill to Limit the Duration of Assemblies had passed through the Legislature as early as 1792, but Dunmore replied to petitions that it was still being considered by the Privy Council in London. After the inevitable delay, the Bill was returned in 1794 with the instructions that it should become law providing the Assembly should never be of less than seven years' duration. Since the House had already sat for nine years, Dunmore was forced at last to dissolve it. The General Election which followed in September, 1794, removed all traces of a pro-Dunmore faction in the House. It also removed all doubt that the Loyalists remained under-represented in the Assembly.

The most lasting monuments to Dunmore's folly were the forts which he built. Massive to the point of impregnability, they never fired a shot in anger. Fort Charlotte, named in honour of George III's Queen, was begun in 1787 and was planned to cost an economic £4,000. By 1789, Dunmore had spent £7,636 and exhausted the local resources. He appealed to Lord Sidney, citing the miseries of the 47th Regiment then providing the garrison, living in palmetto huts and dying like flies. Dunmore had reserved 100 acres around the Fort (which are still public lands) "to prevent houses being built near it, for exercising the troops, and for supplying them with all sorts of Vegetables, which is absolutely Necessary for the preservation of their health in this Climate, more especially as they have no fresh Provisions owing to its high price. It will also be absolutely requisite to erect Barracks for the troops on the Hill adjoining the Fort, first because those they are now in, are in a ruinous State, and Secondly because they are in the Town where the men procure Rum which is their destruction, and thirdly because the present Barracks are at much too great a distance from the Fort, and I will venture to assert that when lodged on the Hill they won't loose one Man where they now loose ten."

Despite a discouraging reply, Lord Dunmore began work on a barracks and added the middle bastion to Fort Charlotte, naming it Fort Stanley after one of his subsidiary titles. In 1791, the Secretary for War sent out a Lieutenant D'Arcy to investigate the dwindling away of money and men. By that time the Governor had begun work on the western bastion, and although he cunningly christened it Fort D'Arcy, the doughty Lieutenant was unimpressed and sent a disparaging report back to his superiors. Among other points, he noticed that the site of the barracks was in direct line of fire between the Fort and the town it was intended to defend. It was with great reluctance that the War Office forwarded the £17,846 required to finish the building of the Fort.

The barracks were completed in 1794 and cost £10,784, bringing Dunmore's expenditure to £32,267, or roughly eight times the original estimate. Designed to accommodate six companies of troops, the barracks were never fully used. Even by the time they were completed, disease had carried off 150 men of the 47th Regiment as well as 109 of their women and children. Unstrategic and unsightly, the barracks were pulled down as insanitary in 1835 and transferred to the site of the dismantled Fort Nassau, where they remained until the West India Regiment left Nassau finally in 1891. Fort Charlotte itself, which in its heyday boasted an armament of 42 large cannon, remains in magnificent but useless preservation, a magnet to wondering tourists.

In spite of his earlier extravagances, when war broke out in

1793, Lord Dunmore built batteries at Winton, on Hog Island and Potter's Cay and began another fort. Placed on the highest point of the ridge overlooking Nassau and shaped like a stranded paddlewheel steamer, this one he named Fort Fincastle after the viscountcy borne by his eldest son. In February, 1794, Dunmore described this fort as "mounting two 24 pounders, two 32 pounder Carronades, two 12 pounders, and one Howitzer, which not only covers the battery on Hog Island but all the Town and Road to the Eastward where the enemy might probably have effected a landing".

Ironically Nassau, which was never to be attacked again, was more strongly fortified than ever before. But superfluous fortification did not satisfy Dunmore's mania for building. Towards the eastern end of New Providence he built a small country house called the Hermitage (now the residence of the Catholic Bishop) and throughout his governorship he expanded and remodelled the Government House on Mount Fitzwilliam, while all the time clamouring for another building on a slightly more elevated site. Lord Dunmore also recommended the erection of an entirely new range of public buildings: House of Assembly, Council Chamber, Courthouse and Gaol. All these improvements came, but gradually, and after Dunmore had left the colony.

Governor Dunmore took an interest in Harbour Island, the second most populous settlement in the Bahamas. There he built a summer house for himself as a refuge from the vapours and gossip of Nassau, with the inevitable fortification, on what became known as Barracks Hill. On October 5, 1791, he laid out Dunmore Town, still the chief township, by splitting up part of his own land into 190 lots and allocating them to each of the leading settlers at an annual quit rent of 2s. 6d. per lot. Since the land of Harbour Island was not very fertile, most of the inhabitants lived there but worked estates across on the mainland of Eleuthera.

The French Revolutionary War, news of which reached Nassau in June, 1793, brought the prospect of renewed prosperity through privateering to the Bahamas, but merely a new set of problems to the harassed Lord Dunmore. A French warship, aptly named *L'Embuscade*, patrolled off Hog Island for weeks, effectively blockading the harbour. Disquieting news reached

Nassau from America that M. Genet, "calling himself the French Minister of the American States", was blowing on the embers of anti-British feeling, recruiting a Legion of American troops and commissioning privateers. In September, 1793, Hammond, the British Minister to the United States, and Bond, the Consul at Philadelphia, warned of a full-scale attack impending on the Bahamas.

The inhabitants, as usual, were hardly awake to their dangers and most unco-operative, blocking expenditure, refusing to support the militia and thinking only of the profits of privateering. Many openly favoured the Americans, who in turn were supporting the French. In May, 1795, for instance, Dunmore had to report that the Chief Justice, Stephen Delancey, whom he had removed from the Council after a dispute in 1791, had deserted the islands for the United States.

Colonel Peter Irving, the senior officer of the garrison, pleaded for reinforcements, while doing his best to man the new fortifications and provide some form of naval defence. The only response of Whitehall was a constant stream of memoranda complaining of Dunmore's extravagance.

George Chalmers had been appointed Colonial Agent in London in 1792, a post which he occupied with success for thirty-four years. With his finger on the pulse of events, he diagnosed Dunmore as the cause of all the troubles in Nassau and did his utmost to have him replaced. In early 1793 a merchant called Inglis reckoned "that the application of almost any reputable Individual interested in the islands could secure his lordship's recall". Colonel Irving reported about the same time that "My Lord Dunmore has lately had several ugly attacks and is at this moment labouring under one of a very serious and alarming appearance". In 1796, John Clear of Harbour Island testified that Governor Dunmore had broken a stick over his head "without the slightest provocation whatever". It came as a surprise to no-one, except perhaps the noble lord himself, when, just nine days after this incident, Governor Dunmore was ordered to return to England by the Duke of Portland. Despite several requests to be allowed to return to the Bahamas, he was never reappointed to a position of responsibility. He died in Scotland in 1809.

John Forbes, a Loyalist with an estate in Exuma, was appointed Acting Governor. He neatly summed up the Opposition view of the unfortunate Lord Dunmore when he said that the Scottish Earl had "at great expense to the British Treasury (concealed under items of Fortifications, Gallies, etc., etc.) packed the Assembly . . . and protected defaulting Treasurers with Handsome Wives . . . the lower order of *whites* here being rather a lawless race, the descendants of Pirates, they have not departed from the principles of their ancestors, though their practices may assume the different names of wrecking vessels and Privateers. Between my predecessor and these People a sort of reciprocity of Abuse was established; and a species of implied compact of mutual conniving at the violation of the law by the one and the Peculation on the British side by the other."

The departure of Dunmore did not bring an immediate improvement in conditions. In late 1796, a disastrous hurricane ravaged the islands and in its wake came a fearful outbreak of yellow fever brought from Santo Domingo by a detachment of 500 troops sent by General White to recuperate. Among the hundreds of dead was Acting Governor Forbes. President Robert Hunt filled the gap until William Dowdeswell arrived to succeed Lord Dunmore in 1798. In that year, John Wells was able to report that Nassau was jogging "along in the old quiescent torpid way".

If anything this was an understatement. The animosities generated by the arrival of the Loyalists and the heavy hand of Lord Dunmore had died away. The story of the remainder of the long French war, which ended in 1815, can be briefly told. The Governors: Dowdeswell, John Halkett, who was commissioned in 1802 and Charles Cameron (1804-20), were so colourless as to be almost anonymous. Despite their oft-repeated expressions of concern, cotton continued to decline. In 1803, Daniel McKinnen noted that in Crooked Island the plantations were "for the most part deserted", and in 1812 a visitor recorded only two planters active on Acklins. These islands were only saved from complete insignificance by the establishment of the General Post Office of the Bahamas on Long Cay, packet boats sailing between London and Kingston calling there on their way through the Crooked Island Passage.

On Long Island, which at the height of the cotton boom

boasted a good carriage road 100 miles in length, "eight or ten plantations were entirely quitted and thirteen others partially given up" between 1795 and 1803. Perceptively, McKinnen observed that the thin soils once worked could never recuperate owing to the lack of stock animals for manuring. Shift planting was used, but once all the available land on a plantation was worked out the plantation perished. In 1800, fifty cotton planters petitioned for relief from the Crown and in 1802 the Land Office was empowered once more to allocate Crown Lands freely. This revived cotton planting to a certain extent and the complete collapse of the industry was postponed until the abolition of slavery in 1838.

Wrecking was a perennial, if somewhat unreliable, standby. The number of ships cast up on the Bahamas in the age of sail, before the publication of accurate charts or the erection of lighthouses, was almost incredible. Whole fleets were sometimes destroyed, as in August, 1800, when H.M.S. *Lowestoft* and eight Jamaica ships she was convoying, were wrecked off Inagua. McKinnen recorded a telling conversation with a "Conch" (white Bahamian) wrecker from "Philimingo Bay, Icumey" (Flamingo Bay, Exuma) who was off on a "racking voyage to Quby" (Cuba). The naïve visitor asked the weatherbeaten old salt if many sailors were employed in the trade:

A. We lay with forty sail four months along *Floriday* shore.

Q. Forty sail? Then certainly you must have had many opportunities of being essentially serviceable to vessels passing the Gulf Stream, by directing them to keep off from places of danger, with which you made it your business to become acquainted?

A. Not much of that—they went on generally in the night.

Q. But then you might have afforded them timely notice, by making beacons on shore, or showing your lights?

A. No, no (*laughing*): we always put them out for a better chance by night.

Q. But would there not have been more humanity in showing them their danger?

A. I did not go there for humanity: I went *racking*.

As in all previous wars, privateering was a more profitable and certain trade than wrecking. This was particularly true after the ill-advised American declaration of war against Britain in 1812, when "all was bustle in Nassau, for these islands flourish most in times of war". As soon as the news reached Nassau, more than a dozen ships were seized in the harbour and the correspondence and newspapers for 1812-14 were crowded with references to confiscations. Between January 14 and March 17, 1814, for instance, the *Royal Gazette* recorded the auction of four schooners, two brigs and a sloop seized from the Americans and Spanish. In the two years of the American War, almost as many vessels were condemned in the Vice Admiralty Court in Nassau (246) as in the previous nine years of war (257).

Britain commanded the seas and despite the proximity of the Bahamas to the hostile States and the paucity of local defences, Nassau did not attract reprisals throughout the War. The only bad effects were inflation and the shortage of supplies usually obtained from the mainland. The Rev. W. Dowson, one of the first Methodist missionaries, recorded that "flour rose to 25 dollars per barrel and corn meal to 26 shillings per bushel Bahama currency". When a prize was brought into Rock Sound, Eleuthera, the inhabitants could not resist seizing the flour it contained, an offence for which seven people were expelled from the Methodist church.

One of the interesting sidelights on the part played by the Bahamas in the War of 1812 was that towards the end of 1813 Governor Cameron received letters from two Red Indian chiefs stating that between 10,000 and 20,000 Indian braves in the South were ready to go on the warpath against the United States if they received aid from the British. The British Government, however, was so slow in taking up this offer that by the time an expedition to support the Indians was planned in August, 1814, the war had ended.

On the profits of privateering, if not the plantations, Nassau gained steadily in stature. Unlike the New England colonies and the puritanical commonwealth proposed by the Eleutherian Adventurers, however, the Bahamas remained until the nineteenth century almost a godless place. The spirit of piracy and wrecking was deeply ingrained and was always likely to resurge. As to the slaves, many of the masters considered that Christianity would demoralise them by teaching them notions of equality, and preferred the slaves to linger on in their dimly remembered African superstitions. In 1802, the Anglican missionary the Rev. D. W. Rose recorded that many of the Negroes of Exuma, presumably Mandingoes, were "followers of Mahomet". *Obeah* practices persisted furtively in backward areas for a further hundred years.

The first of the few ineffective missionaries, the Rev. William Guy, was sent out by the Society for the Propagation of the Gospel in 1731. He found a neat wooden church in Nassau and managed to baptise 128 persons; but although he twice held Holy Communion, there were less than 20 communicants altogether. A second missionary, the Rev. William Smith, was able to report in 1733 the existence of a Church Vestry of 12, and in 1754 the church was rebuilt on the present site of Christchurch. Old prints show a pretty little wooden building with a quaint steeple like a pagoda. In 1768, a new parish was created at Harbour Island and in 1770 Governor Thomas Shirley sent eighteen casks of wine to Boston in order to repair the steeple of Nassau church. In 1782, however, at the time of the Spanish invasion, the incumbent, the Rev. Mr. Barker, was one of the first to desert Nassau. It was significant that during the interregnum a certain Mr. Treibner, an unspecified dissenter, was allowed to preach in the church.

As could be guessed, the coming of the Loyalists had a decided effect upon the religious life of the colony. The American Tories were traditionally firm supporters of the Anglican establishment and except for the Presbyterians who founded St. Andrew's Kirk in 1810, the Loyalists, once they had gained power in the Legislature, did all they could to place the Church of England on a firm basis. In 1789, the Rev. James Brown complained that his thrifty expenditure for the year, £237, far outran his paltry income from fees of £185. In an Act of 1795, however, the church was given the income from liquor licences and the Vestry was granted the supervision of weights and measures and the management of the public market. In the same year another Act created five new parishes throughout the islands.

At this critical juncture the Anglican Church began to lose ground. Acts of the Legislature cannot create religious zeal and this was a period of demoralisation. Besides this, the S.P.G.

was almost bankrupt and was unable to send out missionaries between 1807 and 1835. For most of this time there was seldom more than one minister in the islands. A third reason for decline was the reluctance of the Established Church to proselytise the Negroes. The Dissenters had no such scruples and found among the slaves and free Negroes the eager material for a religious revolution.

It is a matter of dispute as to whether it was Baptist or Wesleyan missionaries who first sowed the seeds of Dissent in the Bahamas. In the 1790s, Negroes from the Carolinas preached both new doctrines at the risk of their lives, and in 1796 a brave Negro called Joseph Paul founded a Wesleyan church in the Western district of Nassau where St. Mary's Anglican church is today. In 1799, Dr. Thomas Coke, the evangelist of the West Indies, pleaded with the Methodist Conference at Manchester to send out a missionary to the Bahamas. On October 22, 1800, the Rev. William Turton, a 39-year-old Barbadian, arrived in Nassau to begin his ministry. Within the same year the first Baptist chapel, called Bethel, was established in Meeting Street, overlooking Delancey Town. The race for converts had begun.

Unlike the missionaries in the other slave colonies, Turton did not face open violence, but rather at first had to endure "slander, petty persecutions and impertinent officialdom". His first public services were held in the open air, since no-one had the courage to rent him a building. His first converts were too poor to build, but by 1804 foundations had been laid for a chapel in Nassau Court, opposite the ruins of Fort Nassau. This modest building was destroyed in the hurricane of 1813 and not rebuilt until 1821. By this time, Turton had been joined by the Rev. John Rutledge and the Rev. William Dowson and flourishing congregations had been established at Eleuthera, Harbour Island and Abaco. Although the first Wesleyan missionaries preached with considerable success to the Negroes, their doctrines were even more attractive to the native whites, especially of the poorer kind. As time went on there came a noticeable social or racial division in the Methodist Church.

Among the Baptists there has never been a racial division for they have always been almost 100 per cent Negro. Unity, however, they have never enjoyed. Baptism spread with the spontaneity of a bush fire but with as little organisation. It was not until 1833 that the Baptist Missionary Society sent out its first mission under the Rev. John Burton, which founded Zion church. By that time there were already at least two flourishing branches, the offspring of the original missionaries and the St. John's group founded by an American called Spence in 1814, which later became nominally Episcopalian. Today although Baptists are the most numerous of the Bahamian sectaries, they are split and splintered into innumerable doctrinal factions.

Though few of the early dissenting chapels were very grand, and none have survived in their original form, Nassau itself was becoming more impressive at the close of the Loyalist period. McKinnen described the town as being "as well built as any I saw in the West Indies" and contemporary engravings depict a far more imposing place than Woodes Rogers or P. H. Bruce knew. Many of the gracious colonial houses which are such a charming feature of contemporary Nassau, were built during the period 1800-15. Most of the public buildings were also built about that time. Vendue House, now the home of the Bahamas Electricity Corporation, where slaves and general merchandise were bought and sold, was built about 1787. The present cathedral was erected on the site of the old parish church in 1840, but St. Matthew's, the oldest extant church, was designed and built by the ingenious Joseph Eve between 1800 and 1804 with money voted by the Legislature.

The present Government House was erected between 1803 and 1806 on land purchased in 1799 from Paul Drumgold by the Legislature for £4,000, although the Governor's residence had been on that site at least since the time of Lord Dunmore. The story that the present Catholic Priory on West Street was once the Governor's house seems to be a myth, since the excellent map of 1788 shows no building there. The total cost of building, or rebuilding Government House, with garden, walls and gates, was £10,000. The well-known statue of Columbus, looking from the steps down George Street, was erected by Governor Smyth in 1830.

The most notable additions to the architecture of Nassau were the public buildings arranged around Parliament Square. The Gaol, now the Public Library, a quaint octagonal building, was raised between 1796 and 1800. Nearby was a workhouse which has since disappeared. The fine buildings on three sides of a square facing Bay Street and housing the Assembly, the Council and the Court, were begun as early as 1803, but not completed until 1812. Their design was based upon that of the public buildings at New Bern, the capital of North Carolina, which many of the Loyalists remembered with nostalgia.

Except for the filling in of the Crown Dock under Governor Rawson (1865), before which boats could tie up on Bay Street itself, and the erection of the new Supreme Court building and Police headquarters (1920), the administrative heart of Nassau has changed little since 1815. Today the buildings possess a dignity and old-world charm so lacking in these chromium-plated days. In 1815, they were all modernity, an immense advance upon the buildings the German Schoepf had described in 1784. "A church, a gaol and an assembly house", he wrote, "make up the public buildings of the town." Looking back at the great, if gradual, progress made since that time, the sons of the Loyalists in 1815 had good cause to be proud of the work of their fathers.

XVII

Slavery

1815-34

It was the hard-won improvements of the years after 1784 that the planter class and their merchant friends saw threatened once the emancipation movement gained sway in England and began to make its influence felt in the colonies. To the ruling class, the plantation system was the foundation of the Bahamian economy and the basis of their own wealth and position. Disgraceful as the concept of slavery is to modern ideas, it must be acknowledged that the cheap labour of slaves was indispensable to the plantation system. The planters fought Emancipation in all its phases because they knew that it meant the destruction of most of what they stood for.

To free the slaves would mean a revolution in colonial life as drastic as the recent upheavals in America and France. To see this revolution in its true perspective, we must examine slavery and the plantation system as it was in the Bahamas before 1834, the desperate but hopeless resistance to the Emancipation movement in the Assembly, and the effects of Abolition in the years that followed.

In 1831, there were 12,259 Negroes in the Bahamas, outnumbering the white inhabitants by three to one. Of this majority, 2,991 were free; a sixfold increase over the total of barely 500 in 1789. But the remaining 9,268, almost two-thirds of the population of the islands, were slaves. In the eyes of the law, slaves were barely human beings. They were termed chattel labourers; the possessions of their masters, liable to be bought and sold and bequeathed like any other property. To us they seem to have been regarded as useful and rather valuable animals. How fair is this assessment?

The vast majority of the slaves came from West Africa north of the Congo. But this itself was an area vaster than Europe, with far more separate races and different languages. The dense forest in which most of the Negroes lived was an effective barrier to communication and they existed in self-contained units of family and tribe. Practically their only common denominator was ignorance and primitive barbarism. They were natural prey to more highly developed (and thus more predatory) peoples such as the Arabs, Ashanti and Dahomey tribesmen, who had learned how to travel from region to region and were comparatively well-organised.

Mandingo, Fulani, Hausa, Ibo, Ijo, Yoruba and many other tribes made their involuntary contribution to the great African migration, which at its peak may have reached 150,000 a year. For good or bad, the institution of slavery gave these Africans their first unity. Very quickly their tribal identities broke down; their babble of tongues before the unity of a single European language; their customs before the unity of a single law; their religion before the attractions or organised coercion of Christianity. Today in the Bahamas there are no names and few customs that can be traced back to Africa with any certainty. A possible exception is the picturesque and exciting *John Canoe* or *Junkanoo* dance still held at Christmas and New Year, to the playing of the *goombay* drums. Similar drums of wood and goatskin are called *gumbies* in Jamaica and *gombeys* in Bermuda. Parsons' "Folk Tales of Andros Island" (1911) showed that superstitions and quaint folklore lingered on in that backward island well into the twentieth century but it is almost certain that the furtive practice of *Obeah*, primitive African magic, has finally died out, although it persists in Jamaica.

Although the migration of Negroes to the Bahamas was continuous, if sporadic, down to 1834 or even as late as the ending of slavery in the United States (1864), many coloured Bahamians today are doubtless descended from the slaves whom the first permanent settlers brought to the islands. By the time the first large group of settlers reached New Providence about 1666, the English West African slave trade was well organised. Six years later, the Royal African Company began its monopoly, which

was reinforced by the granting of the *Asiento** by the Spanish in
1713. As we have already seen, the first authentic list of settlers,
dated tentatively 1671, included 443 unnamed slaves, comprising
40 per cent of the total population.

Taking into account the usual shipping routes, it is probable
that most of the Bahamian Negroes came from the more northerly
parts of West Africa. There were found the brown-skinned
Mandingoes, Fulani and Hausa, with straighter hair, longer faces
and more pointed noses than the purer Negroes of the south.
The black "Coromantyns" of Jamaica and the Dahomey peoples
found in Haiti came from the Ivory Coast and the Gulf of Guinea.

Slave ships destined for Havana often stopped first in the
Bahamas, thus giving Bahamian planters the benefit of pre-
emption. Once in Nassau, slaves would be advertised for auction
and were usually sold at Vendue House. There was also, of
course, a permanent trade in experienced slaves from master to
master. The following advertisement, from the *Bahama Gazette*
for October 1, 1785, proposes such a sale:

TO BE SOLD

AT PUBLIC AUCTION

On Monday next,

At Twelve o'clock,

SEVERAL VALUABLE YOUNG

NEGROES

Among whom are Carpenters, a Cooper, House
Wenches, who are good cooks and washers, a very
handy Young Girl for waiting at table, and several
Boys, who have been accustomed to boats and
fishing, &c. All the above Negroes are undoubted
property, and may be sent to any part of America.
Warranted bills of sale will be given.

STERLING & MACKENZIE

Nassau, September 28, 1785.

Daniel McKinnen was witness to a sale of a large number of
slaves in 1803. His description modifies the extremist view of

---

* The right to supply an annual quota of slaves to the Spanish American
colonies first granted to the British at the Treaty of Utrecht (1713).

slave conditions. The sale, he reported, "was conducted with more decorum, with respect to the slaves, than I had expected. They were distributed mostly in lots from five to twenty in each; but some of the boys and girls were disposed of separately. On the neck of each slave was slung a label specifying the price which the owner demanded, and varying between two and three hundred dollars, according to age, strength, sex, &c. This cargo was composed, as generally happens, of slaves from different nations, and speaking languages unintelligible to each other. Some apprehensions prevailed, notwithstanding all the expedients which had been used to convince them to the contrary, that they were brought over to be fatted and *eaten*. I had an opportunity of observing two or three the day after the sale in the hands of benevolent masters purchased for domestic servants, who seemed much delighted with their kind treatment as well as change of situation. Instead of being naked they were clothed (in this climate as usual) in woollens; their food was much superior to what they had ever known before; they found themselves lodged in habitations abounding in comforts, some of them indeed superior to their comprehension; and in the streets they beheld many of their own colour, whose appearance, friendship and hilarity had the most powerful influence in rendering them contented and happy in their new scene of life."

McKinnen went on to say that although the slaves sometimes arrived from Africa in a condition of wretchedness and were sometimes mistreated by overseers, many "liberal and enlightened strangers in the West Indies" underwent a change in their attitude to slavery once they examined the "actual situation and character of the negroes. . . . Whatever may be the horror we justly feel at the idea of their perpetual bondage", he concluded rather smugly, "it will be recollected that they are not often endowed with that spirit of independence and dignity of sentiment which render it insupportable to a generous mind."

Daniel McKinnen also gave an invaluable account of the working of a cotton plantation on Acklin's Island. He was there in March, when the plants were in bloom and the slaves busy in picking. The species of plant favoured was that from Anguilla in the Leewards, which was reckoned to need the labour of one slave per six acres against one slave for every four acres of the variety from Georgia. McKinnen noticed that, although the men worked under the encouragement of certain incentives, the women were generally far more dexterous. One outstanding female slave carrying a baby on her back, for example, gathered in between 40 and 50 pounds of cotton in a day's work.

Once collected into a store-room, the pods were put through a "gin" to separate the staple from the seeds. This simple machine, the invention of which by Eli Whitney had revolutionised the cotton industry, consisted basically of two parallel contra-rotating rollers which agitated the wool so that the seeds fell through. Joseph Eve of Nassau had invented an improved version of the common gin, for which he was rewarded by the Legislature. In the absence of running water, this machine was worked by a wind vane.

The average yield of cotton per acre seems to have been about 112 pounds, mostly in March, with an unreliable after-crop in the summer. Exceptional plantations could expect to harvest as much as 1,500 pounds of clean wool for each working slave. Others reckoned themselves lucky to get in a sixth as much. Clearly, the productivity of each slave was as important as the comparative fertility of the soil and it must have been obvious to the most naïve observer that the most productive slaves were the most contented.

"The negroes of the Bahama Islands", wrote McKinnen, "discover, in general, more spirit and exertion than in the southern parts of the West Indies. Something perhaps may be attributed to a more invigorating climate as a physical cause; but I believe more is due to the circumstances in which they are placed. Their labour is allotted to them daily and individually, according to their strength; and if they are so diligent as to have finished it at an early hour, the rest of the day is allowed to them for amusement or their private concerns. The master also frequently superintends them himself and therefore it rarely happens that they are so much subject to the discipline of the whip as where the gangs are large, and directed by agents or overseers."

Even before the decline of cotton, few Bahamian estates were very grand. The reader must forget all pictures of fields to the horizon, slave gangs of hundreds and palatial plantation mansions. Only a handful of owners possessed more than one hundred slaves and their plantation houses were hardly substantial, for not one has survived intact to the present day.

A typical Bahamian plantation was that on Watling's Island owned by Charles Farquharson, whose journal for 1831 and 1832 has luckily been preserved. Farquharson's Estate consisted of 2,000 acres, but only a small proportion of this was cultivated. Most of it was pond, scrub or bare rock. In all there were about fifty working slaves, but very rarely were more than a dozen employed at the same task. Cotton was still the most important commercial crop, but only twelve bales were exported in the two years. Otherwise, produce shipped for sale included stock animals, lignum vitae, citrus fruits and some guinea corn. Charles Farquharson hardly expected to become a millionaire.

The most remarkable fact about the Watling's estate was its self-sufficiency. The only imports from Nassau which the journal mentioned were flour, rum, furniture and cloth. Guinea corn, the chief crop, was mostly used to feed the slaves. Other food crops were several kinds of peas, yams, sweet potatoes, snap beans, cabbage and pumpkins. Castor beans, catnip and sage were grown for medicinal purposes. It is unlikely that the slaves often tasted the meat of the sheep, pigs and steers that were raised on the estate, but there was mention of hens and turkeys and the "hauling of seine for bonefish". Mules and horses were bred for transportation.

The tasks at which the slaves were employed were innumerable. With the exhaustion of the soil, new land was always being prepared, in the invariable Bahamian manner of cutting, piling and burning the scrub. Hoes were used for planting and manure from the stock-pens was used whenever possible. When, or if, the crops began to grow, there was thinning and "filling in the blanks", weeding and trimming to be done.

With so many varied crops, harvesting was a complex and almost continuous process. Maize had to be broken and stripped, guinea corn cut and threshed. Peas and cotton were picked, fodder stripped, yams and potatoes dug and catnip pulled. Then, when the crops had been carried on horse or slave-back, the cotton had to be ginned and baled and the castor beans put

Nassau in 1729. From a contemporary drawing by J. Gascoigne

Nassau in 1862, showing a blockade-runner in the left foreground.
From a drawing in the *Illustrated London News*

through the mill. When the work of harvesting was slack, men might be sent to fish or cut wood.

Besides all this, some slaves were employed in tending the cattle, which roamed almost wild over the island, trying to keep them in bounds by building and mending walls and fences. Others were specialists in making roads, thatch and wattles or building the simple wooden houses in which the slaves lived. For more permanent buildings, some men were employed in cutting rock, burning lime, fetching sand and making mortar. A few slaves were competent masons and carpenters. On the infrequent occasions when ships called in or were leaving, slaves were employed in carrying goods the several miles to the dock. All too rarely there was the excitement and profit of wrecking.

As to the actual condition of the slaves, we must gain much from inference. Despite the imminence of emancipation, there was no mention of slave unrest or insolence. Nor was there much reference to wrongdoing or punishment, though Farquharson wryly accused several slaves of feigning sickness to escape from work. Of church-going and education there was no record, though the slaves had the traditional three days free at Christmas and rarely worked on Sundays. Charles Farquharson was reputed to be a good master and most of the simple and ignorant slaves were more than content to jog along under his protection. Drought, fire, hurricane and disease were probably all regarded as worse evils than the state of slavery. But even these disasters, in such a modest and self-contained community, were shared in common.

Laudable as it was, the abolition of slavery (as has already been implied) was not a movement generated from within the colonies but imposed upon them from without. To the ruling whites, abolition was unthinkable. Even the betterment of the slaves would invite discontent rather than gratitude. Certainly, the authorities at home should not meddle in something which they clearly did not understand. "In the language of the Scriptures", wrote ten angry slave-owners to the colonial Agent in 1823, "they *are our money*, and to divest us of them against our will . . . would, in plain language, be nothing less than robbery. . . . The truly disgusting tales of the Abolitionists, of the slaves being, like beasts of burden, flogged out in droves to their work, kept to it with the lash, and then driven back to their stables, have, we solemnly declare to you, not the slightest foundation of truth within these islands."

Nevertheless, despite their moral indignation and employment of biblical texts to support their case, the slave-owners were fighting a rearguard action against moral certitude. After the Somerset Case (1772), which abolished slavery in England, complete emancipation throughout the British Empire was only a matter of time.

The first great victory of the abolitionists was the ending of the slave trade within the British Empire by an Act passed on March 25, 1807. This was reinforced by another in 1811 which decreed transportation the penalty for slave trading, and a third in 1819 which equated slaving with piracy. These Acts effected slight hardship upon Bahamian masters, for the decline of the plantations meant that there was no demand for a continuous influx of new slaves. In fact, the market price of slaves in Nassau declined appreciably between 1810 and 1815, and by 1825 their value was said to have depreciated by 50 per cent. The labour situation was further complicated by the arrival of freed Negroes from seized slave ships who probably totalled 1500 between 1807 and 1830. By the 1807 Act, these were bound to masters as indentured servants.

It was not until the movement for the registration of all slaves, the next campaign of the abolitionists, that the Bahamian slave owners began to resist the British Government. The chief motive for registration was to prevent the illegal transportation of slaves from place to place. Since the 10,000 Bahamian slaves were found on sixteen islands as much as 600 miles apart, this was regarded as a particular hardship. As in Bermuda, many Bahamian slaves were employed as mariners and their status under the registration scheme was not clear. Although registration was first enforced in Trinidad in 1812 by an Order-in-Council and the British Act was passed in 1815, it was not until 1822 that the Bahamian Legislature passed a Registration Act and even then it was inefficiently administered.

The protracted opposition to registration in the Bahamas was closely connected with "The Wylly Affair", which brought

about the most serious rift yet between the executive and Legislature. William Wylly, for a long time Attorney-General of the
colony, had reportedly become converted to abolitionism. He
was known to have asked William Dowson to come out to his
plantation at Clifton and preach to the slaves, and was said to
be in correspondence with the newly formed and hated African
Institute in London. Finally, in late 1816, he openly challenged
the authority of master over slave. In 1809 a slave called Sue
had been brought to Nassau from Georgia. In 1816, her master
came to Nassau with a male slave called Sandy. When he returned
to Georgia he intended to take Sue as well as Sandy and a child
that had been born to them both. The slaves absconded and
when they were seized, Attorney-General Wylly ordered that
although Sandy and the child might be taken back to Georgia,
Sue must remain.

The House of Assembly determined to make an inquiry into
the Attorney-General's conduct and summoned him before a
committee of the House. Wylly refused to appear and was immediately arrested and imprisoned for contempt. The Chief
Justice thereupon obtained a writ of *Habeas Corpus* from the
General Court and Wylly was freed. The House of Assembly
censured the Chief Justice and asked Governor Cameron to
suspend the Attorney-General from his office. Instead, the
Governor ordered the dissolution of the House.

Three days later, on January 31, 1817, a public meeting was
called at which the action of the Assembly was unanimously
upheld and the Governor condemned. The House of Assembly
was said to be the superior court of the islands and the only judge
of parliamentary usage and its own privileges. The situation
remained highly inflammable throughout the spring and summer
of 1817; nor did the situation improve when the new House met
in September. Its composition was almost identical with the
previous one and it began by refusing to accept the censure of
the British Government. A Bill reversing the judgement of the
General Court in the Wylly case was passed by the Assembly but
thrown out by the Council. The Registration Bill was framed
and read three times, but in such a form that it was certain not
to obtain the approval of Governor or Council. The Appropriation Bill pointedly omitted the salaries of the Attorney-General

and the Justices of the General Court. In despair, the Governor prorogued the Assembly and very shortly afterwards left for London to consult with the Privy Council.

The Acting Governor was none other than Munnings, the Chief Justice whom the House had attacked. When he summoned the Assembly to read a message from the Prince Regent upholding the action of the General Court, its only reaction was to order the Attorney-General to appear before it on July 14, 1818. After upbraiding the Members in the Council Chamber, Munnings dissolved the House of Assembly for a second time.

An attempt at harmonisation in March 1819 failed, since the Members of the Assembly were further angered by having been made to serve on juries. It was not until the arrival of Major-General Lewis Grant to be Governor in 1820 that the Wylly Affair began to dissolve. By the single casting vote of the Speaker, a "Healing Act" was passed which stated that neither the arrest of Wylly nor the action of the General Court in releasing him were to be used as precedents to define the relative privileges of the House of Assembly and the General Court. Although the House was dissolved once more in December, 1820, after passing a resolution refusing to pay the Attorney-General and upholding its future right to arrest whom it pleased for breach of privilege, the crisis had passed. In the following session, a workable Registration Act was passed, by which a limited movement of slaves between the islands was allowed.

But the slave-owners were not permitted to relax. After their victory in the Registration dispute, the tireless abolitionists turned their attention to the "amelioration" of slave conditions. A new Slave Code was passed by the Imperial Parliament in 1824, most of which became law in the Bahamas after a delay of only two years. One reason for this comparatively weak opposition was that conditions in the Bahamas were already better than those in the other colonies. Also, it was realised that in such a scattered colony, such Acts could not be very effectively enforced.

By the amended code, which consisted of eight Acts passed between 1826 and 1829, a master's obligations to his slaves were specified for the first time. Every slave over ten years old was to receive a peck of ground corn each week and two suits of "proper and sufficient clothing" per year. Adult slaves were also to be given a small plot of land around their houses on which to grow vegetables. Slaves were forbidden to grow cotton, raise cattle or rake salt in opposition to their masters, but could be given permission to open up trade in dry goods. Thus, a minority of the slaves began to use money for the first time.

Slaves could hold property and make bequests, being subject to the common law in these respects. The permission of masters had still to be obtained before slaves could marry, but after 1827 ministers other than Anglican could legally perform the ceremony. Before restrictions were placed on the movement of slaves, many masters were said to be opposed to the marriage of their slaves finding it more convenient to transfer slaves unburdened by marital ties. By the 1826 law, the separation of husband and wife was made an offence and no children were to be taken from their recognised parents until they were 14 years old.

Although free Negroes had been given the right to vote in 1807, slaves, of course, were never permitted to do so. Nor were they allowed to serve in the militia, although, under the pressure of war, free coloureds had been enrolled from 1804.

The question that excited most controversy was the admissibility of slave evidence in the courts. The majority of the whites were obsessed by the dangers of unfriendly or perjurious evidence against them, either in criminal or civil cases. What an iniquity it would be if they were defrauded out of their lands or even sent to jail on the evidence of the slaves they owned or of Negroes who had recently been slaves! In the Code of 1784 a foothold had been gained by the admission of slave evidence in criminal cases against manumitted persons and against all persons in suits for debt, provided that the slaves were Christians and competent to take the oath.

This advance was consolidated by Acts in 1822, 1824 and 1829, by which time the evidence of slaves in nearly all civil cases was declared admissible. But this was so hedged around with provisos that it is doubtful whether it was ever effective. Native Africans and other slaves who had been in the colony less than five years were excluded. Slaves had to testify that they were Christians and satisfy a clergyman or justice that they could understand the oath. They could not testify in libel cases or cases dealing with slave ownership. As if this were not enough, courts could throw out the evidence of any slave who could be proved to be of bad character. Finally, the penalty for perjury was fixed at fifty lashes and branding with the letter "P".

One of the common defences of slavery, used in particular by Catholic apologists, was that it gave the heathen Africans some chance of conversion to Christianity. With a few commendable exceptions, such as William Nairn of Watling's who held morning prayers which his domestic slaves attended and William Wylly, the masters had been hitherto indifferent or opposed to the spiritual welfare of their slaves. This accounted for the great success of the non-Anglican missionaries thought by many of the masters to be so dangerous. The law passed in 1829 said that "All masters or owners of slaves . . . shall . . . endeavour to instruct their slaves in the Christian religion, and shall endeavour to fit them for baptism, and, as soon as conveniently may be, shall cause to be baptised all such slaves as they shall make sensible of the Deity and of the Christian faith". Doubtless a favourite biblical quotation of the slave-owners was the passage in which St. Paul announced the return of the slave Onesimus to his master, Philemon.

From 1800 until the emancipation of all slaves, manumission became steadily easier and there was a great increase in the number of free Negroes. After 1784, masters could free slaves if they wished, but since there was a manumission fee of £90, very few availed themselves of this privilege. The fee was not removed until 1827, when a nominal registration fee was substituted, but by that time it was recognised that the slaves themselves could purchase their freedom by agreement with their masters. Obviously, many needy owners without a shortage of labour took advantage of this and went through the rigmarole of getting the manumission in writing, under seal, witnessed and registered. The following is a typical example:

Bahama Islands

Know all men by these presents that I, George Brook, of the Island of New Providence, gentleman, for and in, consideration of the sum of one hundred pounds lawful money of these Islands, to me in hand well and truly paid by my negro woman slave named Bell for and on account of herself the receipt thereof, I do hereby acknowledge, having manumitted, made free and released from bondage, and by these presents do manumit, make free and release from bondage, and all servitude, the said negro woman slave named Bell and her issue.

Witness my hand, etc., Jan. 3rd. 1823.

(*Sg.*) GEORGE I. BROOK

A. T. Bethell stated that there were five hundred such documents for the years 1819-34 lodged in the Registry.

A law of 1805 permitted suits for the freedom of slaves to be brought in the General Court, but it was not until a special slave court with two justices and five jurors was established in 1824 that any slaves successfully petitioned for their freedom against the will of their masters. Slaves could sue for damages, but only by bringing a separate suit, and the awards were never more than nominal. A slave could buy or petition for the release of his wife and children, but no children under 14 could be manumitted without the permission of their masters. By a law of 1824, no aged or infirm slaves could be freed, since they might become a burden upon the colony. In 1827 this was altered to allow their freedom, but their ex-masters were held responsible for their support until they died.

Runaway slaves were fairly common in the Bahamas, but since they could never escape far they were usually treated leniently. An absence of ten days and flight of eight miles was decreed as the crime worthy of the maximum penalty of fifty lashes. Masters losing slaves usually advertised and offered a reward for the return of their runaways. The following notice was inserted in the *Bahama Gazette* in January, 1786:

RUN AWAY about the 12th. of October last, a stout made Negro Fellow named *Jackson*, about 30 years of age, a little pitted with the small pox, and is well known about town. He has associated himself with several Runaway Negroes, who are encamped in the bushes somewhere behind the Hospital. Whoever will deliver the said Negro to the subscriber, shall receive *Twelve Pieces of Eight* Reward.

JOHN MORRIS

Subsequent issues of the paper described the flushing out and capture of the small band of runaways in the vicinity of the Blue Hills, one of the Negroes being killed in a scuffle.

The general improvement in slave conditions in the West Indies was accompanied by serious slave rebellions in Barbados (1816), Demerara (1823) and Jamaica (1831). Bahamian masters were always quick to point out that there had never been a successful slave insurrection in the islands and, rather illogically, they attributed this both to their own leniency and the efficient operation of the punishment code. They resisted changes whenever they were proposed and there is evidence to show that the general severity of the masters tightened up to counter the increase in slave restlessness before emancipation. The very first prosecutions of Bahamian slave-owners for brutality occurred under Governor Smyth (1829-31) although the General Court threw out the three test cases he brought, on grounds of insufficient evidence.

The most severe punishments were directed against insubordination. By the 1784 code any white was empowered to disarm a slave and the penalty for the assault of a white person by a slave was death. Even verbal abuse was penalised by a fine of £15 or corresponding corporal punishment. In 1827 this penalty was limited to fifty lashes, but even after 1830 a slave was to be executed for assaulting a white person with a dangerous weapon.

In 1827 mutilation as punishment, the use of iron collars, weights and chains and whips for encouraging work were forbidden, but it is unlikely that this was regarded as a deprivation by the masters. Flogging continued to be the general punishment for crimes. Despite the limitation to thirty-nine lashes in one day and the prohibition of flogging by jailers and workhouse supervisors without the permission of masters in 1824, it is likely that the slave-owners continued to administer their own corporal punishment exactly as they saw fit.

It was over the question of the flogging of female slaves that the slave-owners in the House of Assembly made their biggest protest against the amelioration campaign. In 1829, John Carmichael Smyth, a vigorous abolitionist, was appointed Governor. Although he congratulated the Members on the liberal slave measures they had passed since 1826, he angered them by suspending Assistant Justice Lees and Police Magistrate Duncombe for ordering the flogging of a female slave. In this, Smyth was following an instruction sent out by the Secretary of State. In 1831, he provoked a crisis by asking the House of Assembly to suspend John Wildgoos, a Member, who had ordered the flogging of one of his female slaves confined to the workhouse.

The House appointed a Committee to inquire into the conditions in the jail and workhouse, which reported that Governor Smyth had persistently meddled in cases of punishment and had even interfered in cases before the courts. It was resolved by a vote of 13-4 to petition Lord Chandos for Smyth's recall, a move that was actively supported by the newspaper of the time, the *Bahama Argus*. A large number of names was collected and the petition sent off.

Smyth's reaction was to dissolve the House, prosecute the editor of the *Argus* for libel and to send off to London a sheaf of dispatches defending himself. In one of these, he wrote that "many of the ignorant whites at Abaco and elsewhere signed the petitions against him, because they were under the influence of the store keepers on Bay Street at Nassau".

When the House was reconvened in 1832 the opposition party was even stronger and only two Members dared support Governor Smyth. News of the full plans of the British Government for the amelioration of the slaves' condition had reached Nassau and the temper of the House became truculent to the point of mutiny. The reply of the Governor's opening message was the most disrespectful in the history of the Assembly, the Members passed several bills which Smyth was unable to sign and sent a second petition to London for Smyth's recall. The result was a second dissolution.

From that point until his recall to England in 1833, Smyth governed the Bahamas without the help of the Assembly, despite the fact that neither of the sessions had seen the appropriation bill become law. Governor Smyth reformed and strengthened his Council by dismissing or ignoring those, like Chief Justice Munnings, who were in tune with the opposition or dependent upon the Assembly for their salaries. In the manner previously practised by Lord Dunmore, he revived the salt tax and tonnage duties and was able to announce at the end of 1832 that all colonial officials' salaries would be paid in full.

By provoking the two dissolutions on the comparatively minor point of the flogging of female slaves, the slave-owners served their own cause badly. During the year and a half during which the Assembly did not meet and the Bahamas were ruled quite effectively by the Governor in Council, the British Government moved relentlessly towards the complete abolition of slavery. The Emancipation Act passed into law on August 1, 1833, and when Acting Governor Balfour recalled the House, the disgruntled slave-owners were presented with a *fait accompli*.

XVIII

Emancipation
1834-40

The Emancipation Act, which was designed to come into force on August 1, 1834, did not immediately give the slaves complete freedom. There was to be a compulsory "apprenticeship" similar in all but name, to the old system of indentured labour, which was not to disappear finally until August, 1840. In fact, the ex-slaves became fully free on August 1, 1838.

Nor, in theory, did the British Government impose its will on the colonies. The Emancipation Act was to be ratified first by the colonial legislatures. But since a share in the handsome compensation of £20,000,000 voted by Parliament was dependent on ratification, the slave colonies hastened to accept the inevitable. Jamaica, which stood to gain most, was first, in December, 1833, but the Bahamas were not very far behind. The Bahamian Acts to implement Emancipation and the apprenticeship system were on the statute books well in advance of August 1, 1834.

The amount of compensation paid to the slave-owners was calculated in a most ingenious manner. The Parliamentary commissioners took the value of the total exports of each of the slave colonies and divided this figure by the number of slaves in each colony. This ratio, which represented the average economic value of the slaves to each colony as a whole, was applied to the gross compensation to determine the total amount due.

Since the exports of the Bahamas had been declining over the previous thirty years, the colony fared badly in the share-out, receiving a total of £128,296 for her 10,086 slaves, an average of about £12 : 14 : 6d. a head. This was the lowest average in all the 19 slave colonies, and compared very unfavourably with the average of £52 for British Guiana, £50 for Trinidad or even the £20 for each of the 311,000 Jamaican slaves.

The allocation of compensation within the Bahamas was made by a local commission. Masters were to file their claims and these were to be published in order to resolve disputes over ownership. The eleven lists which appeared in the *Bahama Argus* between August and December, 1834, provide an interesting analysis of the system that was just coming to an end. The 10,110 slaves for whom compensation was claimed had been the property of no less than 946 owners, giving an average ownership of 10·7 slaves per master. Only 11 masters owned more than 100 slaves, Lord John Rolle with 376 possessing almost twice as many as anyone else.

Domestic slaves or craftsmen were assessed as more valuable than the labourers of the Out Islands. The highest sum paid out for a single slave was about £32. "Inferior field labourers" or praedials as they were called, were paid for at the rate of £19 a head. Payments for children below working age and infirm slaves were barely more than nominal. Since most of the compensation money was swallowed up by merchant creditors or mortgage holders, few slave masters, especially in the Out Islands, had any relief from the prospect of impending ruin.

In announcing emancipation to the reconvened Assembly in 1833, Acting Governor Balfour explained that it had been forced upon the Imperial Government by the pressure of public opinion in England. This candour did not mollify the angry Nassauvians, and 15 out of 16 of the proclamations were torn down within twenty-four hours. There was a great deal of confusion over compensation and the operation of the apprenticeship system and it was feared that there would be immediate outbreaks among the slaves. There were alarums in Exuma and the Turks and detachments of troops were sent to those places, leaving Nassau critically weak. Despite this, the actual day of emancipation and the transition to apprenticeship passed by without serious incident. There does not even seem to have been much general rejoicing among the liberated slaves. Uncertainty was probably the most common sentiment.

By the Acts of 1834, the ex-slaves were divided into two categories: "praedials" and "non-praedials". The term of apprenticeship for praedials was to be six years and for non-praedials, four. In fact, all ex-slaves were released after four years. No praedials were to be removed from the soil without the permission of the magistrates, but no children under the age of 12 were to be deemed praedials.

Employers were still responsible for maintenance, though food and clothing could be commuted for good land by agreement. Sick and aged apprentices were the responsibility of their ex-masters. In theory at least all the ex-slaves had full civil rights except in having to adhere to the apprenticeship system. In practice, however, they were subjected to what Smyth had called "the most arbitrary vagrancy law in the West Indies". This was amended in 1835 to forbid assemblies for "no specific and lawful object, loitering and carousing . . . in the liquor shops, loud singing or whistling, flying kites in or near highways, and calling loudly in the markets to attract customers". The maximum fine was five days' imprisonment. Corporal punishment by employers was retained in the law, but permission had to be obtained from a magistrate and in practice it was discontinued. Runaways were to be returned to their employers by force, an unauthorised absence for $7\frac{1}{2}$ hours constituting an offence.

The best and most lasting feature of the new legislation was the provision of contracts between the ex-masters and the ex-slaves. These compulsory documents were usually liberal in their terms, especially in the allocation of task work, and many Negroes voluntarily continued them after 1838. No contracts were to last more than a year, they were to be properly witnessed by two persons and both parties had to understand all provisions. Each plantation had to keep a record book of all contracts, open to inspection by the special magistrates. The maximum work that could be imposed was 45 hours a week, between sunrise and sunset, Monday to Friday. Saturdays and Sundays were completely free for the Negroes to do as they pleased.

The provisions of the apprenticeship system were to be upheld and the rights of the Negroes protected by special magistrates appointed from London. These were the forerunners of the two present stipendiary and circuit magistrates, who are assisted in their legal duties by each of the Out Island Commissioners. In 1834, three special magistrates were appointed and stationed in

New Providence, Eleuthera and the Turks Islands but they were insufficient for the necessary travel and business and were assisted by the local Justices of the Peace, most of whom were themselves employers of ex-slaves. In 1835, Acting Governor Colebrooke declared this system unfair and forced the resignation of eighteen local justices. He reformed the General Court on a circuit basis and asked for more special magistrates. By 1838, there were six and the system was working well.

The ending of the apprenticeship system was hastened by the terrible conditions discovered in the workhouse and jails of Jamaica and other islands. This was not true of the Bahamas, where the houses of correction were underpopulated and the number of punishments declined steadily. For the last month of the apprenticeship system, July, 1838, for instance, special magistrate Winder reported that there had not been a single case in New Providence.

Although the House of Assembly petitioned Governor Cockburn in July, 1838, to continue the apprenticeship system for its full term, it is unlikely that many plantation owners suffered any additional penalty from its discontinuance. The reason for this quiet acceptance of the change was that there was no shortage of cheap labour in the islands. Most of the Out Island plantations had been broken up, leaving the Negroes as independent farmers or squatters, or as eager candidates to sign contracts for whatever work was available. The first contract labourers for work outside the Bahamas, for instance, went to Demerara as early as 1838. This competition in the labour force, so beneficial to employers but uncomfortable for the employed, was aggravated by the continuing influx of Negroes seized from illegal slave traders and planted on the Bahamas between 1830 and 1840.

After the abolition of the British slave trade in 1807, the Royal Navy maintained a special squadron to suppress the traffic. From 1830, slaves seized on the high seas were freed absolutely. The first such cargoes reached Nassau in September, 1832, when 370 negroes were settled on Highborne Cay, 514 at Carmichael, six miles from Nassau, and 134 at Adelaide in the south-west of New Providence. In 1833 there was a serious drought and the Negroes on Highborne Cay were brought back to New Providence and settled at Headquarters, just "over the hill" from Nassau, where Grant's Town is today.

Between 1833 and 1838 at least six further cargoes of freed slaves were brought to Nassau. In March, 1836, for example, the *Vigilante* arrived with 230 sick slaves, to be followed just one month later by the *Creole* with a further 314. In November, 1837, a seized slave ship was wrecked off Harbour Island, only a few of the Negroes being saved. In the spring of 1838, no less than 1,043 were brought in, nearly all being in lamentable condition.

After rest, good food and whatever medical treatment was available all at the expense of the British Government, the freed Negroes were allotted small plots of land in the various new settlements. Carmichael and Adelaide were never popular, being too far from the sources of work, but Headquarters flourished. Swampy land was drained, gardens and streets laid out so that very shortly the settlement had the appearance of a picturesque native village. Further settlements were attempted at Williamstown and Victoria in the Berry Islands, Bennett's Harbour on Cat Island, the Bight and Great Harbour on Long Island and on Rum Cay and the Ragged Islands.

A thin stream of new immigrants from Africa continued to trickle into the Bahamas after 1840, consisting of slaves destined for the southern states of the U.S.A. carried in British ships. The last recorded seizure was in 1860, though British naval vessels continued their vigilant patrol against slavers down to the abolition of slavery in Brazil in 1888.

Except for significant minorities of Greek and Chinese, British West Indians and Americans, the Bahamian melting-pot had received its chief ingredients by 1860. The tale since then has been one of gradual, almost imperceptible, amalgamation, so that within a hundred years only a handful of families can call themselves "pure white" or "pure Negro". This makes any attempt at racial discrimination so fatuous as it seemed to a visitor in the 1880s:

> *God bless the white folks one and all, though hark ye,*
> *I see no harm in blessing too the darky!*
> *But which is the darky and which the white;*
> *God bless us all! That is beyond me quite!*

Except for the inevitable distinctions of class, the only valid classifications for those living in the Bahamas today are "Bahamians" and "Non-Bahamians". A person in the latter category can echo the words of McKinnen, written in 1803: ". . . were I on a slight impression to judge from the present and former characters of the natives I should be almost tempted to attribute something to the assimilating influence in the climate; for I certainly did in some striking instances observe that amiable and beneficent disposition which accords with the representation of the antient *Lucayans*. Their regularity of features is not imperceptible in some modern faces. Perhaps there are few countries more favourable to female beauty than this and adjacent parts of the continent. I have nowhere observed more delicacy united with a spirited expression of countenance."

If the Bahamian Negroes did in fact demonstrate by the 1840s something of the indolent and carefree nature of the Lucayans, these attributes were a great asset to them. For without doubt the lot of the average free Negro during the nineteenth century was worse than that of the average Negro in the latter days of slavery. The logic of events was pitiless. Abolition meant the final collapse of the plantation. The end of the plantation economy meant general poverty and insecurity, for no-one more than the ex-slaves. Even without actual discrimination, the lot of the Bahamian Negroes was bound to be a sad one, for the poor are always underprivileged.

To the Negroes for whom there was no paid employment, subsistence farming was the only refuge. The system of land tenure was extremely confused. The masters were supposed to allocate good land to their ex-slaves and many did so. In most cases, however, their own tenure was far from sure. With such large areas of poor or worked-out soil they had been accustomed to work unoccupied areas to which they had very little title. Moreover, in a colony where cash was in very short supply, the most popular method of holding land was by quit rent tenure. Enormous acreages were theoretically leased from the Crown for the payment of a nominal quit rent, often as little as 1d. an acre per year. In fact, these rents were often not paid, in which cases the lands should have reverted to the Crown and certainly not given to the ex-slaves.

BAY STREET THEN AND NOW

1862: The high-water mark of the prosperity brought by the American Civil War

1962: In the background is the British Colonial Hotel, on the site of Fort Nassau

In 1831, the arrears in quit rent totalled £5,000 and although there was a remission in 1833, it was estimated that by 1835, 100,000 acres had been "re-commuted" by the Crown for non-payment. In 1845, of the £800 a year due in payment of quit rents, only about a quarter was regularly collected. In 1846, the Assembly paid up the outstanding arrears in quit rents for £3,000, which legalised many dubious conveyances and was a boon to most smallholders. It was, however, a poor substitute for absolute freehold. A remission of debt is less valuable than the removal of its cause.

Clearly, the solution to the thorny problem of land tenure lay in the hands of the Crown. With official foresight and generosity, a sturdy class of small farmers might have been established. In fact, for nearly a century, the inhabitants of the Out Islands drifted on miserably at the threshold of starvation. Shackled by counsels of conservatism, the Crown was niggardly in its allocations. The freed Negroes were given no materials and little guidance in their strange new status. The Blue Book for 1864 complained that "there is scarcely a plough or a sickle throughout the islands. The Bahama farmers grow, but don't cultivate the vegetables they require. They neither water nor manure the plants, nor do they prepare the ground, and rotation of crops is unheard of."

The British Government, moreover, was dedicated to the policy, first put forward by Edward Gibbon Wakefield, that Crown Lands could only be developed by those who could afford a "sufficient price" and should therefore not be given away freely. Even today, Crown Land is only granted to those who can undertake to develop it.

The Registry Act, which was re-enacted in 1834, made it very difficult to gain undisputed title to land. Except for the small plots in the settlements laid out for the Negroes seized from the slave traders, the Crown did not disburse any lands free of charge. In 1836, Lord Glenelg ordered that no Crown Land was to be sold for less than £1 an acre. In 1839, it was decreed that 40 acres was to be the smallest lot for an outright sale, and although in 1840 Lord Russell permitted lots as small as 20 acres to be sold for 12s. an acre, these terms were still too exacting for the majority of the ex-slaves.

A considerable number of the new smallholders after 1838 came into the category of squatters. Today some titles to land are based upon the English law of 1847 which allowed possession to any land worked without question for sixty years. That this could occur merely demonstrated the lack of interest on the part of the Crown in the face of the diffusion of the islands, the haphazard methods of farming and the complexities of the legal processes. Nevertheless, the squatters were never secure. As late as 1923 an over-zealous official at the Crown Lands Office was able to dispossess many poor farmers in Exuma on a technicality, and in the 1962 Bowe case, 28 other Exumians were denied squatters' rights for having shared their crops with the owner of the land.

There were some bright exceptions in the gloomy picture of the allocation of lands to ex-slaves. One example was the Sandilands estate in Eastern New Providence, which was divided up generously among the emancipated Negroes in 1838. Today the picturesque rural village of Fox Hill at its centre reminds us of the type of community the abolitionists visualised. The reverse is all too common in the Out Islands. In Exuma, however, Lord Rolle deeded all his extensive lands to his slaves and their descendants in commonage. This, and not a fantastic exploitation of the *droit de seigneur* explains why nearly half the population of Exuma proudly bears the surname of their benefactor. The inhabitants of Rolleville, Rolle Town, Mount Thompson and Ramsey, although poor, have more than sufficient land to farm. Most islands have areas of commonage, and in the Turks Islands also there are over six thousand acres of common land, purchased from the Crown in 1840 for $1,000.

It was perhaps in education that the Negroes were worst served. Cynics will observe that it was to the interest of the dominant whites to keep the Negroes ignorant. But this was less a calculated policy than the combined result of apathy, poverty and the squabbles between the various churches over who should control, or even share in, the education of the general population.

The pioneers of general education were the Methodist Missionaries after 1800. Although Governor Smyth set up schools in the new settlements of Carmichael and Adelaide, it was not until the Imperial Government made a grant of £25,000 for colonial education in 1835 that a real beginning was made. In that year, the Board of Education with the Governor as President was established, local commissioners were appointed and a normal training school for teachers was proposed.

The Board of Education became the focus of a religious dispute, a microcosm of the religious differences then beginning to divide the colony. The Church of England, the established church, was strongest in the beginning. The Anglican British and Foreign School Society became interested in the colony and plans were afoot for correspondence with King's College, London, an Anglican establishment. In the schools, the "Madras" system was employed which included the liturgy and catechism in the syllabus and encouraged attendance at the established church.

In 1839, the Board was made interdenominational, and included senior members of the Wesleyan and Baptist congregations as well as the ministers of the Anglican and Presbyterian Churches. This merely exacerbated the dispute and the Education Act of 1841 decreed that no clergy should be members of the Board, nor should children be forced to learn the catechism if their parents objected. This improved matters for a time, but the appointment of the new Archdeacon to the Board in 1844 at the same time as the post of Inspector of Schools was created, re-opened the wound. In 1847, the Board was composed entirely of lay members once more and an Act of 1864 decreed that it should consist of the Governor and five members of the Legislature. Nevertheless, the dispute over control continued, and long outlasted the disestablishment of the Anglican Church in 1869.

Meanwhile, the condition of education improved at a snail's pace. In 1847, the schoolmaster at Rock Sound stated that although the inhabitants of New Portsmouth were healthy and bright, only about one in twenty could read and write. He opened his school in the only building available, a hut 18 feet by 21 feet leased from the Wesleyans, into which were crammed 85 children, half of those eager to attend. The roof leaked, but neither the Wesleyans nor the Board could afford repairs. There were no school supplies.

By 1859, there were 26 public schools, but only 39 teachers. In 1864, the number of children in the Board schools totalled 1,570, out of a population of 36,000. The entire bill for the salaries of the Board teachers was £1,920 a year. In despair, the Board of Education relied heavily on the "Monitor" system whereby the more advanced pupils instructed those below them in standard. Although this system was rejected in England as inefficient in 1840, it has continued in the Bahamas until the present day.

A compulsory Education Act was passed in 1877, but at first this was confined to New Providence. In 1889, it was considered feasible to extend the Act to the Out Islands, and in 1897 the school leaving age was officially fixed at 14. The attempt to collect fees for public school education had been discontinued five years earlier.

Over the decades, the literacy of the general population increased steadily, until by 1953 it had reached the satisfactory level of 89 per cent. During the nineteenth century, however, there was no attempt by the Government to sponsor secondary education. Nor, despite several promising starts, was a permanent school for training teachers established. A Government High School was not set up until 1925, nor housed in adequate premises until 1960. In 1957 the ratio of primary school children to those in secondary schools was 67 : 1, three times as high as any other area in the Caribbean, including Haiti.

Through poverty and indifference, education allocations never kept pace with the increase of population. As late as January, 1961, a newspaper writer was able to report a primary school where 250 children were taught in a leaky building 50 feet square, with a dearth of books and materials, and sanitary facilities unworthy of a medieval prison. Of the 770 "teachers" in the Bahamas, he claimed, 628 were totally untrained.

The small improvement in education in the 124 years since emancipation is probably the worst indictment that can be made of the governing class in the Bahamas during that period. The degree of actual repression practised upon the Negroes by the whites is far more difficult to assess. It has probably been exaggerated in some quarters. It was none the less real enough, and even into the 1960s considerable bitterness remained, the residue of grievances real or imagined.

It was a long time before the emancipated Negroes served on juries, for the high qualifications effectively excluded the poor. To sit on the Grand Jury a man had to be worth £1,000, and even members of Petty Juries had to have property worth £100. It was significant that lists of jurors were drawn up within weeks of emancipation in 1834, and these showed that in Christ Church parish only 108 men qualified for Jury service and in St. Matthew's parish, 117. Of these 225, only 61 were eligible to sit on the Grand Jury.

As far as justice itself was concerned, zealous judges appointed from London were likely to come into conflict with the establishment in Nassau over discrimination. Ex-Stipendiary and Circuit Magistrate Powles, in his fascinating book *Land of the Pink Pearl* (1888), described the tremendous *furore* he created when, in February, 1887, he sentenced a white man, James Lightbourn, to a month in jail for assaulting a coloured servant. Nothing like this had ever happened before and racial feeling almost exploded in a riot.

"The blacks, of course, were delighted", wrote Powles, "and went about crying that justice had come to them at last from England, whilst on the other hand the native whites were up in arms, and the naïveté or shamelessness, I really don't know which to call it, of some of their remarks was positively startling.

"Just as I was leaving the court, a prominent white citizen came running up to me, saying, 'Of course Lightbourn got off?' 'No,' said I, 'he didn't. I've sentenced him to a month's imprisonment, but he has appealed to the Chief Justice and is out on bail.'

" 'Will the appeal be to a jury?' he asked. I replied in the negative.

" 'What a pity,' said he, 'if it had been to a jury we could have made it all right.' "

On May 3, 1887, the Chief Justice reversed Powles' decision and freed Lightbourn without even a fine. In this summary he went as far as to say that "he should not think of believing the evidence of any number of black witnesses against that of a respectable man like Mr. Lightbourn".

As a result of the Lightbourn case, Powles was as unpopular with the ruling class as he was popular among the Negroes. The House of Assembly refused to vote him certain allowances for which he had petitioned and Governor Blake asked for his resignation on the grounds that he had "started the race question" and that therefore his "usefulness in the colony was at an end".

In fairness it must be mentioned that Powles was an outspoken Irish Catholic who admitted himself guilty to several indiscretions which aggravated an already delicate situation. He was an avid supporter of a Negro radical paper called *The Freeman* and was heard to say on many occasions that he "would not believe a Methodist on his oath". Since Lightbourn and most of the Members of the Assembly were Methodists, as well as subscribers to the conservative *Nassau Guardian*, their antagonism was inevitable. Much of the acrimony seems to have departed with Powles and the administration of justice in the twentieth century has been a model of impartiality. It is interesting to note that there has never been a case of lynching in the Bahamas.

In the franchise it was poverty rather than open racial discrimination which kept the Bahamian Negro from the vote. Moreover, the situation in the Bahamas was never so inequitable as in the other British West Indian colonies. In St. Kitts in 1855, for instance, there were 166 voters out of a population of 20,741; 47 electors having chosen 22 members in the election of 1854. In the Jamaica election of 1863, 1,482 voted, out of a population of 450,000. In all the other British West Indian colonies except Bermuda and Barbados, these years saw the decay of the system of representative government wherever it existed. Between 1866 for Jamaica and 1898 for Antigua and Dominica all these colonies became "Crown Colonies", that is, changed to a single-chamber Legislature consisting entirely of nominated members. It was not until 1884 in Jamaica and 1924 in Trinidad that some form of representative government was reintroduced. It should be a matter of pride, if not surprise, for Bahamians that throughout this period the Bahamas retained her House of Assembly; reactionary perhaps but continuously active, and through its access to the Executive Council and its increasing use of parliamentary privilege and the Board System, actually implementing its power.

In 1864 in the Bahamas there were 5,949 registered electors, or 16.9 per cent of the population of 35,287. This worked out at an average of 214 voters for each of the 28 seats, out of a population average of 1,267 for each seat. It would be instructive to know the proportion of whites to Negroes in the lists of electors, but this is impossible since Bahamian census returns do not include registered electors and the census of 1826 was the last before 1943 to make a racial analysis.

Nevertheless it is certain that the comparatively high property qualifications of the 1806 Elections Act, which was not repealed until 1886, ensured that the white Bahamians occupied a far larger proportion of the voting list than their numbers warranted. It is significant that most of the largest electorates were in constituencies where the proportion of whites was highest. In Harbour Island, whose 1,994 inhabitants were represented by 3 Members, 22·1 per cent of the population voted, whereas in neighbouring Eleuthera, with 3 Members representing 5,209, the percentage was only 9·3. A more serious inequality occurred over the relative sizes of the constituencies. In 1864, less than a third of the population of the Bahamas lived in New Providence, but by the end of the century the proportion was almost a half. Despite this, New Providence, where most of the wealthier and more educated Negroes lived, continued to elect only 8 Members. This was particularly remarkable when it is recalled that after emancipation very few of the 20 or 21 Out Island Members lived in their constituencies. In the twentieth century only 2 Members have lived in the Out Islands. The last was Esekial Bain (Andros) who sat for one year in the early 1920s.

The simple folk of the Out Islands were very susceptible to sophisticated visitors from Nassau, who made them promises and bribed them for their votes. Lack of education kept the poor people ignorant, just as the economic situation kept them poor. "This mockery of representation", wrote L. D. Powles in 1888, "is the greatest farce in the world. The coloured people have the suffrage, subject to a small property qualification, but have no idea how to use it. The elections are by open voting, and bribery, corruption and intimidation are carried on in the most unblushing manner, under the very noses of the officers presiding over the polling booths. Nobody takes any notice, and as the coloured people have not yet learnt the art of political organisation, they are powerless to defend themselves. The result is that the House of Assembly is little less than a family gathering of Nassau whites, nearly all of whom are related to each other. Laws are passed simply for the benefit of the family, whilst the coloured people are ground down and oppressed in a manner that is a disgrace to the British flag."

This was the extreme view of a disgruntled official. Elsewhere Powles was forced to record that the Bahamian Negro, if he were not actually starving, was the happiest man in the world. Nevertheless his accusation contained a kernel of truth. Unambitious, the Negroes were represented, or ruled, by men who were at best paternalistic in their attitude. Throughout the nineteenth century the power of the House of Assembly continued to increase, but it became, if anything, more exclusive. It was difficult for coloured men to break into the charmed circle of those who dominated trade in Nassau and it was impossible for a poor man to maintain himself independently in politics.

Thus the rule of a minority was perpetuated in the Bahamas. It is possible that the ruling class of white Bahamian merchants were sustained by a belief in their own superiority. But superiority is a senseless myth when supported by enforced inequality. Without doubt, for many years, the Bahamian Negro did not enjoy equality of opportunity. As late as 1885, five Negroes at Harbour Island were convicted of brawling and fined 20s. each simply for entering the Methodist church by the door reserved for the whites. Well into the twentieth century these were clubs and churches which Negroes could not join, schools that were reluctant to enrol their children, buildings that they could not enter except as a servant. A law against discrimination of this kind was not passed until 1956 and even today the situation is not perfectly harmonious. No Assembly can legislate against prejudice.

Just as the abolitionists refused to see either the economic necessity of slavery to the West Indies or any of the advantages of paternalism, they fondly imagined that with the achievement of complete emancipation in August, 1838, their long struggle was ended and their work done. As far as the Bahamas and the other slave colonies were concerned, the problems of the full emancipation of the Negroes were only just beginning.

XIX

American Civil War
1840-65

It was disappointment not resignation which was the key note of Bahamian history during the nineteenth century. The colony alternated between tentative hope and gloomy despair while somehow avoiding the ultimate disaster. While Britain was burgeoning into the world's most prosperous nation, this small fragment of the empire over which she ruled so complacently sank deeper into obscurity, like a man struggling in a morass. In the 1850s much was hoped from salt; in vain. The running of the blockade during the American Civil War provided an interlude of prosperity that was as gaudy as it was brief. Later industries; pineapples, sponge, sisal, disclosed prospects of affluence, but these were fleeting and illusory gleams. Only the first faint beginnings of the tourist trade made promises for the future; but none could foretell what wonders the twentieth century had in store. Well into the memory of persons still living Nassau was a poor place almost untouched by the tide of modern progress and the Out Islands were relics of a poverty that was almost primeval.

The actual emancipation of the slaves passed off with the calm of despair and uncertainty. But the inexorable movement and its unhappy results left a wake of bitterness among a section of the inhabitants, who from then on tended to distrust all the actions of the British Government. The first Assembly after emancipation, which met in May, 1839, was sharply and equally divided between those who supported Governor Cockburn and those who opposed the Government on nearly every issue.

Cockburn, wishing to reward and consult the supporters of the Government, suggested the division of the Governor's Council which occurred in 1841. By this Act, separate Executive

217

and Legislative Councils were created, both to consist of nine members nominated by the Governor, except for the Colonial Secretary, Attorney-General and Receiver-General, who were to be members of the Executive Council *ex officio*. In both Councils the quorum was to be three members. Members of the Assembly could sit on the Executive Council, but not the Legislative Council.

The Governor's intention was to increase the power of the executive in the Legislature. In fact, by allowing the admission of members of the Legislature into the counsels of the Governor, he increased the influence of the lower house over the executive. Only by the Governor's jealously guarded right to nominate both Councils, which, uniquely, lasted down almost to the present day, was an uneasy balance maintained. As it was, there was almost bound to be a government faction in the House of Assembly and party strife was certain to increase. This was aggravated by the unusual later provision which permitted the Colonial Secretary, Attorney-General and Receiver-General to stand for election in the lower house.

For the time being, economic depression with its pale shadow, apathy, effectively quietened the temper of the conflict. The 1840s and 1850s were an era of quiet pessimism. Under Governor Matthew, who succeeded Cockburn in 1844, the House of Assembly ran its full term of seven years for the first time in the nineteenth century. Whether for lack of circulation or dispute, or both, the controversial *Bahamas Argus* faded away, to be superseded by the mild, pro-Government *Nassau Guardian*, the oldest of the three newspapers now published in the Bahamas.

The founder of the *Guardian* was a Londoner called Edwin Charles Moseley who was brought out from England as an assistant by the editor of the *Argus* in 1838. Disliking the policy of that newspaper, Moseley soon resigned, but after an unrewarding stint as a school teacher he returned to journalism with a paper of his own. Having served an apprenticeship on the London *Times* and the *Yorkshire Post*, Moseley was able to make the *Guardian* more competent and attractive than its predecessors. The meagre news bulletins in the bi-weekly journal were larded with literary articles, poems or even songs with printed music. Nevertheless, it is unlikely that the *Guardian* would have survived the depression but for the fortunate windfall of the government printing contract awarded in 1845. With this standby, the paper was able to outlast at least a dozen rivals, under the successive editorship of its founder (1844-85), his two sons, P. J. and A. E. Moseley (1885-1904) and his granddaughter, Miss Mary Moseley, o.b.e., who saw it past its centenary. After Miss Moseley's retirement in 1948, the *Guardian* became the official organ of the majority party in the House of Assembly, later called the United Bahamian Party.

A complete history of the Bahamas since 1844 could be written through the files of the *Nassau Guardian* and the official publications which came from its presses: the Votes of the Assembly, the Laws and Rules of Procedure, the Estimates and Expenditures, the Reports on the Censuses and from the various Commissions and Departments, the Civil Service Lists and Blue Books. This study, however, would need years, a professor and a whole gaggle of research assistants. The ordinary historian must stay closer to the surface for fear of being drowned in paper.

Miss Moseley in the Centenary Issue of November 23, 1944, gave an excellent resumé of the myriad of events recorded in her family newspaper, and an illuminating picture of Nassau as it was in 1844. It was a sleepy town of about 7,000 inhabitants still scattered mostly on the northern slopes of the ridge, and not extending west of West Street or east of St. Matthew's Church. Its people were "a population of idlers with maritime tastes". As yet no carriages were seen on the streets, though the infrequent visitors could hire a horse for between 4s. and 6s. a day. There were four small boarding-houses, the most prosperous of which, French's, charged 8s. 4d. a day "without liquors". The proprietor of this grand establishment, which was situated in West Hill Street, "Near Government House", made ends meet by supplying fresh cows' milk from the animals he kept tethered in his yard.

There was no shortage of places of worship. Besides the two churches, there were four Anglican chapels. St. Andrew's Presbyterian Kirk, two Methodist chapels and the Baptist chapels of Bethel and Zion had all been founded some years. There were also many taverns and a good jail, but no secular hall for public meetings and no bank. This last was not surprising, for the entire currency in circulation amounted to £21,069 : 11 : 8d., only £50 of which was in gold. Mexican and Spanish gold coins, however, were freely used.

Trade was at a low ebb. The commodities exported included pineapples, which first appeared at Covent Garden in London in 1844. The remainder made an interesting list, from arrowroot, through hides, horns and hats to wheelbarrows, but since their total value was only £73,533, they were negligible. The value of imports was more than twice as high at £166,741. The entire revenue of the colony was £25,507, much less than the £36,855 which the British Government spent on maintaining the garrison. Government expenditure totalled £23,650.

In his dispatches home, Governor Matthew reposted that "the Statute Book was suited to the eighteenth century, a poll tax on strangers impeded trade, the poor house at Nassau was the sole public institution and the Militia was but a name". In his public speeches he urged the need for retrenchment, and it is a remarkable fact that during his short term he was able not only to balance the tiny budget, but to reduce the public debt. Furthermore, he established a hospital, a dispensary and an inter-island boat service, extended the public library and put the civil service and the militia on an efficient footing. Unfortunately, these improvements were not made without cost and certain economies in government expenditure produced a faction of discontented civil servants, led by the Receiver-General.

The most outspoken critic of the Governor was Archdeacon Trew. Magnifying some personal grudge, this testy cleric accused the Governor of misconduct with a married woman and even went so far as to write to the Colonial Secretary and *The Times*. The dispute festered on until 1848, and although the majority of the Legislature, the clergy and even the Bishop of Jamaica supported Matthew against the Archdeacon, the Secretary of State, Earl Grey, decided that there was no smoke without fire. Hearing that Matthew had used his influence to help the husband of the woman with whom he was accused of having an affair, he decided upon the Governor's recall. On November 16, 1848, he wrote that "the confidence of Her Majesty in the administration of your patronage would be absolutely destroyed by the discovery that you are using it to provide for an unworthy woman. Nor would it be possible after it became known, for you to enjoy the respect of the colonists necessary to your due influence in the government for a proper exercise of the duties of your office." Matthew was curtly informed that he might leave the Bahamas as soon as he wished, since a successor was being sent as soon as possible. He left Nassau in February, 1849.

The most outstanding monument of the regime of Governor Matthew was the separation of the Turks and Caicos Islands from the Bahamas, which occurred shortly before he returned to England. The rule of Nassau in the Turks had never been either popular or efficient. Although the salt tax had produced between 1827 and 1847 about a quarter of the entire revenue of the Bahamas, it was claimed that less than half this money benefited the Turks Islanders in any way. Moreover, although the current price of salt in 1845 had fallen to 3¼d. a bushel, the same tax was collected that had been assessed when the market price was 1s. 3d.

The Orders of 1781 and the Acts of 1824 and 1844 regulating the salt ponds were uniformly detested in the Turks Islands. The abuses which resulted from the inefficient introduction of long-term leases in the latter Act provoked a climax of discontent. Theoretically, the Turks Islands were represented in the House of Assembly, but owing to the difficulties of travel, the Member rarely sat, and when he did he felt an alien in an unfriendly land.

The inhabitants of the Turks and Caicos Islands can be forgiven their sentiment that the only Bahamians they ever saw were tax-collectors. The mail boat from Nassau sailed as far as Long Cay once a month, but only went on to Grand Turk four times a year. Boats going between England and Jamaica, however, often stopped there and it was natural that the islanders should feel more akin to Kingston than to Nassau.

Between 1837 and 1846, the inhabitants of the Turks Islands sent three petitions to the Secretary of State, but these appeals fell on indifferent ears. The colonial agent was even refused a hearing. Governor Matthew was at first opposed to change, but in 1847 he carried out a thorough investigation and reluctantly recommended the separation. By the Act of 1848, the Turks and Caicos Islands were to be governed by a President and Council, directed by the orders of the Crown-in-Council and under the supervision of the Governor of Jamaica.

An interesting by-product of the loss of the salt islands was the search for alternatives. The Heneaga Salt Pond Company was established in 1849, the first joint stock operation floated in the Bahamas, to develop the salt ponds of Inagua. During the next fifteen years the price of salt appreciated slowly to 7½d. a bushel and additional salt pans were opened on Rum Cay, Ragged Island, Exuma and Rose Island next to New Providence. At the peak of production, Inagua exported a million and a half bushels a year, and Rum Cay at least half a million. The slump in the market after the end of the American Civil War, however, stunted these operations. The population of Inagua, a mere 217 in 1847, rose to 1,120 in 1871 but declined in the succeeding three decades.

A great deal of the energy of the people during the undistinguished governorships of John Gregory (1849-54), Sir Alexander Bannerman (1854-57) and Charles Bayley (1857-64) was expended on religious disputes, which always seem to flourish in a vacuum. The years after 1840 saw an awakening of the Anglican Church, spurred on by the Society for the Propagation of the Gospel; but this came too late. The Baptist missionaries had planted strong roots among the freed Negroes and the Methodists had invaded all classes of society. The vigorous new congregations resented and resisted the fact that the Anglicans and Presbyterians alone were "established" and endowed by the Legislature.

After the conflict over the control of the schools already referred to, the next clash occurred over the public burial grounds. Dissenting ministers had been licensed to perform weddings and funerals since slavery days, but they were denied the right to perform burial ceremonies in the public graveyards. In 1851, disgraceful scenes took place at two funerals, and when the Governor chose to ignore a petition presented by the dissenters through the Churchwardens, a riot threatened. A further petition signed by 800 was referred to a committee by the House of Assembly and might have been shelved but for the timely intervention of the Bishop of Jamaica. He recommended a bill to grant equal burial privileges to all recognised ministers and with its passage through the reluctant Legislature later in the year the animosity died down for a while.

It was a time for the rival churches to regroup and increase their forces. Despite the harshness of the times, the sects built and expanded as best they could. Ebenezer Methodist Church, originally erected in 1840, was rebuilt in stone in 1848 and throughout the islands Methodist and Baptist chapels sprang up, often no grander than the poor buildings around them. The established Churches naturally had an advantage and their buildings were more impressive. St. Agnes Chapel in Grant's Town was completed in 1845, the year that the new Christchurch was consecrated by Bishop Spencer. St. Andrew's Presbyterian Kirk, endowed in 1847, was remodelled in 1850 and again in 1863. One of the innovations was the removal of the old high-backed pews, so convenient for sleeping during the sermon. In 1852 the Anglicans, with the help of the Assembly, completed St. Anne's at Fox Hill, enlarged St. Mary's Chapel in the Western District and built a church in the salt-rich island of Inagua.

In 1854, by the will of the Rev. W. L. Woodcock, the first minister of St. Agnes', who died in 1851, an Anglican school was set up in the Negro quarter of Bain's Town which has continued down to the present. In 1857, Bishop Courtney of Jamaica ordained five Bahamian deacons to bring the total of Anglican ministers in the Bahamas up to an unprecedented thirteen. But the most important Anglican gain in the race for religious supremacy was the creation by Letters Patent of the See of Nassau in 1861. Carved out of the old diocese of Jamaica, formed in 1824, the new see included not only all the Bahamas, but also the lately departed Turks and Caicos. By the same Letters Patent, little Nassau was raised to the dignity of a City. Charles Caulfield, D.D., who had been Archdeacon since 1858 was consecrated the first Bishop at Lambeth, arriving back in the colony on May 23, 1862. His was a brief moment of glory. Enthroned on June 17, he died of yellow fever on September 4, doubtless to the wag of many a dissenting head.

In the later 1850s the first muffled drum-beats of the tragic conflict impending in the nearby States were heard in Nassau, but few guessed the sudden focus of attention that was to make the insignificant capital rich and important for the first time. The year 1857 in fact saw official salaries several months in arrears and another Retrenchment Act reduced the pay of civil servants by a total of £2,000. At the same time the infantry battalion of the Militia was disbanded as an expensive luxury.

1857 saw the first sewing machine reach Nassau and the first Eleutheran pineapples canned, but neither of these novelties held out promises of sudden profits. This was the dawn, or false dawn, of the age of steam, and much more was hoped from the new mobility which enabled steamships to run contrary to the prevailing winds. To far-sighted men it was already obvious that it was only the communications problem that prevented Nassau becoming the winter health resort of North America.

An Act to encourage steam navigation between New York and Nassau had been passed as early as 1851, but since the first steamship to attempt the voyage, the S.S. *Jewess*, had arrived on May 20, 1851, burnt down almost to the waterline, the project died. In 1857, a further Act was passed and an enterprising Bay Street merchant, Mr. Timothy Darling, even managed to sell the government a site, just south of the prison, for a hotel to house the potential winter visitors from the chilly north.

In 1859, the year of the first Bahamian postage stamps, a definite contract was made with Mr. Samuel Cunard, the tycoon of the transatlantic run, for a regular connexion between Nassau and New York. For an annual bounty of £1,000, Cunard agreed to carry mails and passengers to and from Nassau at least once a month. In November, 1859, the S.S. *Corsica* made the first of her hundreds of visits to Nassau on the way to Havana, calling in again on her return voyage. The journey normally took between three and five days and cost $50 from New York to Nassau and $95 for the return trip. A government loan to build what became the Royal Victoria Hotel was floated and work began on the site in the summer of 1860.

But this hoped-for connexion with the North was itself contrary to the wind of events. The Royal Victoria Hotel was designed to accommodate winter visitors from the snowbound northern states. Had it relied solely upon these it would very quickly have become bankrupt. Luckily the new hotel was

A typical Out Island settlement—Tarpum Bay, Eleuthera

destined to become the headquarters of the colourful blockade-runners of the South in the Civil War that was about to begin.

On April 12, 1861, the troops of the Confederate States opened fire on the Federal forts in Charleston harbour and four years of bloody civil war began in America. The rebel states were almost devoid of manufactures and thus dependent upon imports to carry on the war. In order to obtain munitions and materials abroad it was essential for the Confederacy to continue exporting cotton, the staple and almost sole product of the southern states.

President Lincoln declared a blockade of the southern ports in the first week of the war. This action was hasty, for not only was the Federal navy totally unprepared to enforce a blockade, but the presidential declaration gave the rebels the status of belligerents which enabled them to obtain support from sympathetic nations in Europe. Except for the diehard abolitionists, England was typically apathetic to the contest, but the cotton interests of Lancashire managed to arouse some support for the South which was accentuated by the high-handed action of the Yankees in the *Trent* affair. As the war progressed, shipbuilders, shipowners and adventurers were drawn by the vast profits of blockade-running.

At first, the running of the blockade was little more than a formality and trade between Europe and the southern ports continued at pre-war volume. As late as 1862 the British Consul at Charleston reported: "The blockade-runners are doing a great business, and no-one seems to think there is the slightest risk". But as the North mobilised, the grip of the blockade tightened. "Vessels of every conceivable variety were brought into service, armed after a fashion, and sent steaming down to take station off Southern harbours: ferryboats, excursion steamers, whalers, fishing schooners, superannuated clippers."

Steamships could still evade these clumsy guards like dogs chased by cart horses. But by the end of 1862 the Federals were building special blockade ships, which eventually included 24 shallow-craft propeller gunboats and 47 "double-enders"—canoe-shaped paddle-boats that had no need to turn round. By 1865 the northern fleet consisted of almost 700 vessels. After

Farragut's capture of New Orleans in April, 1862, the northerners were able to concentrate their operations on a handful of Confederate ports and blockade-running became increasingly hazardous. Over 150 ships were employed in the blockade of Charleston and Wilmington alone.

Only the absolute necessity of foreign supplies and the vast profits, sometimes amounting to $300,000 for a round trip, persuaded the blockade-runners to continue. Europe was scoured for ships fast enough to run before and between the Federals under cover of darkness, and by the end of 1862 ships were even being built at Birkenhead, Barrow or Clydeside on the assumption that if they made three round trips before capture they had paid for themselves with profit to spare. These were "long, lean, shallow-draft side-wheelers for the most part, capable of high speeds, painted slate grey to decrease their visibility, and burning anthracite coal so that smoke from their funnels would not betray them to the blockading fleets".

To be fast enough to dodge the blockade the ships had to be built like greyhounds. Unable to carry large cargoes, it was essential that they find a neutral port within two or three days' steaming. This is where Nassau entered the picture. The busiest ports during the blockade were Charleston and Wilmington, only 560 and 640 miles respectively from the safety of the Abaco Cays. Bermuda was closer to northern naval bases and about a hundred miles farther than Nassau from the blockaded ports.

In January, 1862, the British Government instructed Governor Bayley to safeguard the neutrality of the Bahamas, "preventing as far as possible the use of Her Majesty's harbours, ports and coasts, and the waters within Her Majesty's territorial jurisdiction in aid of the warlike purposes of either belligerent". Belligerent ships were to be denied entry except in cases of extreme distress, such as fire, serious leaking or dismasting. These instructions, proclaimed by the Governor on March 11, 1862, were eagerly misconstrued. Public opinion translated them to mean that warships alone were denied the use of the islands and that all blockade-running merchant ships should be safe as soon as they entered territorial waters in the Bahamas. Governor Bayley in fact, in an address to the Assembly, rejoiced in the

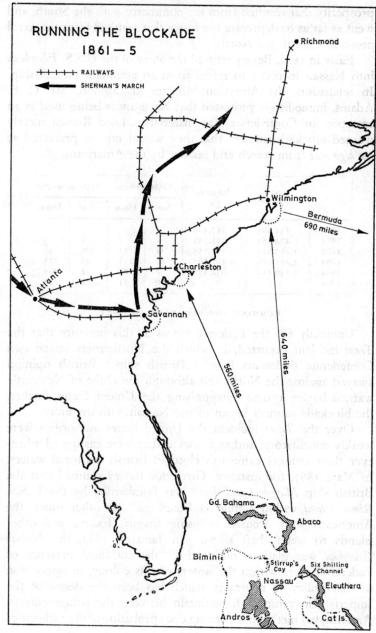

RUNNING THE BLOCKADE
1861 — 5

+++++ RAILWAYS

SHERMAN'S MARCH

Richmond

Wilmington

Bermuda
690 miles

640 miles

Atlanta

Charleston

560 miles

Savannah

Gd. Bahama

Abaco

Bimini

Stirrup's
Cay

Six Shilling
Channel

Nassau

Eleuthera

Andros

Cat Is.

prosperity that resulted from the commerce with the South, and went as far as to deprecate the losses that resulted from the naval predominance of the North.

Early in 1862, Bayley refused the entry of the U.S.S. *Flambeau* into Nassau in order to refuel from an attendant bunker-ship. In retaliation, the American Minister in London, Mr. C. F. Adams, immediately protested that Nassau was being used as an entrepôt for Confederate war materials. Lord Russell merely warned blockade-runners that they would not be protected *on the high seas* from search and seizure by the Americans.

	Imports £s	Exports £s	Ships arriving		Ships departing	
			Sail	Steam	Sail	Steam
1860	234,029	157,350				
1861	274,584	195,584	2	2	1	3
1862	1,250,322	1,007,755	74	32	109	46
1863	4,295,316	3,308,567	27	113	48	173
1864	5,346,112	4,672,398	6	105	2	165
1865			0	35	0	41

RUNNING THE BLOCKADE 1861-65

Unluckily for the Federals it was at this juncture that the *Trent* incident occurred, in which the Northerners seized two Confederate diplomats from a British ship. British opinion swayed against the North and although the Duke of Newcastle warned Bayley against antagonising the United States further, the blockade-runners began to use Nassau with impunity.

Over the *Trent* incident the United States authorities were weakly conciliatory, and as a reward they were castigated whenever their cruisers came too close to British territorial waters. In May, 1863, for instance, Governor Bayley claimed that the British ship *Margaret and Jessie* was bombarded by the U.S.S. *Rhode Island* within a mile of Eleuthera. At other times, the Americans were accused of using Inagua, Exuma and other islands to water their ships. In January, 1864, the *Nassau Guardian* was glad to notice that "the continual presence of Federal cruisers within the waters of this colony, in opposition to that policy of neutrality which has been the desire of the Imperial Government to maintain between the belligerents of America, has met with the strong disapprobation of the authorities at home". Although towards the end of the war anti-British feeling was running high in the North owing to the depredations of the *Alabama* and other British-built Confederate raiders, the Americans never felt strong enough to violate the waters of the Bahamas, and Nassau flourished as long as Charleston and Wilmington remained in Confederate hands.

Bruce Catton has estimated that during the War some 1,650 vessels made about 8,000 trips to and from Confederate ports. Between December 1, 1861, when the first ship arrived from Charleston with 144 bales of cotton, and March, 1865, 397 ships entered Nassau from the blockaded ports. During the same period there were 588 sailings from Nassau to the southern ports, 428 being by steamships.

Losses were tremendous. After 1863, running the blockade with a sailing ship was a conjuring trick. Even with one of the new 15-knot propeller ships it was a gamble. Of the steamships which left Nassau, 42 were captured and 22 sunk. But as long as cotton bought in Charleston for 8c. or 10c. a pound could be sold in Nassau three days later for $1, or stores purchased in Nassau for £6,000 could fetch £27,000 in gold in Richmond there would be men enough to risk the passage. In 1864, it cost about £5,000 to send an 800-bale ship to Wilmington and back. The captain received £1,000 and the right to carry ten bales on his own account; the pilot also received £1,000 and the right to five bales; the purser and first officer were paid £300 and allowed two bales each, and even the ordinary seamen who stood no danger of extra punishment from capture by the Federals were paid £20 a month and a bounty of £10 for each completed trip.

The import and export figures for Nassau between 1860 and 1865 tell the story of the blockade-running. In 1860, the imports were valued at £234,029 and the exports £157,350. By 1862 they had risen to £1,250,322 and £1,007,755, and in 1864 they reached an incredible peak of £5,346,112 and £4,672,398. In January and February, 1864, alone, 20 ships ran the blockade to Nassau with 14,182 bales of cotton worth $2,750,000.

Nassau has never known a more frenzied interlude before or since. Perhaps J. H. Stark did not exaggerate when he wrote in 1891 that "everyone was mad with excitement during these years of the war. The shops were packed to the ceilings, the streets were crowded with bales, boxes and barrels. Fortunes were made in a few weeks or months. Money was spent and scattered in a most extravagant and lavish manner. The town actually swarmed with Southern refugees, captains and crews of blockade-runners. Every available space in or out of doors was occupied. Men lay on verandahs, walls, decks and floors. Money was plentiful and sailors sometimes landed with $1,500 in specie. Wages were doubled, liquor flowed freely and the common labourer had his champagne and rich food. Not since the days of the buccaneers and pirates had there been such times in the Bahamas; success paid larger premiums than were ever attained by any legitimate business in the world's commercial history, fully equal to the profits realised from the Spanish galleons by the buccaneers."

One of the earliest extant photographs shows Nassau harbour, which before the war rarely saw a dozen visiting ships a year, crowded with more than twenty tall-stacked steamers. Perhaps among them were Wilkinson's famous *Robert E. Lee*, which ran the blockade 21 times, a record for a single ship, or Taylor's *Banshee* in which he made 8 of his 28 dashes through the Federal lines.

Although only 20 when the war broke out, Thomas Taylor, author of the exciting *Running the Blockade* (1896), became one of the most experienced of the blockade-runners. Employed by a firm of Liverpool cotton merchants, he was first sent out to Nassau early in 1862 with an old tub of a cattle boat called the *Despatch*. When this boat proved far too clumsy to evade the blockaders, his employers provided him with the *Banshee*, a 214-foot ship of only 217 tons, specially built at Birkenhead. This slender ship, which drew only 8 feet of water, was the first ocean-going steel ship ever built, being constructed of cardboard-thin plates which buckled and leaked with frightening ease.

After several adventures and alarms, the strange new ship arrived at Nassau via Madeira in March, 1863. There Taylor ordered the rigging and superstructure trimmed to two short masts and had the ship painted a light grey that experience had taught would make it indiscernible on a dark night at a cable's length. For captain, Taylor employed a man called Steele who had already been captured and released by the Northerners. "Absolutely devoid of fear, never flurried, decided and ready in emergency, and careful as a mother, he was the beau-ideal of a blockade-runner." The engineer was also a veteran, Erskine: "cool in danger, full of resource in sudden difficulty, and as steady as the tide, he was yet capable of fearlessly risking every-thing and straining to the last pound, when . . . the critical moment had come". Taylor's first pilot was Burroughs, an untried man from Wilmington who turned out to be one of the most remarkable characters produced by the blockade. "He knew his port like his own face, and the most trying situations or heaviest firing could never put him off or disturb his serene self possession. For all his duties he had an instinct that approached genius. On the blackest night he could always make out a blockader several minutes before anyone else; and so acute at last did this sense become, that it used to be a byword that Tom Burroughs at last got to smell a cruiser long before he could see her."

Manned with these intrepid officers, who seem to come from the pages of a boys' adventure story rather than from real life, "and laden with arms, gunpowder, boots, and all kinds of contraband, as soon as the moon was right, the *Banshee* stole out of Nassau for the first time to make the best of her way to Wil-mington". The run could easily be made with two days' sailing, but since the *Banshee* was always extremely cautious, it might take much longer. "As long as daylight lasted a man was never out of the cross-trees and the moment a sail was seen the *Banshee*'s stern was turned to it till it was dropped below the horizon. The lookout man, to quicken his eyes, had a dollar for every sail he sighted, and if it were seen from the deck first he was fined five."

Adventure began immediately out of Nassau, for Federal cruisers were accustomed to lurk as close as Stirrup's Cay and Goat Cay in the Berry Islands. These warships, however, were scattered and easily dodged. The real tension began with the approach to Charleston or Wilmington.

One blockade-runner who sailed with Wilkinson of the *Lee* recorded that "anyone who showed an open light when we were near the fleet was liable to the penalty of death on the spot; a cool, steady leadsman was stationed at each quarter to give the soundings, a staunch old quartermaster took the wheel, and a kedge bent to a stout hawser, was slung at each quarter. All lights were extinguished, the fire room hatch covered over with a tarpaulin, and a hood fitted over the binnacle with a small circular opening for the helmsman to see the compass through the aperture."

Wilmington lies some miles up the Cape Fear River and the two entrances, then guarded by Forts Caswell and Fisher, are less than half a mile wide.

At this time [wrote Taylor] the favourite dodge was to run up some fifteen or twenty miles to the north of Cape Fear, so as to round the northernmost of the blockaders, instead of dashing right through the inner squadron; then to creep down close to the surf till the river was reached. . . . [This manœuvre prolonged the tension and required, of course, an expert pilot.]

With everything thus in readiness we steamed on in silence except for the stroke of the engines and the beat of the paddle-floats, which in the calm of the night seemed distressingly loud; all hands were on deck, crouching behind the bulwarks; and we on the bridge, namely, the captain, the pilot, and I, were straining our eyes into the darkness. Presently Burroughs made an uneasy movement—"Better get a cast of the lead, Captain," I heard him whisper. A muttered order down the engine-room tube was Steele's reply, and the *Banshee* slowed and then stopped. It was an anxious moment, while a dim figure stole into the fore-chains; for there is always a danger of steam blowing off when engines are unexpectedly stopped, and that would have been enough to betray our presence for miles around. In a minute or two came back the report, "sixteen fathoms—sandy bottom with black specks". "We are not as far in as I thought, Captain," said Burroughs, "and we are too far to the southward. Port two points and go a little faster." As he explained, we must be well to the northward of the speckled bottom before it was safe to head for the shore, and away we went again. In about an hour Burroughs quietly asked for another sounding. Again she was gently stopped, and this time he was satisfied. "Starboard and go ahead easy," was the order now, and as we crept in not a sound was heard but that of the regular beat of the paddle-floats still dangerously loud in spite of our snail's pace. Suddenly Burroughs gripped my arm——

"There's one of them, Mr. Taylor," he whispered, "on the starboard bow."

In vain I strained my eyes to where he pointed, not a thing could I see; but presently I heard Steele say beneath his breath, "All right, Burroughs, I see her. Starboard a little, steady!" was the order passed aft.

A moment afterwards I could make out a long low black object on our starboard side, lying perfectly still. Would she see us? that was the question; but no, though we passed within a hundred yards of her we were not discovered, and I breathed again. Not very long after we had dropped her Burroughs whispered,—

"Steamer on the port bow."

And another cruiser was made out close to us.

"Hard-a-port," said Steele, and round she swung, bringing our friend upon our beam. Still unobserved we crept quietly on, when all at once a third cruiser shaped herself out of the gloom right ahead and steaming slowly across our bows.

"Stop her," said Steele in a moment, and as we lay like dead our enemy went on and disappeared in the darkness. It was clear there was a false reckoning somewhere, and that instead of rounding the head of the blockading line we were passing right through the centre of it. However, Burroughs was now of opinion that we must be inside the squadron and advocated making the land. So "ahead slow" we went again, until the low-lying coast and the surf line became dimly visible. Still we could not tell where we were, and, as time was getting on alarmingly near dawn, the only thing to do was to creep down along the surf as close in and as fast as we dared. It was a great relief when we suddenly heard Burroughs say, "It's all right, I see the 'Big Hill'!"

The "Big Hill" was a hillock about as high as a full-grown oak tree, but it was the most prominent feature for miles on that dreary coast, and served to tell us exactly how far we were from Fort Fisher. And fortunate it was for us we were so near. Daylight was already breaking, and before we were opposite the fort we could make out six or seven gunboats, which steamed rapidly towards us and angrily opened fire. Their shots were soon dropping close around us: an unpleasant sensation when you know you have several tons of gunpowder under your feet. To make matters worse, the North Breaker shoal now compelled us to haul off shore and steam farther out. It began to look ugly for us, when all at once there was a flash from the shore followed by a sound that came like music to our ears—that of a shell whirring over our heads. It was Fort Fisher, wide awake and warning the gunboats to keep their distance. With a parting broadside they steamed sulkily out of range, and in half an hour we were safely over the bar. A boat put off from the fort and then—well, it was the days of champagne cocktails, not whiskies and sodas—and one did not run a blockade every day . . .

And not every ship was as fortunate as the *Banshee*, nor every captain and pilot as skilled and daring as Steele and Burroughs. J. H. Stark visited Wilmington in 1873 and found "the beach lined with sunken steamers, the hulls firmly imbedded in the sand, and in several cases with the smokestack and walking beam still standing". Even *Banshee* was captured on her ninth trip after a long chase off Cape Hatteras, Steele and the crew being kept for eight months in a Federal prison. Despite this, Taylor estimated that she had repaid her owners 700 per cent on their investment and she was quickly followed by the *Banshee No. 2*, the *Tristram Shandy*, the *Wild Dayrell*, the *Wild Rover*, the *Stormy Petrel*, the *Night Hawk* and the *Will-o'-the-Wisp*, which once managed the astounding speed of $17\frac{1}{2}$ knots over the measured mile.

Once at Wilmington or Charleston the blockade-runners hastened to load and return. Working round the clock, it was usual to unload the cargo in twenty-four hours and load up with cotton in a further three days. So reckless was the pursuit of profit that even the decks were piled high like hay waggons with bales of cotton often three tiers deep.

Running out of harbour was far easier than making a night landfall and evading the blockade at the same time. Steele's usual stratagem was to sail impudently close to the anchored enemy flagship, usually a 60-ton frigate, knowing that the patrolling gunboats would leave a sufficiently wide berth and hoping that the lookouts on the flagship would think that the *Banshee* herself was a Federal ship. Once daylight came it was a different matter and few ships reached Nassau without having to run from one or more of the second line of Federal cruisers. The pursuit was bound to be keen, for the profits to the blockaders in prize money were scarcely less than those of the blockade-runners. When the U.S.S. *Magnolia* captured the *Memphis* in July, 1862, each of the lieutenants received $38,318 and even the ordinary seamen $1,700 apiece.

Tales of excitement and narrow shaves were commonplace in Nassau. The *Guardian* for January 9, 1864, for instance, told how the British steamer *Hansa* was chased by the Federal paddle-boat *Vanderbilt* from Abaco almost all the way to Nassau. Fired on continuously for two hours, she threw overboard seventy bales of her deck cargo to gain more speed. Then the pressure in her boilers suddenly failed and she only escaped by risking the dangerous passage inside Six Shilling Reef, while the *Vanderbilt* fretted outside in the ocean.

Thomas Taylor told of many desperate chases including the sixth trip of the first *Banshee*, which almost ended in disaster. Still a long way from Abaco they were chased downwind by the *James Adger* under full sail and steam. So close did she get that Taylor could see the Federal officers in uniform on the bridge "each one, doubtless, counting his share of the prize money to which he would soon become entitled". At the last moment Steele ordered the ship turned northwards into the wind, so that the *Adger* had to reef her sails and by frantic efforts on the part of Erskine and the stokers the *Banshee* slowly drew away. For fifteen hours the little boat bucked the waves while her fragile plates groaned and her engine bearings grew red hot. Only by jettisoning her entire deck cargo was she able to shake off her pursuer and by this time she was 150 miles off course. Coal was running low and in the three days it took to reach the shelter of the Abaco Cays, the engines of the *Banshee* devoured every available scrap of wood, including the mainmast, bulwarks and deck cabin, as well as part of the remaining cargo of cotton and turpentine.

The sudden flood of ready money transformed Nassau like a poor spinster just bequeathed an unexpected fortune. Bay Street was widened at a cost of £13,130 and provided with kerbstones and lights for the first time. The north side was filled in with warehouses and a project was put forward for a completely new dock. Other new buildings sprang up like mushrooms after rain. The public debt of £47,786 was wiped off almost over-night and officers' salaries were increased by 25 per cent. The Bahamas Police Force was created by an Act of 1864, and consisted at first of an Inspector, 2 Sergeants, 9 Corporals, 52 first-class and 32 second-class Constables. The value of land, especially on the waterfront, appreciated by 300 or 400 per cent. The Royal Victoria Hotel, completed in the first year of the war at a cost of over $130,000, became the scene of nightly parties at which the colourful characters who thronged the city shut out the strain and boredom of the morrow in a rush of rowdy gaiety. "Confederate military and naval officers; diplomatists using the blockade-runners as a means of ingress and egress from their beleaguered country; newspaper correspondents and advertisers of all kinds,—some rascals no doubt; the very cream of the English navy, composed of officers on half pay who had come out lured by the prospects of making some money . . ."

Nassau had never seen such a band of adventurers at one time and this modern age certainly does not breed their like. There was Captain Roberts who later, as Hobart Pasha, com-manded the Turkish Navy in the Russo-Turkish War; or Hewett, who won the V.C. in the Crimea, was knighted for his services as ambassador to King John of Abyssinia and later became Commander-in-Chief of the Home Fleet and captain of Queen Victoria's yacht. Dean of the war correspondents was the portly Frank Vizetelly, whose drawings for the *Illustrated London News* give us our best picture of Nassau in the war years. Attached successively to the Federal and Confederate armies he came to

Nassau late in 1863, and was destined to die in the Sudan at the side of Hicks Pasha twenty years later.

One factor which added to the danger and uncertainty of those years was disease. Yellow fever, which ravaged Nassau and Wilmington in the summer of 1864, was a particular scourge. Taylor recorded that he once counted seventeen funerals passing his window before breakfast and once buried three intimate friends on the same day. In Wilmington 2,500 died out of the population of 6,000. Taylor himself caught the dreaded disease and was forced to go to Halifax to recuperate.

On his return he ran the blockade and went by rail from Wilmington to Richmond, the Confederate capital. What he saw in the south shocked him and he wrote to his chiefs on January 15, 1865:

"Altogether I think the Confederate Government is going to the *bad*, and if they don't take care the Confederacy will go too. I never saw things look so gloomy, and I think spring will finish them . . ." Lee told Taylor that if Wilmington fell, Richmond would follow and he would be forced to retreat into Tennessee. Strangely enough, it was the same day that Taylor wrote his letter that Fort Fisher fell, after a terrific bombardment, to General Terry. In the following month Sherman continued his famous march from Savannah and knifed his way through the interior of the Carolinas. Cut off from the rest of the Confederacy, Charleston and Wilmington had both fallen by March and the days of the blockade-running had come to an end. Governor Rawson W. Rawson, who succeeded Bayley in 1864, informed the British Government that although in January and February, 1865, 20 ships reached Nassau out of 32 that set sail from behind the blockade, after February only 3 more ships arrived in all.

On Palm Sunday, April 9, 1865, Lee ended the war by surrendering to Grant at Appomattox. Perhaps fittingly, Nassau and the Bahamas, which had prospered from the calamity of the Civil War, were destined to share the fate of the defeated Confederacy.

XX

Forgotten Colony
1865-1914

In Nassau, the ending of the blockade-running deflated the economy with the speed of a punctured balloon. So severe and prolonged was the depression that most Bahamians came to wish that they had never enjoyed the brief interlude of garish prosperity during the war. "What good came of it at last?" asked Surgeon-Major Bacot in 1869. . . . "There was, no doubt, a good deal of drink going . . . many a Dinah owed her ruin to the extraordinary temptations offered by reckless sailors with more money than they knew what to do with, and with the very lowest notions of morality. A few undertakers may have profited, as disease became rather prevalent and fatal; and the Government managed to pay off a small debt, but what became of all the money made is a mystery."

Some men made fortunes from the blockade; but they were mostly foreigners, commercial agents, captains, pilots, who had flocked to Nassau for the duration and began to leave as soon as Wilmington fell. Very few Bahamians profited from the war and they were the worst sufferers from the inflation that followed the flood of Confederate money into Nassau. In a way the Out Islands suffered least, for they gained least from the brief war years. For them life went on like an endless and uneventful dream.

The sudden development of Nassau had been over-optimistic. Once emptied of cotton and war supplies, the new warehouses lay empty for fifty years. Emptied of its wartime profiteers, the Royal Victoria Hotel was offered for sale, but not a single tender was received. In Bay Street the thirty-four new street lamps usually went unlit.

As if to underline the futility of Nassau's hopes, 1866 saw a terrible visitation of tempest and disease. Typhoid, the last bequest of the departing southerners, carried off more people than ever before and the hurricane which struck New Providence on October 1 was the worst in living memory. No building escaped damage and some, such as John S. George's brand-new warehouse, were totally destroyed. Rebuilding and repairs completely drained Nassau's resources, private and public. By 1869 the very credit of the Government was threatened, and despite an official inquiry into expenditure, officers' salaries fell three months in arrears.

Bacot's description of Nassau four years after the Civil War left no echo of the conflict, and shows a town fallen back on its immemorial ways: "The town faces the harbour, the commercial part straggling along the shore; while, sloping backwards and upwards to a ridge of rising ground which shuts in the town from the marshy interior, lie the villas of the wealthier inhabitants, buried in the foliage of palms and fruit trees. Nassau proclaims its maritime character unmistakably. Its stores are full of ropes and pulleys, tar, red herrings, and preserved provisions, and the very rafters of the houses often tell of the dangers of the sea. Ecclesiastical windows, intended for some church, have been secured by wreckers for the windows of a grocer, and monumental urns may be found ornamenting the gate pillars of a comfortable villa. Nassau is a quiet, sleepy, hollow sort of place, with a bright sun always shining on its pure white streets, and the blue sea for ever sparkling and dancing, and generally alive with pretty little schooners just back from one wreck and starting for another."

With blockade running a thing of the past the Bahamian sailors reverted to wrecking, their perennial standby. In 1865 Bishop Venables reported that the inhabitants of Bimini were entirely engaged in the dubious trade and seemed "nearly the most degraded people that I have yet visited". In 1858 there had been 302 licensed wreckers, engaging 2,679 men as crew, and these figures were equalled or surpassed in the first years after the Civil War. Wrecks were considered a regular, almost predictable, resource. In 1864, there were 48 ships wrecked and 19 damaged. In 1865, the figures were 30 and 31, and the hurricane year of 1866, 63 and 31. Between 1855 and 1864, 37 ships were salvaged, valued at £59,988, an average of £1,620 each. In addition, 59 derelicts produced material worth £11,318. These were the official figures and doubtless there were many other ships picked off the rocks but not recorded. In 1866, for instance, of the 63 vessels wrecked, 34 were fully investigated, but the fate of the others was officially cited as "mysterious".

The hurricane of 1866 provided a rich harvest for the wreckers but their days of prosperity were numbered. Despite the most violent opposition, the Imperial Lighthouse Service erected lighthouses and beacons and the Admiralty produced the first accurate charts of Bahamian waters. The familiar white light-house at the entrance to Nassau Harbour had been erected as early as 1816 and three low-power lights were established during the 1830s. The first really powerful lights on the important shipping lanes, however, were those placed on the Great Isaacs (1859), Cay Lobos (1860), Stirrup's Cay (1863), Elbow Cay, Abaco (1863), Castle Island (1868), Inagua (1868) and Bird Rock (1876).

The first I.L.S. tender was purchased in 1857 and the first automatic lights were introduced in the 1870s. Eventually there were thirty-seven automatic acetylene lights among the islands and there were few stretches of dangerous water beyond the range of guiding beacons. Besides this, the general application of steam and motor power progressively reduced the risk of sailing through the Bahamas. Year by year the number of ships aground became fewer and their value less, while the wreckers dwindled, starved and fought over what they could find.

One contemporary writer told an amusing, but probably apocryphal, story of a Bahamian parson who brought his sermon to an abrupt conclusion and raced the congregation from the church when news of a wreck arrived during service time. Generally the churches fought against wrecking and the evils that accompanied it. At their best they tried to promote an attitude of temperance and Christian industry, two concepts foreign to the Bahamian wreckers. Unfortunately, the rewards of the righteous were no more substantial than those of the ungodly.

The brief prosperity of the American Civil War saw an even

Rawson Square, Nassau. On the right is the House of Assembly. In the centre building, over the Post Office, is the executive Council Chamber. The Legislative Council meets in the building on the left, which also houses the Secretariat. The new Court building is behind the Post Office

Cupid's Cay and Governor's Harbour, Eleuthera, the probable site of William Sayle's colony (1648)

briefer spurt of building activity by the rival churches, but the depression that followed provoked a crisis. In 1865, the Legislature voted £2,200 for the building of St. Agnes and even went as far as to vote a similar amount for the building of Trinity Methodist church, which was completed at a cost of £8,000 on April 2, 1865. Zion Baptist church, founded originally in 1835, was reopened on August 27 in the same year.

Among the hundreds of buildings destroyed by the hurricane of October, 1866, was the new Trinity church. By this time many of the Members of the House of Assembly were Methodists, but there was no hope of the Legislature repeating its generosity of the previous year. The Treasury had been suddenly emptied and to the disappointed dissenters in the House the thought of having to continue to endow the Anglican Church through storm and stress was insupportable.

In March, 1867, Mr. R. H. Sawyer proposed the disestablishment of the Church of England in a resolution to the House of Assembly. A committee was appointed and a Bill drawn up which passed through the House with a majority of four votes. It was rejected by the Legislative Council. By another partisan vote the House decided to ask Governor Rawson for a dissolution. The Governor refused and in the angry debates that followed Speaker George Anderson, an Anglican and a Government supporter, resigned. His successor, Ormond Malcolm, Q.C., adjourned the House for three months, an action amounting almost to rebellion.

Luckily for the peace of the colony, Governor Rawson chose this moment to return to England and the change of Governors was followed by a general election. The Disestablishment Bill was reintroduced in March, 1869, and this time passed through both the House and the Council. From that time on, the rival churches were on an equal basis, like swimmers without lifebelts in an angry flood.

Understandably it was the Anglicans who came nearest to sinking. No longer financed by the Bahamian Treasury they were forced to fall back upon the S.P.G. and their poor parishioners. Eighteen years after the disestablishment, Powles recorded the plight of the hard-working Rector of Cat Island, the Rev. F. Barrow Matthews: "Mr. Matthew's predecessor, who belonged to the Establishment, got £250 a year. He only gets £150, half of which comes from the S.P.G., and half from the people. In 1886 they were too poor to pay their dues, and he had to go £30 short. All the clergy appointed since the disestablishment are in the same boat. There are but thirteen Anglican clergy all told in the Bahamas, and they have charge of a large number of parishes, where they visit as best they can, their place being supplied in their absence by catechists (most of whom are coloured) who are licensed to read prayers, preach, baptize and marry. Wherever I went where there was a Wesleyan minister I found him well housed and well cared for, and all mainly through the action of the Wesleyan Conference in England."

But it was not only the spectral hounds of poverty that harassed the Anglican Church. From the disestablishment of 1869 down to the present century, in which apathy has moderated the conflict, the Church was bedevilled by discord over the Ritualist question.

By the Act of 1869 a Church Commission, consisting of the Bishop, the Rectors of Christ Church, St. Matthew's and Harbour Island and five members of the laity, had been created to administer the Church. Since Canon Swann of Christ Church and Parson Saunders of St. Matthew's were Prayer Book men and the laity on the Commission were equally conservative, this body undoubtedly acted as an unwelcome brake upon the majority of the clergy. Dispute regularly broke forth in the annual Synods, at which all beneficed clergy were eligible to vote as well as one lay member of each of the parochial vestries. Between 1871 and 1874 the Ritualist controversy came to a head, with the conservatives maintaining that the Bahamian Church, being subordinate to England, must adhere to the anti-Ritualist judgement in the English Purchas Case. Clearly, the only solution for the Bishop and his fellow Ritualists was to gain independence from the English Church.

The second Bishop, Addington Venables (1863-75) was the most remarkable character in the history of the Anglican Church in the Bahamas. Brought up by Sir Robert Peel, through whose patronage he gained his preferment, he had been a priest at Cuddesdon and Oxford. Consequently he had become an eager convert to the Oxford Movement, and during his regime, vestments, incense and the other trappings of Ritualism made their appearance in the daughter churches, if not in the Cathedral itself. To many it seemed that each new priest who arrived was more "popish" than the last.

One quality that Bishop Venables and the new Ritualist movement had in common was superabundant energy. Bishop Roscow Shedden related that his predecessor once vaulted a five-barred gate to win a bet and 10/- for church funds. Celibate and of indifferent physique, Venables wore himself out in the service of his often ungrateful flock. A miserable sailor, he purchased a missionary yacht which, christened the *Message of Peace*, became a familiar and welcome visitor to the spiritually deserted Out Islands.

In 1874, the Church Commission refused to pay the Out Island catechists and Bishop Venables voluntarily took upon himself the burden of providing for them. In the stormy synod of that year his evangelical opponents accused him of dishonesty over some revenues and forced him to resign the chair. Nevertheless the Bishop and a majority of his faithful priests carried the day against the conservatives. In the following year the Church of the Bahamas became autonomous, owing only nominal allegiance to the Archbishop of Jamaica. A body of Incorporated Trustees with only temporal powers was created to take the place of the Church Commission, and a series of canons was promulgated by the synod. Although nominally opposed to ritualism, these Canons allowed in fact far greater elasticity to individual priests. Venables, however, was not satisfied with the power which the laity continued to wield in the synods and correctly predicted discord for his successors. He himself died in the U.S.A. in 1876 at the age of 48, worn out by the opposition. As Shedden said, he was a true martyr for a noble cause.

Bishops Cramer-Roberts (1875-85) and Edward Churton (1885-1900) consolidated the work begun by Addington Venables, but it was uphill progress. The Ritualist controversy continued virulent down to the 1920s, when Bishop Shedden was forced to go to law to vindicate his spiritual authority. By then the Church was hardly recognisable as the old Establishment. After the death of Parson Saunders of St. Matthew's only the conservatives of Christ Church stuck solidly to the Prayer Book.

Even in the Cathedral itself candles and a cross appeared on the altar and the Bishop was occasionally seen in a cope and mitre. Many of the prominent families of white Nassauvians forsook the Anglican Church about this time and took their notions of segregation and evangelical worship around the corner from the Cathedral to Trinity Methodist Church.

Their places were eagerly filled by Negro converts. "The Ritualists are gaining ground among the coloured people every day", wrote Powles in 1887. "This is not to be wondered at, for whether one agrees with them or not, it is undeniable that their faith is seen in their daily lives. They live among the people and with them. There is no thought of a colour-line in their hearts, and the people have learned to love and trust them." The Negroes were attracted by the colourful ritual just as they had been drawn to the simple message of Christianity in their spiritual void fifty years before. Under a succession of strong Bishops and dedicated missionaries such as Father Weigall the Apostle of the Spongefishers, the Anglican Church regained the popularity it had lost among the common people when it had been associated with slavery and the established regime.

In Andros the Rev. F. Barrow Matthews established no less than twelve churches. In 1901, obviously referring to his work, C. F. Pascoe, the historian of the S.P.G., wrote that "the clergy in addition to their proper work, fill in the office of parish doctor, visitor of the Board schools, Justice of the Peace, public vaccinator, as well as perform the friendly offices of adjustor of private wrangles, writing letters and wills, and giving advice on many matters, for, except the magistrate, they are the only white persons seen all along the shore". When Bishop Henry Churton died tragically by drowning off Long Island in 1904, the people mourned his passing like that of a saint. The noble message of "The Lord Edward" from England to the people of the Bahamas on hearing of the death of his brother was worth a hundred sermons: "Not Orphans". It is significant that only four years before, acrimony in the Church in Nassau had been the cause of the resignation of Edward Churton and had delayed the appointment of his brother Henry for two whole years.

Considering the great success of the Anglo-Catholics, it was remarkable that the Roman Catholic Church was so late in coming to the Bahamas. Occasional Catholic priests visited the islands from 1845 on, including Father Gibbons, later a famous Cardinal, who was wrecked at Grand Bahama in 1853. In 1858, the Pope attached the Bahamas theoretically to the See of South Carolina, but it was not until 1885, that a resident priest, Father George O'Keefe, was stationed in the Bahamas and the foundations of St. Francis Xavier's Church were laid on West Street. Six years later, the Abbot of St. John's Abbey, Collegeville, Minnesota, sent Father Chrysostom Shreiner, O.S.B., to the Bahamas to seek recuperation from a serious bout of tuberculosis. Not only did Shreiner recover from the disease, but in the first year survived a shipwreck off Conception Island. As a result he decided to devote the rest of his life to the Bahamas. He lived until 1928 and is buried on San Salvador near the spot where Columbus celebrated the first Mass in the New World.

In 1893, Father Shreiner purchased Dunmore House next to the Catholic church, which had been the Officers' Mess of the West India Regiment between 1842 and 1891 and may have been the residence of eighteenth-century Governors. This balconied house in the traditional Bahamian style, was converted into a priory. From the beginning the connexion with the Benedictine Monastery of St. John's has been maintained and the Bahamas is still regarded as a Catholic mission field. From 1889, when four Sisters of Charity founded St. Francis Academy on West Hill Street, the mission has been closely associated with education. In 1892, when a second school was opened, there were 280 children enrolled although the Catholic population was only 77. Today the Catholics educate over 5,000 children in more than a dozen schools, including two High Schools.

In the Out Islands the Catholics went about the task of proselytising with the efficiency of a military operation. Doubtless they filled a need which the Anglicans, through dwindling enthusiasm and lack of finances, no longer provided adequately. Selecting certain depressed islands, such as Cat Island and Long Island, and ignoring others, the Roman Catholics built beautiful churches and the priests and sisters laboured heroically to provide educational, medical and social services so badly needed by the people. Their success was phenomenal and their new converts were attracted from all other denominations.

In 1946, the Catholic monastery of St. Augustine of Canterbury was founded at Fox Hill. The impressive buildings were designed by Mgr. John Hawes, better known as Fra Jerome, the Hermit of Cat Island. After finishing the monastery he retired to a hermitage built on the highest hill in the Bahamas, living in a nearby cave until his death in 1952.

Bishop Bernard Kevenhoerster, O.S.B., was appointed the first Vicar Apostolic of the Bahamas in 1932. He was succeeded by Bishop Leonard Hagerty, O.S.B., in 1950. On July 5, 1960, Pope John XXIII raised the Bahamas to the status of a missionary diocese and Bishop Leonard was installed as the first Bishop. By the mid-1960s, there were at least 20 Catholic priests labouring in the Bahamas and the members of seven orders of sisters. It has been estimated that there are at least 20,000 Roman Catholics in the islands today.

During the last quarter of the nineteenth century the Bahamian depression seemed too bad to be true. Sir Augustus Adderley, manager of the West Indies Pavilion at the Colonial and Indian Exhibition of 1886 and one of six Bahamians knighted within twenty-five years for public services, wrote that "the development of the resources of the islands leaves much to be desired. They are much richer, much more productive than their inhabitants imagine." Bahamian produce and handiwork, such as salt, braziletto, ambergris, straw-work and shellwork were shown at the Crystal Palace in 1851, the Vienna Exposition of 1873 and the Philadelphia Centennial (1875) as well as the 1886 Exhibition without evincing more than a passing interest. As the nineteenth century declined, many commercial products were exploited, but a series of setbacks occurred in order, it seemed, to rob the Bahamas of its long-sought economic stability and prosperity.

One peculiarly Bahamian product that had a brief moment of importance was conch shell, which was exported to France and Italy for the making of cameo brooches. The value of exports of conch shell rose suddenly from £790 in 1855 to £2,400 in 1856 and £6,351 in 1857. Then the capricious winds of fashion changed and within another four years export figures were back again where they started. Although cameos have returned to vogue in the twentieth century, mother-of-pearl or plastics have replaced the unfortunate conch.

A considerable amount of tobacco was grown in the Bahamas, beginning in 1875. The first cigars were exported in 1878 but were found to be inferior to those of Cuba or even Jamaica, and never gained popularity. Tomatoes, of which the first dozen boxes were exported in 1876, were found to grow like weeds on the sandy loam of Eleuthera and Cat Island, but shipping presented insurmountable problems. After reaching a peak of 8,130 boxes exported in 1879, tomatoes declined as a crop until the twentieth century.

In comparison with Bermuda, Bahamian shipbuilding never really flourished; but it is difficult to see why. Pine trees were always plentiful in Abaco, Grand Bahama, Andros and New Providence, and Bermudian cedar could easily have been introduced. Between 1855 and 1864, 108 ships were built in Abaco, 59 in Nassau and 63 in other islands. Their combined tonnage, however, was only 5,416, an average displacement of only 23½ tons, and these fragile sloops rarely ventured outside Bahamian waters.

Today it is not generally known that the Bahamas were the first commercial producers of pineapples on a large scale. Before the development of Cuba, Florida and finally Hawaii, the Bahamas grew the best pineapples in the world, and in the mid-nineteenth century the very name of the islands was synonymous in most minds with the exotic fruit. The first Bahamian postage stamp incorporated a pineapple prominently in its design along with a conch shell, and in fact the original engraving submitted from Nassau implied that a portrait of the national fruit should replace the traditional head of Queen Victoria.

McKinnen in 1802 noticed a fine "pinery" west of Nassau and reported with amazement that the fruit, almost priceless in England, were sold for as little as a dollar a hundred in Nassau. A few years later it was found that the red loams of Eleuthera and Cat Island were perfectly suited to the growing of pines and could support up to 36,000 fruit to the acre. The preferred types were the English and Sugar Loaf varieties, though it was found that the smaller Spanish Scarlet travelled better.

In 1898, Sir William Robinson, an ex-Governor, told the Royal Colonial Institute in London that pineapples which sold for 1½d. in Nassau were "far superior to a hot-house pine in England, which cannot be obtained for less than a sovereign". Unfortunately he was preaching a dying cause, for the great days of the industry were already past. The first cargo of Bahamian pineapples was exported to the United States in 1842 and the first canning factory was opened in 1857 at Governor's Harbour by Mr. Henry Evans of Baltimore. By 1864, 229,226 dozens were exported for a value of £21,299. By 1873, these figures had been raised to 381,222 dozen, worth £36,595, and in addition more than a million cans were exported. The Bahamian growers received a great boost in that year by a typographical error in the printing of the U.S. Tariff. In the list of exemptions from duty "fruit plants" was inserted instead of "fruit-plants" and a writer in the *Guardian* estimated that this simple substitution was worth $50,000 a year to Bahamian producers.

Messrs. J. S. Johnson's Nassau factory was opened in 1876 and by 1892 there were other factories at Governor's Harbour, Harbour Island, Abaco and Rock Sound. Lady Brassey in 1885 gave an interesting account of these early canning operations. "The 'apples', as they always call the pines here", she wrote, "are first stripped of their leaves; then they are swiftly peeled; stalk and eyes are dexterously removed; and the best fruit are thrown whole into coppers full of hot syrup, where they are boiled ten times. They are then put singly into tins, which are afterwards hermetically sealed. Those of the second quality are cut into slices and treated in the same manner. The third quality is cut into squares, the fourth is merely scraped; but all are cooked in syrup and are packed in tins decorated with attractive pictures."

The best year for the Bahamian pineapple was 1892; almost 700,000 dozens were exported for a value of nearly £60,000. Although after the glut of 1900 the colossal total of 7,233,012 dozen fruit was exported, their combined value was no more than that of the 1892 crop, representing a drop in the average price of the fruit from 1s. 8½d. to 2d. a dozen. In addition, the McKinley Tariff of 1898, which laid on a duty of $7 per thousand pineapples, helped stifle the Bahamian trade. By 1902, the exports of pineapples had dropped to 521,482 dozens of fresh fruit valued at £36,957, with 47,892 cases of tins worth £9,515. From then on the industry gradually declined still further. In 1946, less than 20,000 dozens were exported for a combined value of £4,820. This figure represented about 1.2 per cent of the total value of exports, as against the 28 per cent of total exports which pineapples represented in 1902.

The pineapple industry was always beset by peculiar hazards. Mr. McLain, the U.S. Consul in 1885, who had made a special study of the trade, told Lady Brassey that "if everything is favourable good profits are realised; but a few untoward circumstances will bring utter ruin. There may be too much rain or a drought; at times armies of rats and land-crabs invade and devour whole fields in a night or two; bush fires not infrequently devastate a plantation; prices may rule low. If none of these things occur, and the fruit is put on shipboard in good order, the gauntlet of an ocean voyage is yet to be run, and adverse winds and stormy weather mean destruction by decay of the whole cargo, whilst the average of loss on the speediest trip is seldom below thirty-three per cent. Again, the ship may be borne on her course by prosperous breezes, and may arrive in port in fine condition, only, alas! to find other vessels just ahead of her, the market glutted, and her perishable fruit saleable only for what it will fetch. Only a small portion of the fruit is shipped from Nassau, vessels preferring to clear direct from the Out Islands, where most of the fruit is grown, in order to save time and hurry the crop to market."

In the cultivation of the pineapple ignorance and disorganisation prevailed. Every producer raced to ripen his fruit at the ideal time and this invited a glut on the market. The soil was grossly overworked, without sufficient fertilisation or rest, or any form of rotation of crops. The result was that land lost 50 per cent of its productivity in five years and then had to be abandoned for 15-20 years. Although in the growing there was some co-operation and certain Nassau business men invested in plantations and the canneries, the shipping of the fresh fruit was wasteful in the extreme. In 1905, C. N. Mooney of the Baltimore Geographical Society, blamed the decline in exports on the Bahamian growers and shippers. "It is evident to them", he wrote, "that shipping in bulk is not a satisfactory way to put fruit on the market. The market demands that a product be put up in an attractive manner, and this can be done only by using suitable packages. Crates can be obtained at a small cost, and if the fruit were carefully packed it would arrive in good condition, better prices would be assured, and the losses would be reduced to a minimum. . . . A few growers whose shipments are small, have tried the plan and received increased returns, more than enough to justify the additional labour and cost."

These suggestions were not generally adopted and gradually the Bahamas were squeezed out of the world trade. Florida, which did not pay duty on her pineapples, could ship to her markets by rail. Cuba had an abundance of cheap labour and sugar to prepare the fruit for canning. Even Jamaica enjoyed the advantage of regular service by cargo steamships more or less free from the whim of the winds. After she was granted preferential duties and then annexed by the U.S. in 1898, Hawaii possessed all the advantages except proximity to her markets. Perfect soils, plentiful sugar and cheap labour were exploited by rapacious adventurers such as Dole and Spreckels. The Bahamas have been spared the evils of such commercial exploitation by outside interests, but anyone who has tasted an Eleutheran Sugar Loaf pine straight from the plant cannot but class the descent into obscurity of the once-famed fruit as a minor Bahamian tragedy.

In 1898 ex-Governor Robinson blamed the "peasant attitude" for the persistent failure of Bahamian agriculture. "I have begged them to remember", he said piously, "the high authority which says, 'If a man does not work, neither shall he eat', but I fear that all such appeals fall on deaf ears. Why!" he added, "Andros alone would supply a great portion of the States with fresh vegetables in winter." In a reply to this naïve assessment, the Earl of Stamford was more perceptive: "The Bahamas", he suggested, "had a great future before them if the inhabitants would only profit by agricultural education and obtain a better acquaintance with a diversification of industries and co-operation." Throughout Bahamian history whenever a crop or industry promised sudden profit, too much attention was concentrated upon it with too little concern for the future. The history of sisal planting illustrates this well.

The first plants of the *agave rigida sisilana* from which rope is made were introduced by the Coloniel Secretary C. R. Nesbitt in

1845. It was, however, not until the governorship of Sir Ambrose Shea (1887-94) that large-scale production was begun. A government commission was set up and sent out to Yucatan in Mexico, which reported that soil and climatic conditions there were very similar to the Bahamas. Acts were passed in 1889 placing a 20 per cent duty on imports of foreign sisal and offering a bounty of 1c. per pound of hemp produced up to 1895. Attracted by these terms and by the fact that the U.S. did not levy import duties on hemp, groups of English capitalists founded plantations in San Salvador and Andros. Prominent among them was the Rt. Hon. Joseph Chamberlain, Secretary of State for the Colonies, whose ill-fated son Neville spent several difficult years as manager of the family plantation on Andros.

By 1899, about 400 tons of sisal were exported annually. The fibre cost about £12 a ton to produce and as long as the market price remained steady at £20-£25, a good commercial profit could be made. Between 1898 and 1902 the effect of the Spanish-American War upon the industry in the Philippines rocketed the price to £38 a ton and no less than 20,000 acres were planted. Fourteen mechanical mills were established to clean the fibre, and by 1902 production had been raised to nearly 1,000 tons, valued at £37,574.

In 1903, Mooney could write that "the fibre industry of the Bahamas promises to become of great importance", but in fact the short-lived boom was over. The Philippines were more than revivified with American capital and the world price fell steadily. The large Bahamian estates, many of them badly sited on unsuitable soils with an insufficient labour force, fell into bankruptcy and the mills closed. Produced uneconomically on smallholdings and beaten crudely by hand in salt water, the quality and price of Bahamian fibre declined even further. The government ordinances supervising the production and grading of the sisal became a dead letter and the Bahamian product became far inferior to that grown in vast quantities in India and East Africa. Although in 1923 over 2,000 tons were exported, the price per ton was less than half that of 1902. Bahamian producers relapsed into general gloom. By 1946, although the world price had soared once more to £38 per ton, they could only muster an insignificant 165 tons for export.

One industry that suffered far less than sisal from fluctuations in the world market, and thus promised the Bahamas a firmer hope for economic stability, was sponge fishing. It also provided employment for the miserable ex-wreckers who existed like driftwood on the fringes of an almost tideless sea of hopelessness. As early as 1841 a Frenchman, Gustave Renouard, who had been wrecked in the Bahamas, exported parcels of Bahamian sponge to Paris, where the varieties from "wool" to "velvet" were found to compare favourably with sponges from the Mediterranean. The export trade was greatly expanded by Mr. Edward Brown, Renouard's son-in-law, and the Great Bahama Bank was opened up to full development. This enormous shoal, nicknamed "The Mud", 140 miles long and from 10 to 40 miles wide, is one of the great sponge beds of the world. The sea-bed is so shallow that the sponges can easily be hooked from their moorings with the aid of prongs and a water-glass, without the additional expense of trawls and complicated diving equipment necessary in other parts of the world.

As Bahamian sponges gained a hold on the world market, further beds were opened on the Little Bahama Bank, off Southern Eleuthera and in Acklin's Bight. A Sponge Exchange was opened in Nassau and many Greeks familiar with the trade emigrated from the old country, bringing their language, religion and customs, which are still proudly maintained. At the risk of being accused of facetiousness, it can be said that the Bahamians were born spongers. Bred to the sea, they alone could interpret the myriad shifting colours of the treacherous waters, the quirks of weather and tides, or could endure the long vigils and labours under a pitiless sun. When Key West was established as a sponging centre in the 1870s, it was Bahamian "conchs" who formed the bulk of the early population of this isolated city. In 1892, there were 8,000 Bahamians at Key West out of a population of 25,000.

In 1901, at the peak of the Bahamian sponge industry, there were 265 schooners of up to 43 tons burden, 322 sloops of up to 16 tons and 2,808 open boats engaged in sponging. 5,967 men and boys, or roughly one-third of the available labour force, were employed. The quantity and value of sponge exported rose steadily. Between 1855 and 1858 the average annual export was 255,000 pounds. By 1869 this had risen to 625,000 pounds and by 1883 the value of sponge exports was over £60,000 a year. In 1900, exported sponge topped a million pounds and the peak of 1,486,000 pounds was reached five years later. Of the £98,000 worth of sponge exported in 1902, half went to the United States and three-quarters of the remainder to Holland, France and Germany.

Until the disastrous visitation of a microscopic fungoid which destroyed 90 per cent of all West Atlantic sponges and all the Bahamian "velvet" variety in 1938, sponge continued to be the major item in the Bahamian economy. In 1917, the value of exports totalled a record £152,000. Although this declined to £112,300 in 1923 and the total weight had dropped to 670,000 pounds by 1938, chiefly because of the development of plastic sponge substitutes, this was still almost as much as the combined weight of the produce of the eight traditional sponge areas of the Mediterranean, and represented 27 per cent of world production.

Although sponging was the backbone of the Bahamian economy for three-quarters of a century, no-one ever became very rich from the trade. Even if the total value of the sponge in the best years had been divided equally among the fishermen this would have produced the lordly average of £25 a head per year. In actual fact, as in the old wrecking days, the ships were owned by Nassau merchants or white Bahamians from Harbour Island or Abaco, who took one-third of the value of the catch, the captain and crew sharing the remainder.

The sponging voyages usually lasted from five to eight weeks. The value of the catch was almost wholly dependent upon the skill of the fishermen and the luck of the weather. Arriving at the beds, where the water was between 8 and 24 feet deep, a boatload of black sponge was hooked up and then left in salt water "kraals" at a nearby island until the dead animal matter was washed out. On the voyage home the sponges were clipped, graded and strung in the rigging to dry. The stench of a homing sponger was unforgettable. Once back in Nassau, the sponges were sold by auction to the Greeks who were agents for houses in New York, London and Paris. When sold, the sponges were further trimmed and baled for export. Sometimes they were bleached.

L. D. Powles, writing in 1887, gave an unforgettably grim picture of the lot of the Negro sponge fishermen. In this account he stored most of his bitterness for the white Bahamian merchant class, whom he blamed for all Bahamian ills. Although his contentions were challenged by Bishop Shedden in his book written forty years later, his arguments certainly carry weight. "Let us follow the career of one of these unfortunates from its commencement", he wrote. "He applies to the owner of a craft engaged in the sponge or turtle fisheries, generally in the two combined, to go on a fishing voyage. He is not to be paid by wages, but to receive a share of the profits of the take, thus being theoretically in partnership with his owner. At once comes into play the infernal machine, which grinds him down and keeps him a slave for years and years—often for life. His employer invariably keeps, or is in private partnership with someone else who keeps, a store, which exists principally for the purpose of robbing employés, and is stocked with the offscourings of the American market—rubbish, unsaleable anywhere else. As soon as a man engages he has to sign seaman's articles, which render him liable to be sent on board his vessel at any time by order of a magistrate. He is then invited, and practically forced, to take an advance upon his anticipated share of the profits."

By an Act of 1885 these advances were limited to 10s., but could be made "in kind or in cash". "These advances, I need hardly say," went on Powles, "are generally made in kind, consisting of flour, sugar, tobacco, articles of clothing, or some other portion of the rubbish that constitutes the employer's stock-in-trade. Probably the fisherman does not want the goods, or, at any rate, he wants money more to leave with his family; and in order to get it he sells the goods at about half the price at which they are charged to him . . ."

Powles cited a case of Negroes paid in flour invoiced at £1 : 16s. a barrel "which was not fit for pigs" and quoted a long extract from the radical *Freeman* in which it was estimated that each of the 60-odd Bahamian owners and outfitters received about £400 a year in the trade, as against £9 for each of the sailors. One unhappy friend of Justice Powles, Sam Gowan, mentioned a voyage in which he and his shipmates fished, cleaned and dried 900 strings of 9 sponges, 8,100 in all, which realised a

grand total of £11 at the Nassau Exchange, an average of about
½d. each. These same sponges would command prices in London
ranging from 6d. to 5s. each.

"The condition of the fisherman is daily becoming more and
more unendurable", wrote the leader writer of the *Freeman* in a
style strangely reminiscent of Powles' own. "The best and most
honest and energetic of them are emigrating to the Southern
States, and a most alarming feature is the steady deterioration in
the physique of the men and their families as a consequence of
the low standard of living which the accursed system imposes
upon them."

Anyone doubting the description of the condition of the
sponge fishermen of Nassau and the Out Islands has only to
look at old photographs of their pitiful shacks and ragged
clothing. To ascribe blame is not so easy. We cannot entirely
share the acrimony of the disgruntled Irishman, Powles, who
blamed everything on the Bay Street merchants, any more than
we can admire the complacency of Sir Augustus Adderley, who
told the Royal Colonial Society that "he was in favour of the
continuance of local self-government as at present obtained.
The Bahamians were good, honest traders, and would be a credit
to any community."

Poverty was endemic throughout the islands from 1865
onwards. No settlement or class escaped the blight. It is even
possible that the merchants suffered most, for theirs was the
greatest fall and they had none of the cheerful resilience of those
to whom bare subsistence was the norm. Nassau was drained of
capital, energy and hope. Small as it was, expenditure usually
outran income and the public debt lengthened. In 1876 government salaries were months in arrears and the *Guardian* even suggested a tax of 3d. in the pound on incomes over £100 a year.
In 1885, the Public Bank, founded fifty years before, crashed into
bankruptcy with a deficit of over £12,000. The hard-pressed
government was forced to come to the rescue. Although a Post
Office savings bank was opened in 1886 and a "Bank of Nassau"
three years later, finance in the Bahamian capital was decidedly
rickety until the Royal Bank of Canada opened its Nassau
branch in 1908.

Despite all the poverty, the population of the Bahamas did

continue to rise, though the general rate of increase was less than 1 per cent a year between 1871 and 1921 and in many of the Out Islands it actually declined. In the decade after 1911 the total population fell by 4,073 or 5.49 per cent and many of the islands lost 10 per cent of their inhabitants to the United States, especially Florida. Inagua lost more than 30 per cent of her people at this time to emigration, though it is hard to see how the unfortunate Inaguans had held on so long. The circuit magistrate visiting Matthew Town in 1887 described the effect of the collapse of the salt trade, caused by the high American protective tariff. "The aspect of this island", he wrote, "is perhaps sadder than that of any other in the Bahamas, for only the other day it seemed on the road to success, and now everything in it savours of desolation. The tramways and canals that carried the salt to the beach are scarcely ever used, and are terribly out of order. Most of the houses are unoccupied, a great part of the town was burnt down a few years ago, and there has been neither sufficient energy nor capital to rebuilt it."

But perhaps the saddest settlements were not those of Inagua but the "all white" townships of Spanish Wells and Hopetown, Abaco. In 1903, a survey team from the Geographical Society of Baltimore visited these islands. Living in hopeless depression, these poor folk, descendants of proud Loyalists, maintained their racial integrity with the tenacity reserved for the retention of the last family heirloom. The results were pathetic. Persistent inter-marriage at Spanish Wells, where negroes were not allowed to build or even spend a night, had produced a population in which dwarfs, and afflictions such as locomotor ataxia and cataract were common. "We noticed also", wrote C. A. Penrose, M.D., laconically, "that the mental acumen of many of the inhabitants of the place was rather low."

At Hopetown, where only 12 negroes lived among 1,000 whites, the situation was even worse. Almost all the inhabitants —Malones, Russells, Alburys and Keys—were descendants of a Loyalist woman, Wyannie Malone, who arrived from South Carolina with her children in 1785. So closely related did the inhabitants become that degeneracy was the inevitable result. "Early in the history of the Malone family these indications of degeneracy were absent", wrote Penrose; "but they began in the fourth generation and rapidly increased afterwards until they culminated by the presence of five idiots in one family. The original stock was apparently excellent, but the present state of the descendants is deplorable."

Besides many examples of idiocy, deafness and dumbness, almost 10 per cent occurrence of locomotor ataxia, and cases of congenital blindness and polydactylism, there was leprosy in the settlement. "At once the idea of bringing in new blood suggests itself", summed up the pessimistic Penrose. "On the other hand, there is no reason to believe that the people, if left to themselves, will do in the future otherwise than they have done in the past. Future generations will sink to even a lower state of degeneracy than at present." Clearly, the isolated white communities, which, ironically, saw themselves as superior to their coloured neighbours, were in danger of extinction.

The first two decades of the twentieth century saw the negro majority in the Bahamas bogged down in a mire of poverty and ignorance from which they could not extricate themselves. The minority of native whites, whom accidents of history and economics had placed in a position of eminence, seemed powerless to lead, and doomed as a class by their narrowness and insularity.

Luckily the future held better things in store. Two World Wars, the Prohibition era and, above all, tourism, gradually produced the changes which the Bahamas needed so badly. Step by step, new elements and ideas, new wealth, revivified the islands. The twentieth century has been characterised by great strides in communications. Nowhere in the world has profited more from this acceleration than the Bahamas. It has produced, in a phrase, the last, and greatest, Bahamian revolution.

XXI

Twentieth Century
1914-45

A thousand miles of gleaming sands, seas of peacock blue and a winter climate which even the staid Colonial Report calls "most delightful", have always been potentially the most valuable Bahamian assets. The first English writer on the Bahamas, George Gardyner in 1651, described the air as "good and wholesome" and this opinion was echoed and amplified by John Graves, George Phenney, Peter Henry Bruce and Daniel McKinnen among the early writers. Surgeon-Major Bacot, writing in 1869, was the first to make a scientific review of the climate and healthiness of Nassau, which he considered almost ideal for tourists. Malaria, to which, along with "rum and overheating" he attributed the awful mortality of the troops at the end of the eighteenth century, had disappeared and yellow fever, cholera, smallpox and typhoid seemed to be on the wane. Indeed, the last serious epidemic of yellow fever occurred in 1864, and of typhoid in 1866.

The chief problem was, and remained for fifty years after Bacot, that of getting the tourists to the islands. There was no lack of hopeful promotion. Acts to encourage navigation were passed in 1851, 1857 and 1879, and contracts were signed with successive steamship companies in 1851, 1859 and 1879. These early efforts, however, were jinxed by misfortune. Besides the destruction of the *Jewess* in 1851, five other tourist boats were burnt or wrecked before 1895. In 1872 occurred the *Missouri* disaster, in which this Atlantic Steamship Company liner burnt out on its way to Nassau with the loss of the lives of 84 of its 96 passengers.* Among these were two of the brothers of President

---

* Casualties tragically duplicated by the loss of the *Yarmouth Castle* by fire in November, 1965.

Grover Cleveland, one of whom, Louis, was on his way to manage the Royal Victoria Hotel. This unhappy affair was followed by the loss of the *Zodiac* on its first trip in 1875, the *Leo* in 1877, the *City of Austria* in 1881 and the Ward Line's *Cienfuegos*, wrecked at Harbour Island in 1895.

The best tourist year before the twentieth century was 1873, when 500 winter visitors came to Nassau. In the 1890s, however, northerners began to discover the attractions of Florida and Governor Robinson suggested that the Bahamas ought to do something to attract some of the 100,000 who were making the annual trip south of the Suwannee River. Accordingly, in 1898 a fourth and the most important Hotel and Steamship Act was passed and a ten-year contract was signed with H. M. Flagler, the founding father and Czar of Miami. Besides buying the Royal Victoria Hotel for £10,000 and the site of the Army barracks at Fort Nassau for an equally reasonable sum, Flagler agreed to build a new hotel and provide a regular steamship connexion with the Florida coast. Begun in 1899, the Hotel Colonial, a structure of surpassing ugliness, was opened in the following year.

The new hotel, like most of Flagler's enterprises, was premature. The hotel never prospered and the company was saved from bankruptcy only by a fire on March 31, 1921, which completely destroyed the building. The government, rich on Prohibition income, repurchased the site, floated a 3 per cent loan of £430,000 and signed a ten-year contract with the Bahamas Hotel Company, a subsidiary of the Munson Steamship Line. Begun in July, 1922, the New Colonial Hotel, constructed in a style that can only be termed Nassau Byzantine, was completed in time for the winter season of 1922-23. Four years later, a similar monster hotel of over 200 rooms was built near Fort Montagu with a locally-raised loan of £150,000.

The vital connexion with New York, maintained from 1879 to 1917 by the Ward Line, was continued after 1917 by the Munson Company. By their ten-year contract they were to provide a weekly service from January to April and a fortnightly service for the rest of the year in return for an annual subsidy of £35,000. In 1921, the Royal Mail Lines began a monthly service between Britain and the Bahamas, and the 1920s also saw the beginning of a regular connexion between the Bahamas and

Canada. Proposals for reciprocal trade agreements and even the adoption of the Bahamas as a Canadian province had been made as early as 1880, but it was not until the Bahamas became a partner in the Canada-West Indies Trade Treaty in 1920 that the link became a reality. By another treaty in 1925, Canada was to provide a steamship serving Nassau displacing 5,000 tons and carrying at least 100 passengers, in return for an annual subsidy of £2,000. Trade between the Bahamas and Canada continued to expand, especially after the Imperial preference legislation of the 1930s. By 1938, Bahamian annual trade with Canada amounted to over £400,000, or almost one-third of the total, though the balance was unhealthily in favour of the northern partner.

By this time, Nassau's horizons had widened enormously. After an abortive measure in 1873, the Telegraph Act was passed in 1891 and in the following year a telegraph connexion was opened between Cable Beach, Nassau and Jupiter, Florida, which made it possible to send messages direct to the United States and even to England. By the time this cable had become defunct in 1914, a wireless connexion with Florida had been in operation over a year. In Nassau itself, the telephone system, after several private ventures had failed, was established by the government in 1907, two years before an adequate system of electricity supply was installed.

But it was probably the First World War which did more than anything else to bring the Bahamas closer to the world outside. Not only did thousands of Bahamians travel away from their narrow shores to undreamt places for the first time, but at the same time many Out Islanders came to and through Nassau and thus widened their outlooks and hopes.

At first, the 1914 War made very little real impact; the issues were too remote. The brief telegram published in the local press concerning the assassination of the Archduke at Sarajevo was lost among a discussion of the new steamship contract, the latest sisal prices and the chances of the British yacht *Shamrock* in the forthcoming America's Cup races in the Solent. News of the British declaration of war on August 4 was a day late reaching Nassau, but was greeted by the conventional attitudes of patriotism. Jingoistic messages appeared in the *Guardian* and *Tribune*; the Governor, Sir George Haddon-Smith, spoke publicly of British war aims and the Legislature rushed through a Proclamations Act and an Emergency Relief Act. By the end of September, the War Relief Committee formed by the Governor had raised £2,000 from the public and 225 Bahamian fishermen had volunteered to act as prize crews for the Royal Navy. These patriotic sponge-men, however, were never called upon to serve, and by the time Haddon-Smith left to be Governor of the Windwards in December, 1914, the initial war enthusiasm had evaporated.

In actual fact, the only exciting home incident of the whole war occurred during the first few weeks, and passed unnoticed. The outbreak of war found the German cruiser *Karlsruhe* lurking around the Plana Cays between Acklin's and Mayaguana. Surprised by H.M.S. *Suffolk*, she was forced to abandon one of her boats, which drifted up at Hopetown, Abaco, some weeks later and was declared a war prize. The 27.5 knot *Karlsruhe* managed by luck and good navigation to elude the slower *Suffolk*, *Bristol* and *Berwick* and even contrived to take on fuel from a German collier at the Grassy Creek Cays on the Tongue of the Ocean before slinking off safely to San Juan, Puerto Rico. In November, 1914, she disappeared mysteriously off Barbados, probably the victim of an accidental explosion.

These facts became known in the Bahamas only after the war. It was not until mid-1915, when the European nations were locked in their death grips in Flanders, that the seriousness of the war became apparent in the distant outposts. Short of men for the first time, the War Office suggested the raising of 1,000 men from the West Indies. The British West Indies Regiment, disbanded in 1891, was reconstituted with a nominal strength of 2,000 men. In all, during the war, 12,000 men served in its ranks. The new Governor, Sir William Allardyce, suggested that the Bahamas raise a platoon and called for recruits. On the first day 11 volunteered, the first man being William F. Albury, later commissioned. In all, 70 men came forward for the first contingent, 30 being selected as fit to go overseas. The Bahamas Contingent Fund raised £1,315 to equip the men and transport them to France.

Hastily drilled, these "Gallant Thirty" were shipped off to Jamaica on a schooner, after an impressive ceremony, on

September 9, 1915, carrying a silk flag presented by the Imperial Order of Daughters of the Empire. They were followed before May, 1916, by two further contingents of 105 and 87 men as well as by five drafts totalling 265 men sent out between August 1916 and September 1917 after the passage of the Bahama Islands War Contingent Act (1916).

In all, 1,800 Bahamians presented themselves for service with the Colours. Besides the 487 sent to Jamaica and from there to Egypt and France with the British West Indies Regiment, some 53 Bahamians joined up from England, 50 from Panama (where they were engaged in contract work on the Canal) and at least 80 in Canada and the U.S.A. With a very few exceptions such as W. F. Albury, all those who served in the B.W.I. Regiment were coloured men, *soldats noirs aimables* as the French called them. Most of the white Bahamians who served, including 36 Old Scholars of Queen's College, joined up with the Canadian forces. Of the 670 Bahamians who went to war, 50 died on active service. This proportion would have been much higher had it been the British policy to use coloured troops more generally in the front line. Most of the Bahamians were used as pioneers on roadworks and gun emplacements just behind the lines, though they saw and shared most of the horrors and discomforts. Wherever they went they gained praise for their physique and cheerfulness, and had particular commendations from Allenby and Haig.

At home, the war did not produce real hardships until it was nearly over. The stringently enforced, and largely superfluous, blackout restrictions were regarded as a severe burden. Although there was a serious recession in trade in 1914 and exports fell by over £40,000, sponge and sisal revived in 1915 and prices remained high throughout the rest of the war. Even the tourist trade did not collapse until the winter season of 1916-17.

The island which suffered most was that which could least afford it; unfortunate Inagua. Immediately before the war, the German ships of the Hamburg-America Line and certain Dutch ships had been accustomed to stop at Matthew Town to pick up stevedores. With the war this invaluable employment ceased abruptly and actual starvation was only narrowly averted in Inagua by the action of the War Relief Committee.

In all, the Bahamas raised over £47,000 for the allied war

effort. Paltry as this amount seemed when compared with the sums raised by Britain herself, it produced a severe strain on the Bahamian economy. The Bank of Nassau failed suddenly in December, 1916, and the entry of the United States into the war in April, 1917, was followed by a grave shortage of food and other essential supplies. At the same time that money was becoming in shorter supply than ever, prices began to rise to unprecedented heights.

In the financial emergency, the Home Defence Force, nicknamed the "Home Expense Force", was disbanded on June 14, 1917. But this did not solve the food shortage. At one time it was estimated that Nassau had flour enough for one week and the bakeries did not produce bread for two days.

Into this crisis the Governor moved with assurance. By virtue of the full emergency powers given him by the Proclamations Act, he used the War Relief Committee to commandeer food stocks, to fix prices of bread, flour and kerosene and to order retailers to conserve supplies. In May, 1918, the Committee ordered that all bread should contain 20 per cent of rye or corn flour, and there were several prosecutions for "Black Marketing". Some relief to the critical situation occurred in July, 1918, when 2,500 contract labourers were recruited to work on the port installations at Charleston, South Carolina. Nevertheless, it was with real jubilation that Bahamians heard the news at 3.25 p.m. local time on Monday, November 11, that the war was over.

"The wonderful news seemed to reach every part of the City at the same moment", wrote Frank Holmes in 1924, "and the bells rang out on all sides—church bells, fire bells, ships' bells and all other kinds of bells. Bunting appeared everywhere like magic, fluttering gaily in the breeze and the streets were soon filled with triumphant and cheering crowds parading up and down with bands playing and flags flying. Market women, their heads garlanded with flowers, danced for joy, and motor cars, cabs and pedestrians were all mixed up in inextricable but hilarious confusion. The Governor and his party were in the thick of it all . . ."

A new Assembly was convened early in 1919, the previous one having sat since 1910, the longest in Bahamian history. The first contingent of Bahamian soldiers arrived back in April, 1919, two months after a visit by two American seaplanes from Miami, the first aeroplanes ever seen in the islands. To the returning soldiers the hard-pressed Assembly voted a magnanimous bounty of £5 apiece. They could do no better; the public debt was £69,423, 50 per cent more than in 1914. With soldiers and contract men returning and a general decline in sponge and sisal prices expected, complete disaster threatened the Bahamas.

Providence, after whom Nassau's island is so aptly named, once more intervened. In December, 1919, the Volstead Act, a war-time measure, was passed by the United States Congress as the Eighteenth Amendment of the Constitution. This ill-judged and ill-fated law, which condemned a large proportion of otherwise innocent Americans to hypocrisy and crime, made it an offence to manufacture, import or sell intoxicating liquors. For the Bahamas it was an undisguised blessing. "Bootlegging" between 1920 and 1933 became a rich Bahamian industry, in the swashbuckling tradition of privateering, wrecking and running the blockade.

The Bahamas, with its nearest land less than fifty miles from the American coast, was a natural base for smuggling liquor into the thirsty States. At first, however, the island economy lacked the necessary complex organisation, and it was by no means certain that the authorities would turn a compliant eye upon such a dubious export trade. Exports for 1920 and 1921 did not exceed by much the steady average of about £30,000 for the previous decade. It was not until the end of 1921 that it became obvious that the Bahamas government would not actively support the United States Excise Service. More than twenty giant liquor concerns sprang up in Nassau almost overnight and speedy motor-boats began to sneak from Grand Bahama and Bimini across the Gulf Stream to the Florida coast, or chartered schooners make the longer and more hazardous journey up to "Rum Row" off New York, Boston and Philadelphia. Even planes were used, taking off from Bimini and landing in secluded lakes deep in the Everglades of Florida.

Re-exports of liquor in 1922 were valued at £1,612,122, an increase of tenfold over the figures for 1921. The total for 1923 was £1,591,538 and the average for the ten years between 1922 and 1932 was well over half a million pounds. The number of ships leaving Bahamian ports rose from 486 of 81,129 tons displacement in 1919, to 1,681 of 718,110 tons in 1922. In that year, 714 cleared from Nassau, 567 from Grand Bahama and 306 from Bimini. All available ships were pressed into service and one of the most amusing events of the period was the seizure by the American customs men of the *Message of Peace*, once the Bishop's yacht, but sold some time before by Roscow Shedden and chartered to bootleggers.

The hard-pressed Bahamas government was one of the happiest profiteers from Prohibition. The Customs Act of 1919 had laid comparatively heavy duties upon imported liquor and, with the fantastic increase in the trade, revenue rose proportionately. Brandy paid 24s. per proof gallon, rum 8s. and whisky 12s., or 24s. for every dozen "reputed quarts". Customs receipts rocketed from £103,492 in 1919 to £313,949 in 1921 and £640,798 in 1923, and this was only a small portion of the wealth that flooded into Nassau. In 1929, when a band of desperate Cubans were rumoured to be descending on Nassau to rob the Royal Bank of Canada, the vaults of the bank, which before 1920 had never seen a million dollars, were said to be crammed with $11,000,000. Police armed with rifles and bayonets were placed on guard around the bank, but the "hijackers" did not appear. Nevertheless, returning bootleggers out on a spree with a "roll" of $50,000 in their pockets, continued to be a magnet for desperadoes and card sharks.

In modern guise many of the picaresque scenes of pirate days were re-enacted during the 1920s. "Up and down streets that buccaneers had laid out rolled a new tide of marked men" wrote H. McLachlan Bell, "bootleggers, gangster leaders, kidnappers, cracksmen, while for contrast there rubbed shoulders with them public school teachers out for a lark and women tourists who never suspected who their passing neighbours might be. There was no roughness to speak of, and no killings, though guns were out time and time again when rival gangs met. The majesty of the British law held trouble in the waterfront bars down to fist fights and the order was 'No guns in Nassau'—meaning that they were not to be pulled there."

"... Bootleggers played poker for $100 bills on the piles of empties, competed at pitch and toss with gold pieces on the wharves, roared loud choruses as they trekked to their boats for outward runs. Timid folk stayed home o' nights, preachers threatened all and sundry with the wrath of God, an attempt was made to draw social lines between the 'best people' and the newly rich liquor families. But money ruled ..."

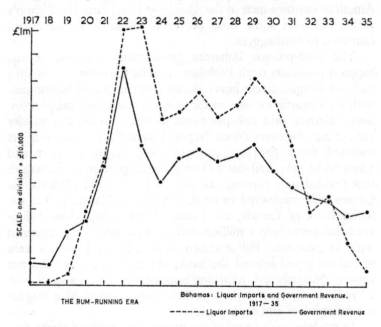

THE RUM-RUNNING ERA

Bahamas: Liquor Imports and Government Revenue, 1917-35

------- Liquor Imports   ———— Government Revenue

The headquarters of the bootleggers were the *Lucerne* hotel, a three-story building still found on Frederick Street, and the well-named *Bucket of Blood* on George Street, burnt down in a block-long fire in 1942. The *Lucerne*, managed by a middle-aged lady from New England whom the rum-runners referred to affectionately as "Mother", was the venue of the annual dance and party now known to legend as the Bootleggers' Ball.

Nassau undoubtedly simmered and boiled in a manner only the oldest could remember. And, to a limited extent, the whole of the Bahamas profited from the Prohibition goldrush. As Bell wrote in 1934: "neglected churches were renovated with liquor money, charities were refinanced, life in general took on a splendour and a spaciousness". The public debt was liquidated and salaries in the Civil Service raised. Wages for coloured labourers rose to $6 a day. Besides the building of the two new hotels, the harbour was deepened and the wharves lengthened. The electricity, water supply and sewerage systems were modernised and cars began to crowd the re-made roads. If the Out Islands, as always, lagged behind, Nassau began to take on for the first time the appearance of a modern city, while losing little of its "old colonial charm".

Nevertheless, it would be idle to pretend that it was more than a tiny minority which gained most from the years of plenty. Some gauge of the profits to be made by the fortunate few can be made by the figures provided by F. Van de Water in his entertaining book *The Real McCoy* (1931). A schooner-load of 5,700 cases of Scotch whisky cost $170,000 duty paid in Nassau. Delivered to the ships stationed off New York or Boston, it was worth $342,000. Landed in the States, its value had doubled again to $684,000, and by the time the actual drinker received the precious fluid it might have cost $2,000,000. William McCoy of Seneca, New York, estimated that in four years he shipped 175,000 cases of liquor out of Nassau. On one voyage alone he cleared a profit of $130,000. But perhaps the men who made the biggest fortunes "never sailed a ship nor sold to any person in the United States a pint of booze. They did not have to go so far; buyers flooded their offices, took the liquor direct to chartered ships and sailed away."

With stringent laws governing the investment of foreign capital, the ranks of the liquor magnates were filled from the existing Bahamian merchant class, prominent among them being the names of Bethell, Christie, Collins, Kelly, Sands and Symonette. As we have already seen, this class was dominant in the colonial Legislature. It would have been short-sighted indeed if an Assembly of any composition had legislated against such a windfall, but one of the least happy aspects of the Prohibition boom was that it produced an even deeper separation between the "haves" and the "have-nots".

The Tariff Amendment Act (No. 2) of 1920 allowed an 80 per cent drawback on liquor re-exported from the colony, provided proof could be shown by the merchant that the liquor had been landed outside the Bahamas and would not be adulterated with other spirits. In addition, the Tariff Act of 1923 decreed a 50 per cent rebate on whisky produced within the British Empire. Falsification of returns and manifests became a commonplace of Bahamian business practice. By a convenient myth, most of the liquor re-exported from the Bahamas was sent to the tiny French island of Miquelon off the coast of Newfoundland. Bahamian exports to Miquelon, nil in 1920, were £25,000 in 1921 and £1,208,718 in 1922. This figure represented 66·2 per cent of the total Bahamian exports for that year. Needless to say, the official figures for liquor re-exported only represented a proportion of the trade. An unknown quantity not only left the colony but also entered it, as contraband, and was never assessed at the bond warehouses.

From the very beginning there was a close correlation between the liquor magnates and the exploitation of real estate. During the 1920s, the Bahamas enjoyed a boom in land investment that was really but an extension of the almost insane speculation in Florida land during the Jazz Decade. Pan American Airways instituted a daily flight, taking $2\frac{1}{2}$ hours, from Miami in 1929, and rich American visitors began to buy up land and build homes they could reach in a few hours from anywhere in the States. It was a significant coincidence that one of the chief pioneers of aviation in the Bahamas made his first money in the liquor trade and then consolidated his fortune in real estate.

In New Providence during the 1920s, the Eastern Road, the Grove, Prospect Ridge and Cable Beach (once the site of J. S. Johnson's pineapple farm) became dotted with the stucco palaces of American *nouveaux riches*. A new hotel, the Rod and Gun Club, and modern houses were built at Bimini, and many small cays were bought and sold and bought again by optimistic speculators. In all, it has been estimated that between four and five million dollars were invested in Bahamian land and building during the ten years that followed the passing of the Eighteenth Amendment.

It was a brittle affluence and was designed to vanish almost as swiftly as it had arrived. The world-wide slump which began in October, 1929, brought new investment in the Bahamas to a standstill, but while Prohibition was still in force, there was always a steady, if declining, inward flow of liquor money. Only upon the repeal of Prohibition by the Twenty-First Amendment in the first year of Franklin D. Roosevelt's first term as President did the source dry up. "Unclassified re-exports" for 1935 had fallen to a paltry total of £121,000. As H. M. Bell in 1934 quoted Tom Lavelle, the Irish barman of the old *Lucerne*, saying as he mixed a sorry last "Coast-to-Coast Flip": "Boys, those days are done, we've got to go to work now!"

The years between the Twenty-First Amendment and the American entry into the Second World War in December, 1941, were a tale of savage depression in the Bahamas, made none the more bearable by its familiarity. Although home-produced food was cheap and plentiful, wages fell to starvation levels even where work was available. A labourer was regarded as fortunate if he received a steady 10s. a week and domestic servants often worked hard for their board alone. New building ceased and land prices tumbled as fast as they had soared. New houses deserted, crumbled and peeled. The ever-energetic bush encroached on newly cleared land. Total exports for 1938 amounted to barely £182,000. When the sponge industry collapsed early in 1939, to be followed so shortly by the outbreak of another World War, it seemed that the Bahamas, hitherto so tenacious of life, had received a double death-blow. In the Out Islands cases of actual starvation were not unknown.

At least one man did not lose his faith that the Bahamas would magically regain their lost prosperity. Born in Nassau in 1896, H. G. Christie, who served in the Royal Canadian Air Force in the First World War, was one of the pioneers of land development in the islands. First elected to the House of Assembly as a Member for Cat Island in 1927, he was one of the founders of Bahamas Airways and the first Chairman of the Development Board. His burning ideal, which never swerved, "was nothing less than to turn this insignificant community into the new Mecca of the world's rich, a metropolis gorgeous enough and luxurious enough to draw the international set away from the Riviera and Biarritz and Palm Beach".

During the lean 1930s there seemed small hopes of attaining

this ideal. But even in the worst of the depression years, Harold Christie achieved a minor triumph. In 1934, he managed to attract to the Bahamas as a resident and huge investor the richest citizen of the country he had served in the 1914-18 War—Mr., later Sir, Harry Oakes. The years between 1934 and 1943 could almost be called The Oakes Era; no man has left such a deep imprint upon twentieth-century Bahamian life.

Oakes was an enigma; an enigma compounded of paradoxes. A hater of publicity, he became a legend in his own lifetime. A thousand tales were told of him but the true man was seldom discerned. A philanthropist, he could be viciously mean. A discriminating art collector, he could be dramatically uncouth. Although he often affected the manner and dress of a Klondike sourdough, Oakes was in fact a Maine Yankee of good family, educated at Bowdoin, one of the best colleges in the eastern United States. Born in 1878, he determined while still at school to make a fortune by gold mining. For fourteen years he prospected the goldfields of the world, from Alaska to the Congo and from Australia to northern Ontario. These backbreaking years bred in him a self-dependence that became ruthlessness when transmuted by success.

One myth attributed Oakes's fantastic success to the action of chance. Penniless, he was said to have been put off a train by the conductor in the Ontario wilds, and there stumbled upon his long-sought private goldmine. In fact, his discovery and exploitation of the Lake Shore Mine from 1914 onwards was the result of experienced calculation backed by a determination bordering on insanity. Lake Shore, the second richest goldmine in the western hemisphere, made Harry Oakes a multimillionaire. By 1930, besides a mansion in Bar Harbour, Maine, he owned houses at Kirkland Lake, Ontario, Niagara Falls, Palm Beach, Kensington (London) and Tottingworth Park, Sussex.

Although he gave generously to charities of his own choosing, Harry Oakes bitterly resented the heavy taxation laid upon his fortune by the Canadian government. After the Conservative administration of Richard Bennett came into power in 1931 Oakes estimated that 85 per cent of his income was being filched from him. Although he had become a Canadian citizen in 1924, the year after his marriage at the age of 48, he threatened to leave

Canada. In 1934 he carried out his threat. Having met Harold Christie at Palm Beach, he was persuaded to transfer his enormous wealth to the Bahamas, a country parched for new investment. His departure brought forth the following bitter headlines in a Canadian paper:

MULTIMILLIONAIRE CHAMP TAX DODGER
Santa Claus to Bahamas. But Heart like Frigidaire to the Land that Gave Him Wealth.

Harry Oakes bought up more than 7,000 acres in New Providence alone, to the south-west of Nassau and overlooking Lake Cunningham. Of many houses which he purchased, his favoured residence was Westbourne, a luxurious mansion now part of the Bahamas Country Club. With the enthusiasm of a young man he threw himself into ambitious projects costing in all over $400,000 and employing many local labourers who had been on the point of starvation.

A lover of trees in his youth, Oakes became known as a savage destroyer of unwanted timber in New Providence. Near Westbourne he cleared a magnificent new golf course. Two miles south-west of Nassau, doubtless persuaded by Christie, his closest confidant, he levelled and paved Oakes Field, the first aerodrome in the Bahamas.

None of Oakes's projects appeared more quixotic than his purchase of the ailing New Colonial Hotel, which he rechristened the British Colonial Hotel. If legend is true, he was denied admittance or served badly one day when he appeared there in his prospector's rig, and bought the hotel the following day so that he could sack the man responsible for his embarrassment. The truth of the matter was that Oakes, like Christie, had his gaze firmly on the future. When he died in 1943, Oakes' property in Nassau was valued at £3,671,000. Had he lived another dozen years he would have seen his land in New Providence appreciate at least a dozen times.

Even in his philanthropies, Harry Oakes was not guiltless of a certain calculation. By his steady engagement of some 1,500 labourers otherwise unemployed, he became very popular in Nassau. In 1938 he was elected a Member of the House of

Assembly. A close confidant of the Governor, he was already one of the most powerful men in the Bahamas. Later he was made a Member of the Legislative Council. In England in the late 1930s he gave parties to the right people and money to the right charities. To St. George's Hospital, for instance, he gave the princely sum of £50,000. On June 8, 1939, while King George VI was in the country of his birth, Oakes was made a Baronet.

Less than three months later, Britain declared war on Germany and the Bahamas once more was fighting an enemy with whom she had no personal quarrel. Considering the microscopic aid which Britain had found herself able to give the Bahamas through the depression years, the unfeigned loyalty of Bahamians to the Allied cause was remarkable.

Although only one contingent was raised during the war, in 1944 for overseas service with the North Caribbean Regiment, and only 14 Bahamians lost their lives on active service, nearly 1,100 served in uniform, mostly in local defence. In addition, the financial contribution of the Bahamas to the war effort was certainly not less than half a million pounds, in the form of interest-free loans, funds for wartime charities and the purchase of tanks and planes, and the twenty shipments of useful articles collected by the War Materials Committee.

Nevertheless, it must be admitted that the Bahamas were spared the horrors of war, and the economic effects were almost wholly beneficial. The tourist trade, for example, depressed in the uncertain year of 1939, enjoyed a minor boom in the winter season of 1940-41. With rationing non-existent until 1942 and never severe, the life-and-death struggle going on in Europe, Africa and Asia was like a distant storm; violent with thunder and lightning, but bringing only marginal showers.

The first direct effect of the European war was the descent of a swarm of rich refugees, eager to escape the shortages and dangers of a beleaguered Britain. Real estate and building received their first faint hints of future inflation, and Nassau cocktail society took on a fresh lease of life. Nothing aided this more than the arrival as Governor of ex-King Edward, Duke of Windsor, and his wife, the former Mrs. Wallis Simpson.

The first year of the war had found the Duke in Portugal,

where he had been the innocent focus of an intrigue among the Axis diplomats in Lisbon. Fearing that he might be seized as a hostage, or even set up as a puppet king, Winston Churchill sent out Sir Walter Monckton to persuade the Duke to return to England. A few weeks later he was appointed Governor of the Bahamas, a post which he occupied from August, 1940, until May, 1945.

In her memoirs, the Duchess of Windsor has written of the sojourn in Nassau of the Duke and herself as an involuntary and somewhat distasteful exile and in personal correspondence has even spoken of the New Providence in terms of Elba and St. Helena. This attitude, as can be imagined, was not well received in Nassau. Nor was it fair to the popular Governor, Sir Charles Dundas, founder of the Dundas Civic Centre, who was forced to leave the Bahamas before his term was completed. Although in public he nobly hid his disappointment, his private feelings were understandably bitter. A Nassau editor has told of a conversation with Sir Charles shortly after he had received news of his summary recall. He had been appointed to Uganda, on the other side of the globe.

"Why don't you turn down the offer?" he was asked when he expressed his disappointment at leaving.

"I can't," he replied. "I'm being moved to make room for someone. I can't tell you who it is but it will be announced in a few days' time and then you'll know why. It will be big news."

After a pause, he added, in a brief explosion of acrimony, "I don't know why I should be pushed out to make room for him."

Although the colony had been divided over the abdication controversy in 1937, it gave its loyalty willingly to the handsome new Governor, who arrived on a steamy August day in the Canadian *Lady Somers* with a destroyer escort. Personally the Duke remained much more popular than his sometimes outspoken wife throughout their stay, and undoubtedly he worked his hardest at the unexpected and unfamiliar minor role of colonial Governor. Paradoxically, however, the post, unprotected by Ministers of the Crown, proved to be beset by more pitfalls than the occupation of the English throne.

Before the arrival of the Windsors, the House of Assembly

had voted £1,500 to modernise Government House. The Duchess called in a famous New York decorator of her acquaintance and gave him *carte blanche*, while she and the Duke remained the guests first of Sir Frederick Sigrist and then the Oakes at Westbourne. By the time Government House had been stripped of its Victoriana and made more habitable, the bill had reached £5,000. It was with rather a grim smile that the House of Assembly paid up.

The most valuable work performed by the Duke of Windsor was in the formation and chairmanship of the Economic Committee, which, as the Out Island and Economic Committee, lasted until the early 1960s, the only governmental body or board presided over by the Governor. In preparation for a food crisis, which never actually arrived, the Duke sponsored schemes to raise the productivity of the Out Island farmers. He also founded a much-needed Infant Welfare Clinic on Blue Hills Road.

Perhaps embittered by his treatment in some quarters during and after the abdication crisis, the Duke did not relish criticism in the local press. On one occasion he reminded Étienne Dupuch that in England it was not usual to criticise members of the Royal Family, to be told quite firmly that it was not as royal prince but as colonial governor that he was being criticised. After this, on more than one occasion, the Duke used his privileges under the Emergency War Powers Act to deny access by the press "for security reasons" to several non-military functions, including the memorial service to the Duke of Kent, killed in 1941.

A discreet veil of secrecy was drawn, for better reasons, over serious riots that occurred on June 1, 1942, which were without parallel in the history of the colony. Despite a parliamentary inquiry under Sir Alison Russell, K.C., and a White Paper, this incident has been largely forgotten or glossed over. In August, 1940, it had been announced that in return for fifty superannuated destroyers, the imperial government had leased to the Americans for 99 years among other places in the Bahamas a substantial site at Georgetown, Exuma, to be used as a naval base. Shortly afterwards the United States Navy began work on a seaplane base there, employing native labour at almost American rates, greatly to the benefit of the depressed Exumians.

Early in 1942, these benefits were greatly extended when the U.S., now at war, decided to expand Oakes Field and to establish a new air base at the western end of New Providence. The Pleasantville Company was granted the contract and was prepared to employ 2,400 Bahamians at American Negro rates at least as high as $2 a day. This, compared with the average Bahamian labourer's wage for 1936 of 2s. a day, was something of a revolution. The contractors were besieged by practically every able-bodied Bahamian.

Facing economic anarchy, the Government, probably advised from London and Washington, pegged wages for unskilled labour at 4s. a day. On the "Project", coloured Bahamians were driving trucks for 1s. an hour while white Americans were receiving at least $1.50 an hour for the same work. The result was chaos. After some days of muttered discontent, a swirling, snarling mob of some thousands of angry men gathered "over the Hill" and descended on Bay Street, breaking windows and looting the shops of the merchants they regarded as the authors of the "double cross". The Company of the Cameron Highlanders then in the garrison were called out, the Riot Act was read and martial law declared. In dispersing the crowds and maintaining order over the next two days 2 people were killed and 25 injured. Sullen but subdued, the men returned to work. Two weeks later, their pay was raised to 5s. a day.

The riots had one unexpected and tragic repercussion. Less than four weeks later, while discontent was still in the air, an ingenuous arsonist, himself a merchant in financial straits, set fire to his shop at the western end of Bay Street. With frightening speed, the flames roared up George Street, jumped the road and threatened the entire business section of Nassau. Only by heroic efforts on the part of the fire engines from the Air Force base was the holocaust contained. The Duke of Windsor, working like a slave in a chain to empty the shelves of the Island Shop, regained some of the prestige lost at the time of the riots. Appalled at the extent of his nefarious work and apprehended, the incendiary was given a sentence of seven years in gaol.

It was ironic that the most exciting events in Nassau during the period 1939-45 bore little or no relation to the war. Another such occurrence was the murder of Sir Harry Oakes. This ghastly affair, which shocked war headlines from the newspapers of the world and remains to this day a tantalising mystery, occurred on the windy night of July 7, 1943.

Oakes, whose wife was away at Bar Harbour for the humid summer months, had spent the evening quietly at Westbourne with Harold Christie and two others, who left the house for home about 11 p.m. Christie, a bachelor, stayed on and was given a spare bedroom next but one to Oakes's. The two friends said goodnight at about 11.30. There were no servants in the house. When Harold Christie awoke at about 7 a.m. he discovered Sir Harry Oakes brutally murdered. His head battered, he had been thrown on the bed, sprayed with inflammable spirit and set alight.

The Duke of Windsor's first reaction to the news was to apply his powers of censorship; but he was too late. Étienne Dupuch, with whom Oakes and Christie had had an early appointment, had been the first to hear of the murder and the story had already been telegraphed to the far corners of the world. Next, the Duke, ignoring the local C.I.D., American F.B.I. or the very competent criminologists attached to the forces in Nassau, telephoned to Miami and requested the services of two police officers of his acquaintance, Melchen and Barker. Melchen was an experienced if somewhat unimaginative detective; but Barker, the strong man of the two, was a scoundrel who became a drug addict and himself died a violent death in 1952.

Shouldering aside the local police, Melchen and Barker went resolutely to work. On the evening of July 9, "Count" Marie Alfred Fouquereaux de Marigny, the Mauritian husband of Nancy Oakes, was arrested and charged with the murder of his father-in-law. The case against de Marigny seemed clear. Notoriously estranged from Sir Harry and Lady Oakes, whose daughter he had married without their consent, he was without an unimpeachable alibi for the night of July 7. In fact, he was known to have been in the vicinity of Westbourne after midnight. When his house was searched, he was unable to trace the shirt he wore on the night of the murder. Barker examined de Marigny's arms and beard and declared that the hairs were singed. When, six days later, Barker announced that he had discovered de Marigny's fingerprints on the screen in Sir Harry Oakes' bedroom, the unfortunate Mauritian seemed headed straight for the gallows.

The sensational trial opened before Chief Justice Sir Oscar Daly and an all-male jury on October 16, 1943, and lasted almost three weeks. Defending de Marigny were Mr. Godfrey Higgs with Mr. W. E. A. Callender as his Junior. The crux of the trial was the three-day cross-examination of Barker, in which Higgs practically reduced the Miami detective to an admission that he had forged the incriminating fingerprints. In a dramatic scene, at 7.20 p.m. on November 8, after being out for only an hour, the jury returned a verdict of Not Guilty 9 : 3, though, inconsistently, it recommended that de Marigny be deported from the colony.

Almost unnoticed during the murder trial, both New Providence airfields had been completed during November, 1943. Despite the official cutback on wages, the contractors had spent £629,978 on labour in eighteen months as well as spending nearly £250,000 with local merchants. The end of the Project was not followed by the usual depression, since between 1943 and 1945 some 5,000 Bahamian labourers were permanently engaged on agricultural work in the United States, and even after the war this flow of temporary labour continued sporadically.

In Nassau many people prospered by catering for the two new Air Force bases. Between 1943 and the end of the war, New Providence acquired an unfamiliar importance, as a school of operational training by the Royal Air Force, as a staging-post on the trans-Atlantic ferry service and as a base for ocean patrol and air-sea rescue work during the anti-submarine campaign in the Caribbean and West Atlantic. For perhaps the last time, the Bahamas occupied a position of strategic importance in time of war. Nassau itself, crowded with thousands of off-duty airmen, took on the appearance of a garrison town.

The ending of the war, which had brought so many benefits to the Bahamas, must have been received by some with somewhat divided feelings; but the celebrations were convincing enough, and on V.J. Day, August 14, 1945, many of the tumultuous scenes of November 11, 1918, were re-enacted.

XXII

Present and Future
1945-67

The end of the war, so joyfully celebrated, was not followed by
the traditional slump. Indeed, the years since 1945 have seen a
period of practically uninterrupted expansion and success. Soar-
ing tourist and investment figures and a corresponding rise in
government revenue have been accompanied by huge improvements in living standards, education and political sophistication.
Serious problems remain, but they are largely the problems of
prosperity and the phenomenal post-war expansion.

In many ways the recent developments have come too fast
and their benefits distributed unevenly. Selfish men have tended
to consider only their own profit, and government to legislate
only for the present while thinking in terms of the past. There is
promise of change and a more forward-looking policy with the
accession to power in January, 1967, of the party representing
the Negro majority; but there is also danger that under the
banner of "Equality", reverse discrimination may be practised
and the very great achievements of the somewhat oligarchic
former regime smothered under a blanket of recrimination.
Again, the beguiling slogan of self-government may lead
Bahamians to forget the benefits of the British connexion and
place the Bahamas in the situation of a very small boat on the
stormy ocean of international affairs. Moreover, the recent
period has seen a growing and potentially dangerous economic
dependence upon the nearby United States, with company
racketeers and gambling syndicates insinuating themselves like
sharks in the inflowing sea of more responsible investment.
A failure to control such predators, as to diversify the economy
and to spread the benefits of prosperity more evenly, could, in

the long run, be as fatal as an attitude of rigid non-compromise in politics.

The startling rise in tourism has been the result of a combination of factors. The vast improvement in air transportation, helped in the case of the Bahamas by the wartime bequest of two modern airports, has brought the beautiful islands much closer to a teeming population riding on the crest of an economic wave of prosperity. Overcrowding in Florida, revolution in Cuba, the comparatively unspoilt charm of "old" Nassau and cheap luxury goods, also attract holidaymakers from the nearby continent. Today an average of 65 aircraft take off and land in Nassau each day in the year, most of them shuttling to and from Florida in 35 minutes for as little as $25 return fare, and throughout the islands there are no less than 43 airfields. Over 40 hotels and residential clubs, 32 of them built since 1949, provide accommodation for 7,500 visitors a day in Nassau and an additional 4,000 in the Out Islands.

Undoubtedly the largest single factor in attracting tourists to the Bahamas has been the promotional advertising undertaken by the Development Board, which became the Ministry of Tourism in January, 1964. Led by Sir Stafford Sands, a brilliant Bahamian lawyer and business man who combined the portfolio of Minister of Finance with that of Tourism until his government's downfall in January, 1967, the Bahamas entered the bitterly competitive world of American advertising on its own terms. The adventure has been costly, but the tourist figures can be used as ample justification. In 1949, when 32,018 visitors came to the Bahamas, the Development Board spent less than £100,000. In the same year there was a General Election and the new House voted almost to double the allocation to the Board. In 1950, the tourist figures rose to 45,371 and the following year to 68,502. Except for a slight recession in 1958, the phenomenal increase has been maintained. In 1966, more than three-quarters of a million visitors came to the islands, with an expenditure by the Ministry of Tourism of about a million and three-quarter pounds.

No longer is the Season restricted to two or three winter months, leaving the hotels shuttered for the rest of the year. Following a similar development in Florida, the Bahamas now attract a new class of visitor during the hot summer months, drawn by special "economy" rates in the hotels. Already by 1959, there were 22,247 visitors to Nassau in July, only 7,500 less than in March, the best month. In recent years also, the Out Islands have attracted an increasing proportion of the total of tourists. From about a tenth in the 1950s, this had reached more than a third by 1965, in which year Grand Bahama alone attracted 196,000 visitors.

Parallel to and probably more remarkable than the tourist boom has been a surge in investment, mostly American, in the Bahamas. Besides hotels, which enjoy very advantageous tax and customs concessions by the Hotels Encouragement Act of 1949, untold millions have been poured into Bahamian building and real estate. With no income, corporation or probate taxes, the Bahamas enjoy what has been called "a salubrious financial climate". Catering for tax refugees has become the most lucrative Bahamian industry. Competition among land speculators has sent real estate prices to undreamt of heights. Land in downtown Nassau now costs almost as much as in Manhattan or Central London, and Cable Beach land which in 1924 sold at £200 for lots 100 x 400 feet now changes hands at about as much per front foot. Seafront land in little New Providence has become so scarce that huge co-operative apartment blocks, in which prices of apartments range from $17-100,000, are mushrooming where once an acre of surrounding land was not regarded as extravagant to provide privacy for a beach *cabaña*. Most enterprising of all New Providence developers has been E. P. Taylor, the Canadian brewery magnate, who has spent over $9,000,000 developing Lyford Cay, where lots of 1½ acres cost as much as $66,000 each. Lyford Cay achieved its ultimate cachet in December, 1962, when it was the site of the momentous Nassau Conference between President Kennedy and Prime Ministers Macmillan and Diefenbaker.

Even in the Out Islands, land values have appreciated by as much as ten times in the last decade, though one of the more unfortunate developments of recent years has been the minute subdivision of some of the less attractive tracts for small down payments. One developer has sold 20,000 adjacent lots on the disingenuous slogan "a place away from it all"; though in his defence it must be remarked that in five years less than a dozen of the lots have actually been built upon. Far more advantageous to the Bahamian economy have been the attempts to tap the natural resources of the Bahamas through infusions of American capital. So far none of the ubiquitous concessionaires have struck oil, but Diamond Crystal have revivified the salt-pans of Long Island and in Andros and Abaco, enormous acreages have been cleared to grow strawberries, okra, egg-plant and cucumbers. In Abaco, Owens-Illinois, having stripped the island practically bald for pulpwood, have switched, improbably, to sugar-cane, having lobbied a 10,000-ton sugar quota for the Bahamas out of the United States Congress.

At the same time, Nassau itself has been transformed. In 1959, Huntingdon Hartford bought Hog Island for $10,000,000, rechristened it Paradise and began the development that will change the island into a glittering offshore resort rivalling Miami Beach, joined to the mainland by a high-flying bridge. In Nassau Harbour, an artificial island was begun in 1965, with wharfage that would allow the largest cruise liners to dock, rather than to anchor off the bar as before. It was perhaps typical of the "wheeler-dealing" that went on behind the scenes that hotel concessions and building lots were spoken for before plans were made public and the enabling Bill went before the House of Assembly.

The most ambitious and exciting of all Bahamian projects is Freeport, Grand Bahama, the brainchild of Wallace Groves. In the early 1950s, Groves, who was then running a lumber concern on Grand Bahama, conceived the visionary plan for a great free port and industrial centre in the wasteland of scrub and mangrove swamp around Hawksbill Creek. In 1955, the Bahamas Government granted Grove's Grand Bahama Port Authority 50,000 acres of land with an option over a further 50,000. An Act of the same year guaranteed freedom from taxation of income, capital gains, real estate or personal property until 1985 and from all customs and excise duties (except on goods for personal use) until 2054.

Attracted by these generous conditions, about forty enterprises, mostly American, have taken options on land and several have started building. D. K. Ludwig the oil tanker magnate cancelled his plans to establish a mammoth shipyard at Freeport

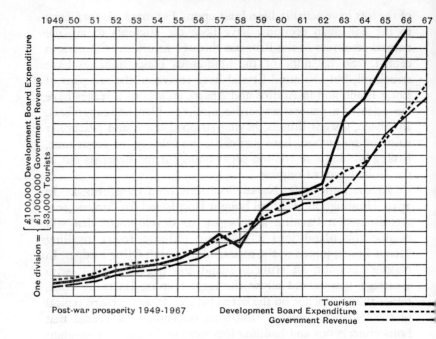

One division = { £100,000 Development Board Expenditure
£1,000,000 Government Revenue
33,000 Tourists

Post-war prosperity 1949-1967

Tourism
Development Board Expenditure
Government Revenue

when he obtained more favourable conditions in Japan, but not before he had spent $5,600,000 on giving the project a 30-foot harbour with a 600-foot turning basin.

By 1966, Freeport, with its residential section, Lucaya, boasted 214 miles of roads and hundreds of buildings, including six hotels, two casinos, a hospital clinic, modern schools, an international shopping centre and a model airport already handling the giant jets. The new port, helped by a huge cement factory and an oil bunkering facility, cleared 1,873 vessels in 1965, importing 332,389 tons of goods and exporting 406,930 tons. Wallace Groves, who claimed that $400,000,000 had already been invested in Freeport, dreamed publicly of a city doubling the population of the Bahamas, pointing out that the water-table could support a population of 500,000 and that the concession area was approximately the same size as the island of Singapore with its two million people. Freeport, however, was not without its growing pains, the most obvious being a series of labour disputes largely triggered by *de facto* housing segregation, producing the absurdity of the population of Freeport's plush acres being outnumbered by the labour force jammed into the shanty town of Eight Mile Rock, outside the Port Authority boundary. This anomaly has largely been remedied by the building of a company town nearer to the centre of Freeport.

Just as important for the Bahamas, though not as flamboyant as Freeport, has been the development of "offshore" or "suitcase" companies in Nassau. These companies are legal fictions designed solely for the purpose of evading United States, British or Canadian taxation. The extent of this traffic can only be guessed at, for one of its most alluring advantages is its secrecy. As one investment broker has candidly expressed it: "Because no treaties provide for the exchange of financial information between the Bahamas and other governments, the accounts of such corporations carried on the books of a Nassau bank or stockbroker are not subject to scrutiny by foreign authorities". Nor does the Bahamas Government require financial statements to be filed by these largely imaginary holding companies, though after a few scandals such as the collapse of the Canadian Atlantic Acceptance Corporation, the Bahamas Government passed a more rigorous Companies Registration Act in 1965.

One certain indication of the growth of offshore companies is the tremendous proliferation of banks in Nassau. Whereas in 1946 one bank, the Royal Canada, was all that was required to handle the finances of the Bahamas, today there are no less than 70 banks and their branches or trust companies. Although President Kennedy made some important alterations in American tax laws in 1963, Nassau bids fair to become one of the great financial centres of the world, occupying as it does a favoured no-man's-land between the dollar and sterling areas. Nassau has for years operated on an unofficial dual currency; prices in shops and hotels being more often quoted in dollars than sterling, and even the Post Office permitting payment for stamps in American cash. By 1960, the official interchange of dollars for pounds had made the Bahamas the biggest single dollar earner in the British Empire, with an annual total in excess of $30,000,000. As was perhaps inevitable, in 1966 the Bahamas, while remaining within the sterling area, switched to a decimal coinage at par with the United States dollar. The pretty new coinage, aimed at attracting the tourist, included a knobbly "dime", a square 15c. and a three-dollar bill.

But as Bacot said in the 1960s concerning an earlier influx of American money, what good came of it all? Who has profited, or profited most, from the post-war surge? It is often stated that "the greater the wealth domiciled in Nassau, the greater will be the prosperity of the whole population of the Bahamas". This is questionable in the extreme. The most obvious result of the pressure of so much foreign money has been almost frightening inflation. Business men and speculators riding the boom, lawyers living on fat fees, indubitably profit from the flow of foreign capital through the islands. The benefits to the average Bahamian are far less obvious.

As is usual, salaries and wages have barely kept pace with the inflationary whirlwind. The cost of living in Nassau is higher than in New York, a fact carefully disguised in a survey of comparative living standards in the Caribbean produced by the Development Board in 1958. Although the average Bahamian does not have to pay the tourist rate of $22 or more a day in the hotels, or $300 or more a month for a modern apartment, his cost of living index rose by about 100 per cent in the decade after 1950, though it appears to have levelled off somewhat since 1960. In 1966, the hourly rate for unskilled labourers was still only 78c. and a maid earned an average of about $17 a week. Salaries in the lower echelons of government service were pitiful.

The one advantage which the ill-paid civil servant enjoys over his wage-earning brethren is the guarantee of continuous employment. A very large proportion of the Bahamian labour force, perhaps 50 per cent, is engaged in catering for the tourists and in the building trade. This employment is lucrative but transitory. Generally since 1950 employment has been so full that any well-mannered boy could get hotel work, and semi-skilled labourers could call themselves craftsmen. At the first sign of a recession, however, labourers and hotel staff tend to be laid off without compunction or delay. An American economic slump would be an immediate disaster for the average Bahamian. Nevertheless, while he continues to make good wages he will give no thought to the future.

As we have seen so often, the Bahamian attitude of living only for the present is all-pervading. The worst sufferer from short-sighted policies is the Bahamas Government. It is a poor government in a rich country. Since there is no direct taxation in the Bahamas, a very high proportion of government income is derived from import duties. Although government revenue has risen steadily since the war, from £840,000 in 1946 to the equivalent of an estimated £18,400,000 in 1967, it has not kept pace with the rise in tourism, let alone the fantastic increase in foreign investment. With the single exception of the Development Board, government departments have been shackled by conservative attitudes and estimates. Only since the introduction of a petrol road tax in 1962 has the Public Works Department been able to graduate from patching potholes to laying new tarmac, and as late as 1959, *The Economist* Intelligence Unit reported that the Bahamas was the only British territory with no government scheme for low-cost housing. Recently this has been remedied, but private interests are still heavily involved in the new housing schemes and the mileage of new government roads continues to be outstripped by those laid privately. Despite its hundreds of millionaires, New Providence does not possess an adequate sewerage system or water supply. In 1959, only 13 per cent of Bahamian dwellings had flush toilets and 77 per cent did not have piped water, and this situation has not been improved greatly in the years since. Besides this, many of the ambitious public projects undertaken since 1962 have been financed by the expedient of floating government loans, thus giving the Bahamas the novelty of a substantial National Debt as the cost of her new independence, the interest repayments for 1967 alone amounting to more than the total revenue for 1950. Clearly, some alternative system of raising revenue is inevitable if the Bahamas is to match her national ambitions with a viable national economy.

As always, the lot of most of the Out Islands is far worse than that of New Providence. Tourism has only touched a few fortunate islands. The submarine testing base established on the Tongue of the Ocean in 1965 did bring some local employment in Andros, but the American missile tracking stations established on Grand Bahama, Eleuthera, San Salvador and Mayaguana by a treaty signed in July, 1950, brought little local benefit since they are entirely self-contained units, and in the mid-1960s they were drastically cut back. Agriculture and fishing are still the mainstay of most of the islands, as they must be for the entire Bahamas in the event of an economic collapse. And yet there is little more planning and co-operation than there was a century ago. The giant farms in Andros and Abaco have shown that the Bahamas will grow practically anything in any season, given only the irrigation of invested capital and a well-planned distribution system; but at least until 1964 the Agricultural and Marine Products Board was the poorest department in a poor government. A fruitful comparison could be made with Jamaica and Trinidad, where for years the agriculture departments have been the best served of all.

The explanation given in some quarters for the lack of support for Out Island agriculture was that the commercial interests dominant in the Legislature were no more willing to foster a flourishing farming economy than they were to support advanced education for Bahamian Negroes. The "Bay Street Boys" were held to be unwilling to subsidise agriculture while rich profits were to be had from importing fruit and vegetables from the United States. The answer to this charge was usually that the Out Island farmer was too lazy, jealous and unco-operative to benefit from what had already been done, let alone what might be done.

This type of charge and counter-charge has been typical of Bahamian polemics in recent years, and to some it has seemed that Bahamians are readier to criticise than to make decisions; more willing to discuss an easier solution than actually to work. Certainly, in the years of comparative ease since the war, politics have become the most popular Bahamian hobby, with political activity rising gradually towards a bubbling climax in the General Election of January, 1967, with its dramatic tie.

Past elections have been notoriously corrupt, especially before the universal application of the secret ballot in 1949.* Bribery, intimidation and the tiny electorates made Bahamian elections similar to those in England during the eighteenth century. The formation of the Progressive Liberal Party to fight the General Election of 1956 on party lines was a great step forward. Dedicated to reform and spurning corrupt practices, the

* It was introduced into New Providence in 1939.

P.L.P. obtained six seats and by its united front provoked the formation of the majority United Bahamian Party in 1958, which commanded 19 seats in the Assembly. Unfortunately, the party division was made on racial lines, with only three Independent Members "sitting on the fence", and the subsequent years if anything saw a heightening of racial tensions.

The leader of the extreme left wing, though a moderate in any but a Bahamian context, was Randol Fawkes, an ebullient Negro labour leader. In 1957, Fawkes, then a P.L.P. Member, formed his own splinter party, the Bahamas Federation of Labour, which was largely responsible for the serious general strike of January, 1958. This arose out of a dispute concerning the conveyance of passengers from the new Nassau International Airport at Windsor Field, but was really the result of general dissatisfaction over labour conditions which had been boiling up for some time.

On the morning of January 12, 1958, the day the new airport was scheduled to open, members of the Taxicab Union, which objected to airline passengers being carried by tour company cars, blockaded the approaches to the airport. Airline traffic was immediately halted. The B.F.L., which for months had been busily unionising, called a general strike in sympathy. Although only a proportion of building and hotel workers "came out", they were sufficient to bring the tourist trade and all building to a standstill. After a hectic two days in which guests helped to wash up and serve meals, all the hotels closed.

Mutterings of violence and rumours were loud in Nassau. Doubtless bearing in mind the riots of 1942, the Governor, Sir Raynor Arthur, telegraphed Jamaica and in the early hours of January 14, a heavily armed detachment of the Worcester Regiment was flown in from Kingston. This action, which shocked all sections in Nassau, was indubitably hasty. There was no actual violence and the presence of the troops was generally resented among the Negro population and the taxi negotiations went on under a cloud of mutual distrust.

After nineteen days the strike folded up. The taximen gained most of the disputed points, but at first it seemed that the B.F.L. and the whole economy of the Bahamas had taken a bad beating. Deterred by the Florida radio stations and press, which exaggerated the disorders in Nassau, the tourists continued to stay away from the Bahamas. The tourist total for 1958 showed the first decrease since 1945. Building employees who had joined the strike were in many cases laid off and hotel workers continued out of work because there was no employment for them. The B.F.L. and its leader were temporarily discredited.

The longer term effects of the strike were far more salutary, and January, 1958, may well be looked back to as a turning point in Bahamian history. Newspaper reports and the Governor's dispatches brought home Bahamian problems to the dilatory Colonial Office in London. In April, Mr. Alan Lennox-Boyd, then Secretary of State for the Colonies, flew out to Nassau and in a series of crucial interviews made it clear that H.M. Government would support majority opinion in the Bahamas despite the composition of the House of Assembly. Following the suggestions of the Colonial Office, an important series of labour bills was passed through the Bahamian Legislature, providing a Labour Board and a Labour Liaison Officer. Important electoral changes were also strongly recommended. Property qualifications and plural voting were abolished and Nassau was given four more seats in the House of Assembly. When the by-elections were held in 1960, P.L.P. candidates were elected to all four extra seats. With another P.L.P. candidate successful in the disputed by-election at Grand Bahama, the Opposition party had almost doubled its representation in the Assembly.

In 1960, an Act was passed to give women the vote and the right to sit in the Legislature. In the same year, two important Colonial Office-sponsored reports were published; the Houghton Report on Education and the Hughes Report on Medical Services. Both recommended sweeping changes. In 1962, the Septennial Act of 1795 was repealed and a Quinquennial Act passed, making an immediate General Election necessary. Clearly, this election would be a testing ground, and since the Progressive Liberal Party had remained clearly identified with the Negro majority, it was felt by many that the P.L.P. would gain a decisive majority in the House of Assembly.

The election held in November, 1962, in which women voted for the first time, produced a shock for the radicals. The ruling U.B.P. was returned with an increased majority, a result that has been variously attributed to the Cuban crisis, the fickleness of the female vote and the fears of the economic effects of a complete change in government. Despite the victory of the conservatives, however, a breeze of reform immediately appeared to waft through public affairs. This became concentrated into a movement for a greater degree of self-government for the Bahamas, though the form that this should take provoked much discussion.

In May, 1963, a delegation representing all sections and parties accompanied the Governor, Sir Robert Stapledon, to London for constitutional talks at the Colonial Office. After three weeks of talks it was announced that as from January 1, 1964, the Bahamas would enjoy complete internal self-rule.* The proposals provided for a bicameral Legislature, with responsible government consisting of a Prime Minister and at least eight other Ministers. The Governor was to act on the advice of this Cabinet, except in matters of foreign policy, defence and internal security. The Legislative Council was to be reconstituted as a Senate of 15 members, of whom eight would be appointed by the Governor, five on the advice of the Prime Minister and two on the advice of the Leader of the Opposition. The House of Assembly, with its 33 Members, was to continue until the next General Election in 1967, when its numbers would be increased to 38.

If the 1962 election surprised and disappointed the radicals, the 1967 election astounded everyone. The years after the U.B.P. victory of 1962, particularly after the achievement of internal self-government, had continued to bring material prosperity to the Bahamas, a prosperity that was claimed by the ruling party to be a result of its paternalistic policies. The Opposition party, however, claimed that the burgeoning prosperity was a natural reflection of the continuing American boom and that the ruling Bay Street clique were apportioning an unfair share of the profit as well as the credit. More sinister, the P.L.P. charged that the U.B.P. was maintained in power by gerrymandered constituencies, that there was strong conflict of interest in the operations of Ministers and that some were even in the pay of shady American casino operators active in Grand Bahama and eager to extend their activities to New Providence. Delegations were sent both

* In fact, this came into effect on January 7, 1964.

to London and to the United Nations, though with little apparent result. Far more effective were factual reports appearing in many American magazines, beginning with the respected *Wall Street Journal* late in 1966, that itemised the extent to which Ministers, including the Premier and his son, the Speaker of the Assembly, had received "consultancy fees" from the Grand Bahama casino operators, who at the same time were shown to be strongly under the influence of Meyer Lansky of Miami Beach. In the case of Sir Stafford Sands, these "fees" were said to be in excess of a million dollars.

Despite these revelations, the Government party went into the General Election on January 10, 1967, full of confidence, reinforced by the knowledge that three of the eight P.L.P. Members in the Assembly had split away and been expelled from the party. The campaign was fought with unparalleled enthusiasm. For the first time the P.L.P., realising its strength in the capital, campaigned hardest in the Out Islands, where the movie idol Sidney Poitier—himself born in Cat Island—made several telling appearances on behalf of the party. Besides this, an enterprising Nassau preacher reminded his congregation that it was on the tenth day of the first month that the Israelites were led out of captivity in Egypt, and the P.L.P. voters went to the polls singing the theme song from *Exodus* as their anthem.

The result of the election was a tie between the two major parties, with U.B.P. and P.L.P. returning 18 Members each. The balance was held by Randol Fawkes, the sole Labour Member, and Alvin Braynen, an Independent. After some hours of tumultuous suspense, it was announced that the Governor had sent for the leader of the P.L.P., the 36-year-old lawyer Lynden Pindling, to form a government, that Fawkes had been offered the Ministry of Labour and Welfare and that Braynen had agreed to act as Speaker.

For the first time, the power of "Bay Street" had been humbled and the Negro majority had come to rule. Yet the new government was obviously on trial. For a few weeks the tide of investment appeared to be on the turn, and unemployment soared. Prime Minister Pindling's public reassurance that his government would "foster the climate of free enterprise" and that their "plans for the pleasures of tourists call for more not less", however, gradually restored confidence. With such a slender majority, Lynden Pindling would have to tread warily, restraining the extremists in his party who demanded punitive reprisals. The investigation into irregularities over the casino concessions, however, were inevitable (they had indeed been promised by the U.B.P.) and the Commission of Inquiry that opened in April, 1967, was generally welcomed. More practically, the Government announced a Budget in March, 1967, in which the allocation for the promotion of tourism, while still princely, was exceeded for the first time by that for education and health.

Sources and Further Reading

A. GENERAL

1. *Primary*

BELL, H. C. and PARKER, D. W. *Guide to British West Indies Archive Materials in London and the Islands* (Washington; Carnegie Institute, 1926) is the indispensable guide to the wealth of documents in the Public Record Office in London, making a complete list and giving synopses of the more important items from the Board of Trade Original Correspondence (1717–80), the Secretary of State's Original Correspondence (1696–1815), the Board of Trade Entry Books (1717–1784), Bahamian Acts (1729–81), Sessional Papers (1721–94) and Shipping Returns (1721–55). This invaluable book also lists the documents to be found (in 1925) in Nassau, in the Registry, in the offices of the Governor, Colonial Secretary and Surveyor, in the libraries of the Executive Council, Legislative Council and House of Assembly and in the archives of the Supreme Court and Admiralty Court. Lamentably, a large proportion of these papers have gone the way of all untended documents and disappeared since 1926.

ANDREWS, C. M. and DAVENPORT, F. G. *Guide to Manuscript Materials for United States History to 1783 in the British Museum, etc.* (Washington; Carnegie Institute, 1908) also lists many valuable Bahamian documents found at the Royal Society, the Bodleian Library, the House of Lords and in the King's, Egerton, Sloane and Additional MSS. at the British Museum.

Nearly all the papers listed in these two books dating from before 1737 are also found listed and summarised in the many volumes of the *Calendar of State Papers; Colonial* (1574–1660) and *America and West Indies* (1661–1737).

MALCOLM, (SIR) H. *Historical Documents Relating to the Bahama Islands* (Nassau, 1910) is useful because it gives certain key documents in full.

The chief series of Bahamian materials lodged in the Public Record Office, London, are:

Original Correspondence (C.O. 23), 1696–1943. 324 volumes.

Register of Correspondence (C.O. 333), 1850–1930. 18 volumes.

Register of Out-letters (C.O. 508), 1872–1926. 9 volumes.

Entry Books (C.O. 24), 1717–1872. 34 volumes.

Acts (C.O. 25), 1721–1939. 130 volumes.

Government Gazettes (C.O. 564), 1894–1940. 11 volumes.

Miscellanea (C.O. 27), 1721–1940. 138 volumes.

Of the documents found in Nassau, those at the Registry are the most important and the most readily available. Originally they were in folios numbered A-Z; A1-Z1 etc., as far as A23-Z23, when a "New Series" began, about 1850. The first index, of conveyances, was made in 1815. All extant Registry records, which include conveyances, land grants, deeds, wills, inventories, records of the Courts of Ordinary and Chancery, lists of freed slaves (1740–1834), records of slave trials (1785–89), the minutes of Executive Council (1789–1802) and the Colonial Secretary's book (1733–51), were microfilmed in 1956. Unfortunately, the original folios are inadequately housed and safeguarded and some early volumes have disappeared even since they were microfilmed. There is as yet no official archivist for the Bahamas.

The Statute Law of the Bahamas (Nassau, 1956), in nine volumes, is the revised list of operative Acts. Earlier codifications were made in 1803, 1843, 1850, 1862, 1877, 1901 and 1929.

The Votes of the House of Assembly, which are the printed minutes of that body, were first published at the end of the eighteenth century and are continuous from 1729 down to the present day, but unfortunately do not give details of bills nor lists of voters.

Newspapers have been published continuously in the Bahamas since John Wells the Loyalist brought out the *Bahama Gazette* in August, 1784. The following is a provisional list of Bahamian newspapers and periodicals. Those asterisked are found on file, complete or in part, in the Nassau Public Library.

1784–1857	*Bahamas Gazette**	1849–77	*Bahama Herald**
1804–13	*Royal Gazette**	1850s	*Bahama Times*
1831–c. 40	*Bahamas Argus**		*Parthenon*
1838	*The Bahamian*, later	1861–65	*Nassau Advertiser*
	the *Observer*	1864	*Young Punch*
1844–	*Nassau Guardian**	1868–93	*Nassau Times**

1879–80	*Our Jem*	1935	*Bahama News*
1886–89	*The Freeman*	1938–40	*The Mirror*
1898–1901	*Bahama News**	1940–	*Nassau Herald*
1901–06	*The Watchman*	1940s	*The Voice*
1904–	*Nassau Daily Tribune*	1944	*The Liberator*
1908	*The Witness*	1951	*Bahamas Digest**
1922	*Observer Weekly,*	1955–	*Nassau Magazine*
	later *Nassau Leader*		

Out Island Newspapers: *Inagua Record*
Bimini Bugle

Eleuthera Palm (Governor's
Harbour)
Searchlight (Inagua)

2. *Secondary*

BAIN, G. L. *The Early History of the Bahama Islands to 1730* . . .
(MA London, 1959)

BELL, H. MCL. *Bahamas; Isles of June* (London, 1936)

BURNS, (SIR) A. *History of the British West Indies* (London, 1950)

CULMER, J. *A Book of Bahamian Verse* (London, 1930)

CURRY, R. A. *Bahamian Lore* (Paris, 1928)

LUCAS, C. D. *Historical Geography of West Indies* (Oxford, 1905)

MCCUTCHEON, E. S. *The Island Song Book* (Nassau, 1927)

MOSELEY, M. *Bahamas Handbook* (Nassau, 1926)

PARRY, J. H. and SHERLOCK, P. M. *A Short History of the West Indies*
(London, 1960)

PARSONS, E. C. *Folk Tales of Andros Island, Bahamas* (Boston, 1918)

PEGGS, A. D. *A Short History of the Bahamas* (Nassau, 1955)

SHARER, C. *Population Growth in the Bahamas* (PhD Michigan, 1955)

STARK, J. H. *History and Guide to the Bahamas* (New York, 1891)

WAKEFIELD, A. J. *Report on Agricultural Development in the Bahamas*
(Nassau, 1942)

B. PARTICULAR PERIODS

Chapter I

There is as yet no comprehensive natural history of the Bahamas,
though there is a fairly extensive bibliography to draw upon. The
following is an abbreviated list:

AGASSIZ, A. *A Reconnaissance of the Bahamas* (New York, 1894)

CATESBY, M. *Natural History of the Carolinas, Florida and the Bahamas* (London, 1731)

CORY, C. B. *General Catalogue of the Birds of the Bahamas* (Boston, 1890)

DOLLEY, C. S. *Provisional List of the Plants of the Bahamas* (1889)

FRICK, G. F. and STEARNS, R. P. *Mark Catesby. The Colonial Audubon* (Urbana, di Illinois, 1961)

KLINGEL, G. C. *Ocean Island* (New York, 1940)

NORTHROP, A. R. *A Naturalist in the Bahamas* (New York, 1910)

"REBUS" *Official Guide to Bahamanian Fisheries* (London, 1883)

RIGG, E. L. *The Bahama Islands* (New York, 1957)

ROSEN, A. *Contribution to the Fauna of the Bahamas* (1911)

SAVILLE-KENT, W. *Report on the Sponges of the Bahamas* (London, 1883)

SHATTUCK, G. B. (Ed.). *The Bahama Islands* (Baltimore, 1905)

THOMPSON, A. *A Short Geography of the Bahamas* (Nassau, 1944)

WAKEFIELD, A. J. *Report on Agricultural Development in the Bahamas* (Nassau, 1942)

WALTON-SMITH, F. G. *Atlantic Reef Corals* (Miami, 1948)

ZAHL, P. A. *Flamingo Hunt* (New York, 1952)

Chapter II

There is a great need for a full archaeological and anthropological work on the Lucayans. It is an almost untouched field.

BROOKS, W. K. *On the Lucayan Indians* (Washington, 1899)

DE BOOY, T. *Lucayan Remains in the Caicos Islands* (Washington, 1912)

FEWKES, J. W. *The Aborigines of Porto Rico and the Neighbouring Islands* (Washington; Smithsonian Institution, 1907)

JOYCE, T. A. *Central American and West Indian Archaeology* (London, 1916)

LAS CASAS, B. DE. *Historia de las Indias,* translated in English as *The Tears of the Indians* (J. Phillips, London, 1655) and *An Account of the First Voyages and Discoveries of the Spaniards in America . . .* (London, 1699)

LOVEN, S. *The Origins of the Taino Culture* (Goteburg, 1935)

MARKHAM, C. R. *The Journal of Christopher Columbus . . .* (London, 1893)

MARTYR, PETER. *De Orbe Novo* (1511), trans. by F. A. McNutt (New York, 1912)

Chapter III

Out of the multitude of books on every aspect of the career and discoveries of Columbus I have taken as my almost invariable guide the masterly

MORISON, S. E. *Admiral of the Ocean Sea* (New York, 1941)

Those who wish to explore the voyages and the landfall controversy more fully should consult

BECHER, A. B. *The Landfall of Columbus* (London, 1856)

COLUMBUS, F. *Life of the Admiral Christopher Columbus* (London, 1867)

CRONAU, R. *The Discovery of America and the Landfall of Columbus* (New York, 1921)

JANE, C. (Ed.). *Select Documents Illustrating the Four Voyages of Columbus* (London, 1930–33)

MURDOCH, J. B. *The Cruise of Columbus in the Bahamas* (New York, 1884)

Chapter IV

There is obviously a great deal of work to be done on the Spanish archives, especially the General Archive of the Indies at Seville. Unlimited time and patience and a knowledge of Spanish would be essential. The following are the most likely sources of relevant documents:

MONTOTO, S. (Ed.). *Colección de documentos inéditos para la historia de Ibero-América* (Madrid, 1927)

NAVARRETE M. F. DE (Ed.). *Colección de documentos inéditos para la historia de España* (Madrid, 1842–95)

Colección de los viajes . . . (Madrid, 1825–37)

PACHECHO, J. F. (Ed.). *Colección de documentos inéditos relativos al descubrimiento, conquista y colonización de las posesiones españolas en América y Occeania* (Madrid, 1864–84)

HERRERA, F. DE. *Historia general de las Indias occidentales* (1601), translated into English by:

STEVENS, (CAPT.) J. *The General History of the Vast Continent and Islands of America . . .* (London, 1726)

LAWSON, E. W. *The Discovery of Florida and its Discoverer Juan Ponce de Léon* (St. Augustine, 1946)

WRIGHT, I. A. *The Early History of Cuba, 1492–1558* (New York, 1916)

Chapter V

ANDREWS, C. M. *The Colonial Period in American History* (New York, 1937)

BELLIN, J. N. *Description géographique des Isles Antilles possédées par les Anglais* (Paris, 1758)

CUMMING, W. P. *The South East in Early Maps* (New Jersey, 1958)

HAKLUYT, R. *Principal Navigations, Voyages, Traffics and Discoveries of the English Nation* (1589)

WILKINSON, H. *The Adventures of Bermuda* (London, 1933)

WRIGHT, I. A. (Ed.). *Spanish Documents Concerning English Voyages, 1527–68* (London, 1929)
Documents Concerning Voyages 1569–80 (London, 1932)
Further English Voyages to Spanish America, 1583–94 (London, 1951)

The Dictionary of National Biography has useful articles on Sir Robert Heath and Samuel Vassall.

Chapter VI

With the Adventurers the English documents previously listed begin and these are the essential basis for the entire history of the Bahamas down to the nineteenth century.

BETHELL, A. T. *The Early Settlers of the Bahamas* (Nassau, 1914 and 1937)

LEFROY, (SIR) J. H. *Memorials of Bermuda (1515–1685)* (London, 1877–79)

MILLER, W. H. *The Colonisation of the Bahamas, 1647–70* (William and Mary Quarterly, January, 1945)

WINTHROP, J. *History of New England* (Boston, 1825)
Dictionary of National Biography for William Sayle.

Chapter VII

OLDMIXON, J. *History of the British Empire in America* (London, 1708 and 1741); part reissued as
History of the Isle of Providence (London, 1949)

Chapter IX

CHRISTIE, H. C. *Blackbeard; A Romance of the Bahamas* (Nassau, 1930)

GRAVES, J. *A Memorial* (London, 1708)

JOHNSON, C. *The History of the Pirates* (London, 1726)

SEITZ, D. C. *Under the Black Flag* (New York, 1925)

SNOW, R. E. *Pirates and Buccaneers* (New York, 1944)

WILKINSON, H. *Bermuda in the Old Empire* (London, 1950)

WOODBURY, G. *The Great Days of Piracy in the West Indies* (London, 1951)

Chapters X and XI

LITTLE, B. *Crusoe's Captain* (London, 1960)

ROGERS, W. *A Cruising Voyage Round the World* (London, 1712), reprinted in 1928 with good introduction by G. E. Mainwaring. Introduction reissued as

Woodes Rogers, Privateer and Governor (Nassau, 1957)

Dictionary of National Biography for Woodes Rogers

Chapter XII

The *Cambridge History of the British Empire* is the best general work on the Old Empire

BEER, G. L. *The Old Colonial System, 1660–1754* (New York, 1912)

HALL, M. G. *Edward Randolph and the American Colonies, 1676–1703* (Chapel Hill, 1960)

MALCOLM, (SIR) H. *History of the Bahamas House of Assembly* (Nassau, 1921)

PENSON, L. M. *Colonial Agents of the British West Indies* (London, 1927)

TOPPAN, R. N. etc. (Eds.). *Edward Randolph . . . letters and official papers . . .* 7 vols. (Boston, 1898–1909)

WRONG, H. *Government in the West Indies* (Oxford, 1925)

Chapter XIII

BRUCE, P. H. *Memoirs* (London, 1782), reissued in part as *Bahamian Interlude* (London, 1949)

SCHUTZ, J. A. *William Shirley, King's Governor of Massachusetts* (Chapel Hill, 1961)

Dictionary of National Biography for P. H. Bruce, Thomas Shirley and William Shirley

Chapter XIV

ARMYTAGE, L. F. *The Free Port System in the British West Indies: A Study in Commercial Policy, 1766–1822* (London, 1953)

MORISON, S. E. *John Paul Jones* (New York, 1960)

Chapters XV and XVI

CLIFFORD, (SIR) B. E. H. *Historic Forts of Nassau* (Nassau, 1952)

MALCOLM, (SIR) H. *Historical Memoranda Relating to the Forts in Nassau* (Nassau, 1913)

SABINE, L. *Biographical Sketches of Loyalists of the American Revolution* (Boston, 1847 and 1864)

SCHOEPF, J. D. *Travels in the Confederation, 1783–4* (Philadelphia, 1911)

SIEBERT, W. H. *The Legacy of the American Revolution to the British West Indies and Bahamas* (Columbus, Ohio, 1913)

WYLLY, W. *A Short Account of the Bahama Islands* (London, 1789)

Dictionary of National Biography for John Murray, 4th Earl of Dunmore.

Chapters XVII and XVIII

Anonymous. *Living in the Sun; A Brief History of the African Tribes Who Came to the Bahamas* (Nassau, 1939)

BURN, W. L. *Emancipation and Apprenticeship in the British West Indies* (London, 1937)

KERR, L. and others. *An Official Letter from the Commissioners of Correspondence of the Bahama Islands to Geo. Chalmers Esq., Colonial Agent* . . . (London, 1823)

LORRAINE, A. DE. *Letters from the Bahama Islands* (Philadelphia, 1827, and London, 1948)

MCKINNEN, D. *A Tour* (London, 1804)

MATHIESON, W. L. *British Slavery and its Abolition, 1833–38* (London, 1926)
British Slave Emancipation, 1839–49 (London, 1932)

RAGATZ, L. *The Fall of the Planter Class in the British Caribbean, 1783–1833* (New York, 1928)

WRIGHT, J. M. *History of the Bahamas* (Baltimore, 1908), part of Shattuck, *op. cit.*, published separately and dealing particularly with the Amelioration and Emancipation period.

Chapter XIX

Anonymous. *Baptist Missionary Society, Centenary Volume, 1792–1892* (London, 1893)

COKE, T. *History of the West Indies* (London, 1810)

HOBART ("PASHA") *Sketches of My Life* (London, 1886)

MOSELEY, M. (Ed.). *Nassau Guardian, Centenary Edition* (1944)

PEGGS, A. D. (Ed.). *Dowson's Journal* (Nassau, 1961)

PETERS, I. *Blockade Running* (London, 1946)

TAYLOR, T. E. *Running the Blockade* (London, 1896)

Chapter XX

AUSTIN, H. W. *Ten Years Chief Justice of the Bahamas, 1880–90* (London, 1890)

BACOT, S. *The Bahamas: A Sketch* (London, 1869)

BRASSEY (LADY) A. *In the Trades, the Tropics and the Roaring Forties* (London, 1885)

CHURTON (BISHOP) E. T. *The Island Missionary of the Bahamas* (London, 1888)

DEFRIES, A. D. *In a Forgotten Colony* (London, 1917)

KING, W. F. H. *Memoirs of Bishop Addington Venables* (London, 1877)

LANGTON-JONES, R. *Silent Sentinels* (London, 1946)

LESTER, G. *In Sunny Isles* (London, 1897)

MACMILLAN, A. (Ed.). *West Indies Illustrated* (London, 1911)

MORRIS, D. *The Sisal Industry of the Bahamas* (London, 1896)

Nassau Guardian Almanacks (annual, 1876–1911)

NORTHCROFT, G. J. H. *Sketches of Summerland* (Nassau, 1906)

PASCOE, C. F. *Two Hundred Years of the S.P.G., 1701–1900* (London, 1901)

POWLES, L. D. *Land of the Pink Pearl* (London, 1888)

RAWSON (SIR) R. *Report on the Bahamas* (London, 1865)

ROBINSON (SIR) W. *The Bahamas* (London, Royal Colonial Institute, 1900)

SHEDDEN, E. *Ins and Outs of the Bahama Islands* (Norwich, 1930)

SHEDDEN (BISHOP) R. *Ups and Downs in a West Indian Diocese* (London, 1927)

STRACHAN, W. *Autobiography* (London, 1855)

Chapter XXI

BACON, E. M. *Notes on Nassau* (Nassau, 1926)
BOCCA, G. *The Life and Death of Sir Harry Oakes* (New York, 1960)
BURNS (SIR) A. *Colonial Civil Servant* (London, 1954)
DEFRIES, A. D. *Fortunate Isles* (London, 1929)
DE MARIGNY. *More Devil than Saint* (London, 1946)
DUPUCH, EUGÈNE. *The Oakes Murder Trial* (Nassau, 1958)
HOLMES, F. *The Bahamas in the Great War* (London, 1924)
HORNER, A. E. *From the Isles of the Sea* (Nassau, 1919)
RUSSELL, A. *Report of the Commission appointed to enquire into disturbances in the Bahamas which took place in June, 1942* (Nassau, 1942)
WATER, H. VAN DE. *The Real McCoy* (New York, 1923)
VANDERCOOK, J. W. *Caribee Cruise* (New York), 1938)

Chapter XXII

COTTMAN, E. *Out Island Doctor* (London, 1962)
DUPUCH (Ed.). *Bahamas Handbook, 1960–67* (Nassau, 1959–66)
DUPUCH (Ed.). *Sun 'n Sixpence* (Nassau, 1964)
HINES, N. C. *The Truth about Freeport* (Miami, 1964)
RICHARDSON, J. H. *Review of Bahamian Economic Conditions and Post-War Problems* (Nassau, 1944)
Anonymous. *The Bahamas, a Diplomatic Press Survey* (London, 1953)
Anonymous. *Comparative Living Levels in the Caribbean* (London, E.I.U., 1959)
Annual Reports: Bahamas; 1946; 1947–48; 1949–50; 1950–51; 1952–53; 1954–55; 1956–57; 1958–59; 1960–1; 1962–3; 1964–5 (London, H.M.S.O.)
Barclay's Bank D.C.O. *Economic Surveys: The Bahamas* (London, 1965)
Burns Report on Bahamian Civil Service; Houghton Report on Bahamian Education; Hughes Report on Medical Services.

List of Governors of the Bahamas

1. *Charter Colony*

1648	William Sayle
1661	Nathanial Sayle

2 *Proprietary Colony*

1670	Hugh Wentworth
1671	John Wentworth
1676	Charles Chillingworth
1680	Robert Clark
1682	Robert Lilburne
1687	Thomas Bridges
1690	Cadwallader Jones
1693	Nicholas Trott
1696	Nicholas Webb
1700	Elias Haskett
1702	Edward Birch
1707	Robert Holden

3. *Crown Colony*

1718	Woodes Rogers
1721	George Phenney
1729	Woodes Rogers
1733	Richard Fitzwilliam
1738	John Tinker
1758	William Shirley
1768	Thomas Shirley

1774	Montfort Browne
1780	John Maxwell
1787	Lord Dunmore
1796	William Dowdeswell
1802	John Halkett
1804	Charles Cameron
1820	Lewis Grant
1829	Sir J. C. Smythe
1835	William Colebrooke
1837	Sir F. Cockburn
1844	George Matthew
1849	John Gregory
1854	Sir A. Bannerman
1857	Charles Bayley
1864	Sir R. W. Rawson
1869	Sir J. Walker
1873	Sir J. Pope Hennessy
1874	Sir W. Robinson
1881	Timothy Callaghan
1882	Sir C. C. Lees
1884	Henry Blake
1887	Sir A. Shea
1895	Sir W. Haynes-Smith
1898	Sir G. T. Carter
1904	Sir W. Grey-Wilson
1912	George Haddon-Smith
1915	William Allardyce
1921	Harry Cordeaux
1927	Major H. Orr
1932	Sir Bede Clifford

1937	The Hon. C. C. Dundas	1951	Major-Gen. Sir Robert
1940	H.R.H. The Duke of		Neville
	Windsor	1953	The Earl of Ranfurly
1945	Sir William Murphy	1957	Sir Raynor Arthur
1950	Sir George Sandford	1960	Sir Robert Stapledon
		1964	Sir Ralph Grey

APPENDIX B

Bahamian Currency

There was no standard coinage in the Bahamas during the seventeenth and eighteenth centuries. There was a great shortage of sterling and French, Spanish and Dutch silver and gold coins were used, their value being determined by weight. The most commonly used coins and prices at the middle of the eighteenth century were the *penny*, the *ryal* (corruption of *real*), the *piece of eight*, the *dollar* and the *guinea*.

In 1786 a *ryal* was held to be worth 9d. Bahamian or 5¼d. sterling. A *piece of eight* was worth eight *ryals* or 3s. 6d. sterling. A *dollar* was worth one *piece of eight* and 2½ *ryals*, or 4s. 8d. sterling. A *guinea*, of course, was 21s. sterling, that is, six *pieces of eight* or 48 *ryals*.

The *moidore* (about 27s. sterling), *Johannes* (36s.) and *doubloon* (66s.), being high in value, were much rarer in the Bahamas.

By 1790 serious attempts had been made to standardise the coinage and align it with sterling. Bahamian currency, however, did not correspond with sterling until modern times. As late as the 1920s unwary tourists were offered wares by street vendors for "threepence sterling" that turned out to cost sixpence "currency", i.e. in Bahamian money. At the same time the expression "check" was still used for 1½d., an obvious derivation from the old Spanish *chequeen*.

John Wells and the *Bahama Gazette*

The *Bahama Gazette*, first published on August 7, 1784, was the original Bahamian newspaper. Its motto, *nullius addictus jurare verba magistri*, is still used by the *Nassau Daily Tribune*. The publisher of the *Gazette* was John Wells, a Loyalist from Charleston who first ran a paper in East Florida before migrating with his press to Nassau in 1784. In front of his printing house in George Street, Nassau, John Wells kept the only bookstore and stationery shop in the Bahamas. Besides the *Gazette*, Wells also published an annual *Bahama Almanack* and several educational handbooks.

The *Bahama Gazette* was a four-page folio size newspaper published weekly until 1790, when it became bi-weekly. Subscription cost a guinea a year delivered until 1790 when the cost was raised to £3 a year. European news, often four months old, took up about a page. "American Intelligence", a little more recent, but still often two months stale, generally filled more space than the items of Bahamian news. Advertisements took up about a quarter of the space. The fourth page was usually devoted to a piece of literary work culled from English periodicals.

Hungry for news and contributions, the *Gazette* paid people to print letters from America and England, and the arrival of any ship, duly announced in the paper, was usually followed by a small spate of news items gleaned from the Captain and passengers. Sometimes, as on November 28, 1789, when the details of the French Revolutionary Constitution reached Nassau, the *Gazette* issued a free two-page supplement.

The Population of the Bahamas 1648–1960

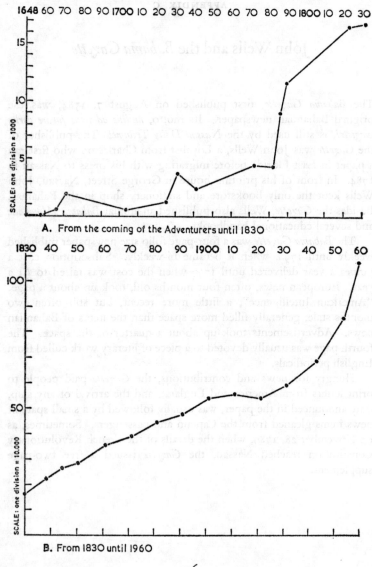

A. From the coming of the Adventurers until 1830

B. From 1830 until 1960

INDEX

Abaco (also called Habacoa, Habakoe or Lucayonique); 43, 44, 45, 46, 55, 62, 63, 66, 97, 127, 137, 154, 164, 165, 166, 168, 184, 201, 226, 235, 240, 247, 248, 253, 256, 281. *See also* Carleton, Elbow Cay, Green Turtle Cay, Hole-in-the-Wall and Hope Town.

abolitionists, 194, 210, 216

aborigines, 17

Acklins, Island and Bight; 15, 36, 180, 190, 252, 261

Acts, Bahamian: under Gov. Trott 85, against adultery and Piracy (Webb) 89, under Woodes Rogers (1729) 115, in Old Empire generally 123, revenue (1734) 130, Slave Code (1784) 165, Electoral (1799) 127, Militia (1782) 158, Liquor Licences (1795) 183, Abolition (1807) 194, Registration (1822) 194, "Healing" (1810) 196, New Slave Code (1826-29) 196, Emancipation (1834) 203, Registry (1834) 209, Education (1841) 211, Agency (1850) 132, Compulsory Education (1877) 212, Elections (1806) 215, Retrenchment (1857) 224, Salt-Ponds (1824-44) 221, Encouragement of Navigation (1851-57) 224, (1879) 258, Police (1864) 236, Disestablishment (1869) 242, Sisal Duties (1889) 251, Sponge Advances (1885) 254, Hotel and Steamships (1898) 259, Telegraph (1873-91) 260, War Relief (1914) 261, Proclamations (1914), 261, War Contingent (1916), 262, Tariff (1919-23) 265, Emergency War Powers (1939) 274, Hotels Encouragement (1949) 280, Anti-Discrimination (1956), 216, Labour and Electoral (1959) 288, Female Suffrage (1960) 289

Adams, Mr. C. F., 228

Adderley, Sir Augustus, 246, 255

Addison, Joseph, 101, 102

Adelaide, New Providence, 206, 207, 211

Admiralty Court, 76, 85, 89, 90, 91, 104, 110, 140, 145, 157

Africa, West, 120, 188

Agents, Colonial, 132, 174, 179

agouti, 25, 58

Agricultural and Marine Products Board, 286

agriculture, 24, 170, 181, 192, 209, 286

Aix-la-Chapelle, Treaty (1748), 142

Alaminos, 44

Albemarle, Duke of, 65; 2nd Duke, 80

Albury, William F., 26

alcos, 25

Alexander VI, Pope, 47

Alfroad, Tabitha, 92

Allardyce, Sir William (Gov.), 261

Allyon, de, 45

Amadas, Philip, 49

ambergris, 59, 67, 71, 84, 94, 133

Amy, Thomas, 87

Anderson, Sir George (Speaker), 241

Andros, 11, 13, 17, 20, 44, 75, 127, 244, 247, 250, 251, 281, 286

Andros, Gov. Sir Edmund, 76

Anglican Church, 183-4, 211, 219,

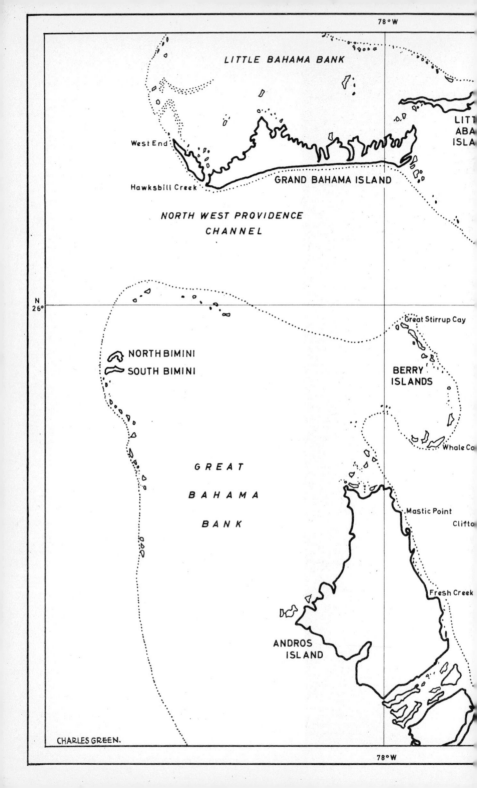